TO BRENDON

LIFE IS A JOURNEY.
WE ALL HAVE A STORY!
I HOPE YOU ENJOY
MINE ♡
   FOLLOW YOUR PASSIONS,
& KEEP SMILING :)

MAY '22

Praise for
THE ONE WINGED PHOENIX

"Motivated by a transformative experience with childhood cancer, Larsen shares her formula for resilience that is grounded in strong family support, a positive attitude, and exceptional resourcefulness and creativity in overcoming personal challenges associated with survivorship. The *One Winged Phoenix* offers a tale of hope that will resonate with cancer survivors of all ages."

-- **Melissa M. Hudson, MD**, Director Cancer Survivorship
Division, Department of Oncology
St. Jude Children's Research Hospital

"A remarkable journey of positivity and perseverance...   Sylvia paints a vivid story of her parents' emigration from Denmark, her youth in classic 1970s California, and her young adult adventures in Europe. She's an inspiration to readers of all ages who believe travel and experience can be life's best teachers."

- **Maryann Jones Thompson**, Editor-in-Chief,
ROAM Magazine

The One Winged Phoenix is a story of survivorship. It takes you through the early life of someone who endured significant challenges and overcame those challenges with Danish pride, family love, shared laughter, and determined independence. Sylvia's story reminds us that life is about the gifts you have and share. Her experiences with cancer are vivid and moving. But her determination and positive attitude are even more powerful. If you are not Danish, you will wish you were part of this community after reading this book. The strong sense of pride and connectedness — being together despite being apart — is a theme throughout. While you read her story, you will often forget she is missing an arm, because that is the way she has lived her life — it is what I can do, not what I can't do. This story has many valuable messages to help others facing significant adversity and provides encouragement for a "can do" attitude.

– **Robert Goldsby, MD,** Professor of Clinical Pediatrics,
Hematology/Oncology,
Director, Survivors of Childhood Cancer Program
UCSF Benioff Children's Hospital

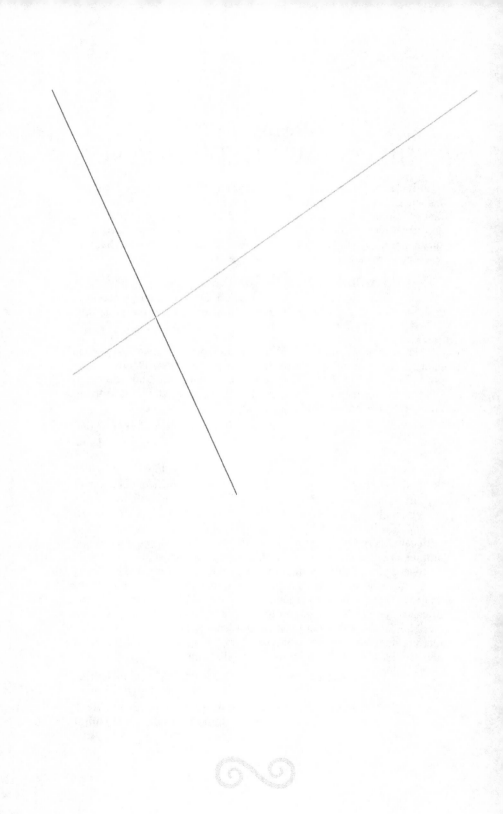

THE ONE WINGED PHOENIX

THE ONE WINGED PHOENIX

A True Story of a
Young Girl
with
One Arm
and a
Fighting Spirit

Sylvia Larsen

Cover illustration © 2021 by Sasha Sagan
Cover design by Sylvia Larsen & Sasha Sagan
Book design and production by SlyFox Productions
Manuscript compilation and setup by Staci Ericson
Story authentication and structure by Teresa Coffman, and Norman Rogers
Editing by Kristianna Bertelsen
Author photograph by Ghitta Larsen ~ Ghitta Larsen Images

San Francisco, California ~ First Printing 2021

Library of Congress Cataloging in Publication Data

LCCN 2020916831

ISBN 978-1-7357106-0-0
EBOOK ISBN 978-1-7357106-1-7

FIRST EDITION

~ Dedicated to ~

All my family and friends for their continual, unwavering support and love. Special thanks to my mother and my uncle Hermann, who taught me independence, problem solving, and that the support and trust of family can give you the courage and strength to carry on as no other.

&

My two incredible children, Ghitta and Anthony, who have allowed me the good fortune to pass these traits on, and teach them to stand on their own and follow their passions.

CONTENTS

CONTENTS

Part Three: Moving Forward

Part Four: Making It Happen

CONTENTS

~ I Did It! ~

~

∾

~ PREFACE ~

In the fall of 2014, I was driving past the Larkspur ferry as it set sail toward San Francisco loaded with commuters. I was headed towards the Richmond–San Rafael Bridge on my way to my new job as Chief of Staff for a prestigious architectural firm in downtown Oakland. The sunrise was glimmering off the bay and the glare was so bad, I could barely see where I was going.

It was at that moment I thought, what a beautiful place it is that I live in. I had a huge smile on my face, and even though I was squinting to see where I was going, I felt as if I had a twinkle in my eye. Because now I realized that I really was the true definition of a survivor.

I had recently had to give up the small architectural firm I had started nearly twenty years ago in Sonoma, along with my beautiful home after my marriage of twenty-five years fell apart in the most horrible way. I had survived cancer twice already and was now a mother flying solo. I had just returned from getting my two children settled into their dorm rooms. They were both starting at NYU.

It was a new beginning for all three of us, and I knew in that instant, everything was going to be okay. I really was a survivor in the best way, and it was time for me to tell my story.

PART ONE:

~TRAGEDY STRIKES~

A woman is like a tea bag ~ you never know how strong

she is until you dunk her in hot water....

Eleanor Roosevelt

Chapter 1

A Man Who Only Knew Good

My father was six feet tall, with a slender build and a strong jawline. When he slicked his hair back like James Dean, it looked almost black to me — surprising, considering he was towheaded as a child. He was very clever and had a playful sense of humor. If he wasn't building forts or tents for my little brother and me in the backyard, he was slingshotting his underwear at us. We would run screaming and giggling from his antics. He was the best of fathers. He was my best friend. Sadly, my story begins with his sudden death when I was almost ten years old.

My father had the most generous nature possible. He would be the first to lend a helping hand to anyone, from family members to complete strangers. I remember many of our neighbors coming by to visit, and when he heard of a project they were working on, he would always have to go check it out and help them without ever expecting anything in return. My father also took his civic duty seriously and devoted countless hours to our local Lions Club, in Corte Madera, California. There he made many friends. People were drawn to him, with his charismatic personality, and the Danes who were members of the club banded together to form a regular poker game. My father loved playing cards. We all did. Growing up in Denmark in the long winters, folks spent a great many hours playing cards while gathered with family. My father had the perfect poker face while smoking his pipe. It was a Canadian straight pipe. He took this pipe just about everywhere, even to the beach. There he'd be in his swim trunks, knee-deep in water, with his pipe teetering on his lip as he talked.

Saturday mornings were for cartoon-watching with Dad. His favorites were Tom and Jerry, Roadrunner, and Popeye the Sailor Man. Weekends were wonderful because I could be his constant companion. He often worked on the weekends, but if I was lucky he would take me with him on landscaping jobs, and I was put to work piecing together sprinkler systems, carrying supplies, and putting in plants. He made everything a game. Nothing made me happier than hanging out with my father.

My father's favorite hobby was fishing — how that man loved to fish! My little brother Steven and I would get up extra early on weekends to go out with him. Breakfast was raw oatmeal with milk and lots of sugar. Later, when I found out that most people cooked their oatmeal, I couldn't believe they actually ate that lumpy mush. My father's younger brother Jens (pronounced Yens), who would also immigrated to California, would join us, and sometimes we would invite a few of the neighbor kids. If we had a whole day, we would drive the winding roads out to the rugged California coastline just north of Bodega Bay. There my dad and Uncle Jens would stand, perched on the black and blue mussel-covered rocks, and cast their poles into the ocean. If we had only the morning, we would head to the nearby shoreline of the San Francisco Bay, usually somewhere near San

Quentin State Prison or Paradise Pier on the north side of the Tiburon Peninsula.

Wherever we went, Dad got us kids set up first. He would open a plastic container of worms and declare, "Look at those beauties!" before inserting his fingers into the squirming mass. "Here," he would say, handing me one. "Try him." After pressing the slimy thing onto my hook, I would cast out my line in the sincere hope of not catching a fish. I didn't like fish. I didn't like the smell. I didn't like the taste. But it never occurred to me not to go because, more than anything else, I wanted to spend time with my dad.

The summer before I turned ten, we took our last trip together as a complete family, to Southern California. Our 1970 Toyota Corolla station wagon had a standard rooftop luggage rack and was painted a mustard color that looked like baby poop; we called it the "Kaka" car. As families did in those days, we sang and played games along the way. At my mother's request, we also stopped and toured every California mission, possibly because the stucco buildings with red tile roofs reminded her of her earlier years in Argentina. We also visited the San Diego Zoo, Sea World, the Botanical Gardens, and the Hotel Coronado.

On our way back, when we reached Orange County, my father mentioned he had a cousin in the area. We decided to stop and visit. Not knowing where our cousin lived, we drove to a grocery store with a phone booth and looked him up. Imagine our surprise to find only one Arvid Bollisen listed — with an address. We headed back out and drove around for nearly two hours looking for that address until my mother, who had been holding her tongue, finally said, "Why don't you just ask someone?" Apparently my father found this suggestion sensible, and we located a mailman who informed us that our cousin was just around the corner — in a court we had driven past multiple times. Why we didn't simply telephone ahead remains a mystery.

Upon finding the house, we parked and went up to knock on the door, earnestly hoping after all our efforts that our cousin would be in. He was! But he and his wife Joanna had never met us before, so my father explained who we were and how we were related. Arv immediately opened his arms. With a big smile, he ushered us inside to the family room where he pointed to a framed black-and-white photograph on the wall. My father recognized it instantly. It was his great grandparents, Laust Rolighed Andersen and Maren Hansdatter, who were, as it turned out, also Arv's great grandparents.

By the time we finished with coffee and getting acquainted, they had invited us to stay on for the next few days. Their two daughters, Debbie and Randi, both in their late teens, worked at Disneyland. We were delighted to discover this. We got escorted with special passes through the Happiest Place on Earth — not once, but twice! The remainder of our time was spent swimming in their fabulous pool that had a diving board, with vines drooping over the water and potted geraniums rimming the edge. It was like our own private Garden of Babylon. All I could think was, "This is the best thing to ever happen to us!"

Upon our return to Northern California, we found orientation information had arrived from my school. I had my fingers crossed that my best friend Tess and I would get the same teacher. We had been in the same class since kindergarten, and I hoped that the school hadn't figured out our antics and would not separate us. We were excited because now we would be in fourth grade and at recess could play in the back quad, which had a snack bar.

Once in school (and yes, in the same class), the autumn moved quickly for us. "Alright," said Mrs. Johnson one day in November. "Let's see who's going to take care of Tigger (the class guinea pig) over Thanksgiving break." There was stiff competition for this honor that could only be decided fairly by chance. Therefore Ms. Johnson reached into a bag full of paper slips, where we had all written our names and stirred them around with great drama. A hush fell over the room. When she announced "Sylvia Larsen," there was a chorus of disappointed groans, but I was grinning. I knew I was the luckiest girl in the world, though I didn't want to rub it in — too much. Thanksgiving break was going to be great.

Two days later I waltzed out of class with a bag of supplies and a large cage that held my temporary houseguest. The little guy scurried and squeaked when I placed him on the car seat next to me, but I soothed him with lilting words and two wiggling fingers stuck through the bars. It looked like this was going to be one of my best holidays ever; little did I know my life was to be shattered in just a few days.

My memory of what came next is blurry, but with the help of family and photos I have been able to rebuild the events of the next week.

Thursday: Thanksgiving Day, we drove inland to Vacaville, just as we had done every year. There was no dispute over who would host this holiday, as Uncle Jens was the only family member married to an American, and Aunt Joan was the only one who knew how to make a traditional Thanksgiving meal. She was, and still is, a fantastic cook with a warm and welcoming home.

Friday: My parents had friends over, and they all ended up playing old records and dancing in the living room. My dad wore his maroon pants and floral striped shirt. My parents were great dancers. After much food and drink, they would pair up and throw themselves into dramatic tangos across the living room. I have great memories of the parties my parents hosted. Ours was a loud and boisterous clan. The children watched with awe as our parents cut a rug on the dance floor.

Saturday: My father went out early to check on one of his masonry jobs and returned mid-morning holding his chest.

"What's wrong?" my mother asked.

"I don't know," he replied, sounding puzzled. "My chest, it's just — tight." He then did something extremely unusual at that hour of the day, and it frightened my mother. He went to lie down.

My mother picked up the phone and called our neighbor, a good friend and local firefighter named Jack Newberry, whose wife said he had already left for the station. Mom started to dial the firehouse to locate Jack, but Dad stopped her. "Don't bother Jack at work," he called from the bedroom.
"I'll be fine, really. Just let me rest awhile."

But after fifteen minutes, my father admitted that the pain had not subsided. It was then that my mother called the firehouse, and Jack came immediately with sirens blaring, and lights flashing, followed by the ambulance, fire truck, and paramedics. There was a lot of commotion, and then they took my father away. My mom went with him, leaving Steven and me behind with a neighbor. I never saw my father again. He had suffered a sudden massive heart attack. He was only 36.

Hours later, my mother and Uncle Jens attempted to explain all of this to my brother and me. After I tried to take it in, my shock changed to apprehension. I was afraid of how my little brother would react.

Steven was only five years old. So I put my arms around him and said, "Don't be sad; we'll just pretend that dad has gone away on a long trip."

But our lives would never be the same. My father would never walk through the door again. He would never kiss my mother or sweep her into a dance. He would never wrestle with Steven, laugh with us, or caress my cheek. As the next couple of days passed and the realization sank in, a void began to form and grow deeper until our little family was staring into a black hole.

I tried to stay occupied and distracted by caring for Tigger, the guinea pig. One of my responsibilities was to clean his cage. So I took the little guy out and put his shoebox over him so he wouldn't run away and get lost, then I proceeded to remove the soiled bedding. My poor mother — exhausted, nerves shot — came around the corner and saw the box creeping across the carpet as if by magic.

"Jens!" called my mother in a loud whisper. My father's younger brother rushed over.

"Do you see what I see?" she asked. Jens stared in amazement.

"Is that box moving?" she continued, implying Tell me I'm not delusional.

The two of them stood there watching, and waiting. Did their eyes deceive them? Was it the stress? Then I came back into the room and saw them staring wide-eyed at the floor.

"What are you doing?" I said.

"Look! That box is... moving."

"I know. That's Tigger." I calmly walked over, lifted the box, and plucked up my furry charge. A brief pause was then followed by a burst of laughter that filled the air like a giant balloon being deflated. We all heaved a huge sigh of relief. I can't say that our grief abated, by any means, but I can say that, at that moment, we saw a glimmer of hope that there would be joy again — not now, or tomorrow, or a week from now — but in time. I always wanted a guinea pig after that. I never did get one, but to this day guinea pigs alway put smile on my face.

The flag at Jack's firehouse was lowered to half-mast on the day of my father's funeral. My mother had chosen Monte's Chapel of the Hills in San Anselmo for the service. Every seat and aisle was packed. Our family sat in an alcove off to the side of the podium, the casket up in front. It was a long service because so many friends and family came up and spoke about how much my father had meant to them. He had touched many with his generous and caring spirit. The admiration and love people had for my father was evident with all the stories and speeches. It was a beautiful service.

Afterward, the large gathering made the sad procession up the winding hill to the Mount Tamalpais Cemetery. I didn't want to go and didn't think Steven should either, so Jens's mother-in-law kindly took us home. I was emotionally shut down. All of this was too much for me to process. A quiet house and some time was what we needed.

My father was buried, his resting place marked with an engraved stone under a newly planted pine tree:

Albert R. Larsen

A Man Who Only Knew Good

1937-1973

Anne-Grethe, my father's older sister who had helped raise him and Jens, couldn't find a flight out of Denmark in time for the funeral, but she arrived a couple of days later. She stayed for six weeks helping my mother and consoling her youngest brother Jens, who was taking the loss very hard. Anne-Grethe had a fun personality and teased us in an effort to lighten the mood. She spent a lot of time with us children playing games and talking.

My mother was besieged by responsibilities: the children, the house, the yard, the business — now she had to manage them all by herself. As there had been no life insurance, and my father's business was too much for her to manage by herself, she would have to return to work as a seamstress. Anne-Grethe didn't think my mother was capable of dealing with the added responsibility of working on top of managing the home and taking care of two young children. So, she tried to persuade my mother that Steven and I would be better off going back to Denmark, where she and her husband could look after us and raise us. She even offered my mother a large antique Danish silver coin that she claimed was priceless. Anne-Grethe had not been able to have children of her own, and she probably convinced herself that her motives were pure, but she clearly underestimated my mother. There was no way in hell my mother would have ever given us up.

For months after my father's death, I existed in a state of disbelief, unable to grieve, simply going through the motions of living. I didn't cry, I didn't act out, I didn't ask why, I just went around cocooned in a fog. My protective shell cracked one evening on Highway 101 as we were driving home from visiting friends. We passed an exit that we had passed hundreds of times before, Seminary Drive, but on this occasion in my mind it registered as CEMETERY! A knot formed in my stomach. My throat tightened. A tremble began in my chest and quickly spread, shaking my small frame until I had no choice but to give up all my control to the wail that so desperately needed to get out.

Sometimes, we just need a good cry. Because once the floodgates had opened, I felt a weight being lifted. I tried to tell my mother why I was crying, but I couldn't communicate my pain at that moment. Once I was finally able to express myself to her, I realized that in my attempt to be brave I had only been hurting myself. Of course, everyone goes through emotional trauma or grief in their own way, but the best healing process is being able to share this information and realize you are not alone.

A few days later, I carried my Sylvia doll with me into the kitchen, where my mother was sitting at the round table drinking her morning coffee, my younger brother sitting beside her eating his Eggo waffle. I took a seat on the other side and placed my Sylvia doll on the remaining chair. This doll had become my comfort object ever since my mother's mother — my mormor — had stitched her for me when I had the flu on Christmas.

I said "God morgen" (good morning) to my mother, and asked if she could make me a bowl of oatmeal the way Dad liked it?

She stood up with a smile on her face and said, "With extra sugar on it?"

"Selvfølgelig!" I answered. Of course! And the three of us began to laugh and reminisce about the way Dad used to pile sugar on anything and everything. Including a slice of pumpernickel. We all knew it wouldn't be the same around here without him. But in that moment I think we also realized that his memory would forever live on in our hearts.

I still hold that thought inside me. He is my guardian angel.

Chapter 2

~ More Bad News ~

Three months passed. Christmas came and went, and a new year began alongside my tenth birthday. Having been born on New Year's Eve, I felt each New Year's held a special significance. We spent the holidays staying with relatives in Vacaville to get away from the loneliness of our own home. The hustle and bustle of a full house and the holidays was a good distraction for us. After we returned home, my mother, my brother, and I were doing our best to try and resume some kind of normal life.

Normal would become a moving target.

It was a cold winter, one that seemed to linger. My mother was attempting to keep my father's business afloat and collect his unpaid invoices. Steven and I had returned to school and were trying to reconnect with classmates. One day in early February, while playing catch with my friend Kristin during recess, I reached to grab the ball and felt a sudden sharp pain in my right arm. When I complained to Mrs. Johnson, she said I had probably strained a muscle.

This happened again a few days later at my Aunt Nanna and Uncle Hermann's house. I was playing outside with my brother and our cousin Bruce. We climbed in the tree branches, scrambling along, using all four limbs, enjoying the freedom of the backyard. That's when I felt the sharp pain in my arm again. Once more everyone assumed I had pulled a muscle.

The pain, though! It did not subside as it had previously. I went inside and complained loudly. Wait until your uncle gets home, have him take a look at it. A few hours passed, and as soon as Hermann walked in the door, I exclaimed how much my arm was still hurting. Since my uncle had a surgeon friend living next door, he brought me over to his house to take a look.

Dr. Long gently probed my arm with his fingers and then suggested, "Just as a precaution, we'll have it X-rayed."

Dr. Long was warm and comforting to me, but as we were leaving and saying our farewells, his eyes teared up. My uncle knew then that Dr. Long was concerned that there might be something seriously wrong, although he kept it to himself for the time being.

In the days that followed, an X-ray showed a growth on the upper bone in my arm. It required further exploration, so on what would have been my father's 37th birthday, February 24, 1974, I went in for a biopsy. My family was completely unprepared for the diagnosis.

Osteogenic Sarcoma is a rare form of bone cancer. The doctors explained to my mother and Uncle Hermann that, to try to save my life, there was no option other than the amputation of my right arm and shoulder followed by chemotherapy.

The two grappled with how to break this news to a wide-eyed, ten-year-old girl still reeling from the loss of her father. Uncle Herman would later say that without a doubt, it was the hardest assignment he ever faced. I've been told that Aunt Nanna took Bruce and Steven out for a drive so my mother and my uncle could talk to me in private. I have only a visual memory: me, sitting in a brown leather chair in my aunt and uncle's living room, my mother and Hermann facing me.

I don't remember their words, but, apparently, I shook my head in disbelief, refusing to accept what I was hearing. I imagine the tortured look on their faces as eventually the truth of the matter was brought home to me. They sat with me through my shock and tears until I realized that I had no choice but to proceed with amputation because I wanted to live.

Uncle Hermann put up a strong front but later wept in his wife's arms, recalling that only days before my dad passed away, the papers were buzzing with news of Senator Edward Kennedy's young son losing his right leg to the same insidious disease. My uncle stepped in and became essentially a surrogate father to me through what was to come. He did extensive research on my cancer and the treatment of it. His assistance in communicating with doctors and providing support was invaluable.

I was immediately put under the care of a renowned cancer specialist and pediatrician, Dr. Arthur Ablin, at the University of California San Francisco Medical Center (UCSF). I was fortunate that he also had a local office only a few minutes away. Even now, when I think of him, 45 years later, I chuckle. He was a tall, thin version of Santa Claus, with silvery white hair, half glasses perched on his nose, twinkly eyes, and a merry laugh. This man's gentle persona, however, belied an uncompromising determination to lead the development of pediatric oncology and change the face of childhood cancer. He was a champion in his own right, defeating the odds, helping children survive.

Up until the late 1960s, a diagnosis of bone cancer was almost certainly fatal. The only remedy was amputation. While this dealt with the disease locally, more than 80% of patients later experienced spreading of the cancer to their lungs. At the time of my diagnosis in 1974, most doctors would have agreed that, statistically, I had about a 10% chance of survival, and this is what they told my mother. There was, however, an emerging treatment — chemotherapy. It was still considered an experimental treatment for pediatric cancer, but Dr. Ablin and a handful of other doctors had recently completed clinical trials and were applying it with promising results. That being said, they had yet to determine what amount could be applied without causing damage to the patient they were trying to save. The main objective was to kill the cancer, meaning douse it with chemo and don't be shy.

The results could be a prolonged life, but side effects might include reproductive sterilization, an increased chance of developing other kinds of cancer, and destruction of the body's ability to fight infection. In spite of these risks, we proceeded, hoping for the best possible outcome.

As was the protocol in those days, the amputation was to precede my chemotherapy treatment. The surgery was scheduled for just two weeks after my diagnosis, on March 8, 1974, my mother's birthday. It was what they called a fore-quarter amputation, where the entire arm and shoulder, including the shoulder blade and collarbone, are removed. It took my surgeon, Dr. Schwartz, over eight hours to complete. When he was done, my torso sported 102 stitches that started at my collarbone, continued around my rib cage, then curled back up around the midpoint of my back.

Afterward, the doctors tried to explain that I would have phantom pains, but until you experience them you have no idea what that really means or how truly painful they are. My arm was taken away, but my brain could not understand this. Signals were still sent to my arm and hand to move. The impulses would go to the cut-off nerve endings and then backfire to my brain where it reacted with a shock of excruciating pain. It felt like I was being stabbed repeatedly with a knife in my missing arm. Every four hours a nurse came in to give me a shot of morphine, which helped, but even that was painful. One nurse discovered that if she gave my leg a quick, hard slap before injecting the needle, it seemed to help with the pain of the shots.

For the next four weeks, I stayed in the pediatric ward of our local hospital - Marin General. During this time I lost 16 pounds, eight of which had been my arm. I received an outpouring of support from the community. Flowers, cards, and even money came from teachers, friends, neighbors, and strangers. There were literally mounds, carloads really, of stuffed animals and gifts. I was especially touched when my neighborhood "big brother," Kevin Nichelini, who I was sure regarded me as a little pest, gave me a book full of pictures of dachshund puppies. Aunt Nanna came by every day and lovingly brushed my hair into pretty pigtails.

Uncle Hermann was wonderful with the doctors, helping us to get our questions answered and to understand the treatment. When there was nothing more he could do, he wrote to the President of the United States. I subsequently received a letter from the White House, signed by President Nixon, expressing his sympathy for my situation and hoping to cheer me up. It included a signed photograph of his dogs sitting on the White House lawn.

In the hospital, I had hours upon hours of free time, and I spent them doing puzzle book after puzzle book. I loved riddles, math, and logic problems. They required my complete concentration and took me away from my troubles, for a while. My best friend Tess visited often, riding her bike to the hospital after school and sitting with me, keeping me company and bearing witness to my pain. She was keenly observant and noticed how the nurses fought back their own tears when they came in to give me my shots. She was good at distracting me with stories of what was happening at school.

When I first came home from the hospital, Nanna and Hermann suggested that we come and live with them so they could provide more constant love and support. Everyone was so patient and kind. I was set up in their family room on their sofa bed surrounded by hundreds of new stuffed animals. If my brother and cousin Bruce came in to watch television with me, they had to be careful not to jostle the bed, as any movement caused me pain. The days were long and hard, but the nights were harder. The phantom pains were worse at night.

My mother knew what I needed: a live, soft, and furry friend to keep me company through my ordeal. When she suggested getting me a dog, my heart leapt. There is nothing quite as good as a puppy to lift the spirits. Uncle Hermann's old friends living in San Luis Obispo could bring me up a miniature dachshund puppy from a litter that had just been born in their neighborhood. They were willing to pick one out and drive the puppy all the way up in their RV to deliver it to me. This was the type of kindness that was showered on me at that time. So many people went out of their way to help us, and it was encouraging.

When I saw the RV pull up, I ran outside with eager anticipation for the door to swing open and my new companion to jump out. But she didn't. She was so little that they had to carry her, as the steps were three times her size. They carefully placed her on the lawn. I dropped to my knees to pet her and introduce myself. Her large brown eyes stared up at me with trusting vulnerability. She was so small, she could fit in the palm of my hand. Before I even had time to consider it, I was asked what I was planning to name her? Steven and Bruce both started calling out names. I realized how grateful I was to Nanna and Hermann, and I wanted to call her Vivi after Nanna's middle name. Nanna protested; she wasn't about to share her name with a dog. So we named her Fefe, which was my spin-off from Vivi. Fefe became my constant companion, always by my side.

Once I had sufficiently recovered from my surgery, I began a two-year course of chemotherapy. Each of my weekly sessions started with my mother and me checking in at Dr. Ablin's office. We waited in the lobby along with other mothers and their children, all of us battling cancer. They looked thin and tired, and many wore hats to cover their hair loss, but none was missing a limb like I was. Bone cancer was rare.

Sometimes Steven or Tess came with me for my weekly chemotherapy treatments. After I waited my turn, a nurse, usually Debbie Ablin (Dr. Ablin's wife), took me back, checked my height and weight, and had me sit up on the examination table. There she would prick the end of my finger to squeeze a drop of blood onto a glass slide, which she then examined under a microscope to get a cell count. Because my fingers quickly became tender and sore from this routine, the nurses had to alternate which finger they drew from. Unfortunately, since I had only four fingers to work with, we always came back around before any of them had had time to heal. I hated waiting for the cell count, hated anticipating the chemotherapy shot. I just wanted to get on with it. If the blood count was acceptable, the nurse would come in and say, "You're good to go," and a short while later Dr. Ablin would appear.

Dr. Ablin was always upbeat and would have something funny to say to break the ice and lighten the mood. Because he was always teasing me, the first time he said, "Bend over and touch your toes," I thought he was being funny. It turned out I would do this every week to make sure my spine wasn't curving from the displaced weight caused by the loss of my arm. Then he'd check my scar to see how it was healing, and listen to my lungs and heart, before having me lie back on the table where he began thumping at my veins.

He started with the inside of my elbow, usually an uncooperative location, but worth a try, then moved on to my hand. If he couldn't find a good vein, he would move on to my feet, and they almost always obliged. Meanwhile, the nurse would set up the portable instrument table and lay out the needles, tubing, saline, and chemotherapy medication that Dr. Ablin would be administering. By the time the nurse was ready, he had tied an elastic band around my arm or leg to help build up the vein. I didn't like to be surprised by the needle; it made me jump and scream, so I reminded Dr. Ablin every time, firmly, sometimes more than once: "Tell me when you're going to do it."

Kindly he would say, "You're going to feel a little stick now."

Once the needle was in, he attached a small tube. He first injected a vial of the saline solution, sending it very slowly through the tube to make sure the vein was unobstructed and flowing. This caused an unsettling, cool sensation as the liquid entered my system. Next, he detached the saline and replaced it with the chemotherapy, pushing slowly on the syringe until it was completely empty, then switched back to finish the treatment with a saline flush. He tried to be very careful when switching vials because whenever even a drop of the chemotherapy medication dripped onto my skin, it would leave a burn mark for years to come.

Please remember that the treatment I went through was 46 years ago, from 1974 to 1976. They did not have central-line catheters or the ability to install ports for easier infusion of treatments. They also had not developed anti-nausea medicine to help control vomiting. I realize that medicine has made a lot of progress in these areas to ease the pain for patients going through cancer — though, of course, it by no means takes away the physical and mental challenges of facing cancer. It is a difficult task, but it can be done. I hope my story helps everyone to realize that.

After treatment, I would go home, nauseated and weak. For several days all I was able to do was sit in bed, heaving into a bucket. After hours of dry heaving, actually vomiting would be a relief. I could not stand any movement or loud noise. If anyone so much as sat on or wiggled my bed, it made my skin crawl. My poor brother must have felt so guilty for causing me to cry out, but I'm sure he also felt unfairly accused for doing nothing more than trying to sit with me and watch TV.

Between bouts of nausea, narrow windows of opportunity would occur where I could give in to my voracious hunger. I could handle only bland, salty foods, probably because of dehydration and also because they weren't so bad if they came back up. My diet was pared down to mostly french fries and buttered corn, everything with lots of salt.

The nausea was so bad, it often denied me any benefit from my pain medicine. Night after night I woke, screaming from the agony of my phantom pains. My mother would come to my bed, gather me to her and hold me, rocking gently, nonstop through the night, speaking softly, reassuring me until exhaustion or relief finally set in.

Every three months, I would pause my weekly treatment and go in for five consecutive days of a second chemotherapy medication. Additionally, every six weeks I had to swallow ten large pills (a third type of chemotherapy medication) per day, for five days straight. This was in addition to my weekly chemo. I felt that the five days of pills on top of the weekly shot of chemo was particularly unfair. Those were the most horrendous days, retching all day and all night. This was my life now — what I did every week of every month, and the month after that, and so on for the next two years. It left me completely wiped out.

Somehow through it all, I managed to keep a fighting spirit. My family knew I had cleared the first hurdle when after one particularly rough chemo treatment and the inevitable time spent with my bucket, someone made a comment and I let out my penetrating, signature laugh. Realizing that I hadn't lost my sense of humor, they redoubled their efforts to cheer me up.

The neighborhood kids on the street outside my house were always playing games of stickball, kick the can, hide-and-seek, and, best of all, capture the flag. I wanted back in. On the days I was feeling good, I was right back out there playing with them. But as one of the youngest, a girl, and now a kid with only one arm, I was picked last for teams. I had good coordination, though, and gained the respect of the older kids when I hit the ball out of the park — or, in our case, down the block — during stickball. I quickly moved up in the ranks.

We all needed a break from the day-in, day-out struggle with my fight against cancer. The family wondered if a change of scenery would do us good. Dr. Ablin approved, so Mom and Nanna took us kids and drove up to Lake Tahoe for a few days to stay at a friend's cabin in the Sierra Nevada. Big mistake. As soon as I started my pill regimen, it was all over. I became sick as a dog. My mom just wanted to get me home, but we could not leave right away because Nanna had taken Bruce and Steven skiing. To complicate the situation, a big storm was blowing in. The challenge was to leave early enough to make it down the mountain before the heavy snow and nightfall arrived.

By the time we finally hit the road, a flurry had begun, and it quickly progressed into a blizzard. It wasn't long before my mother had to pull over. While Bruce, Steven, and I huddled in the car, she and Nanna got out to put chains on the tires. At that point we really didn't have any choice but to continue down the mountain. As we inched along in anxious silence, no one was saying what we were all thinking, that it was getting dark. Bruce and Steven were uncharacteristically silent, sitting stone-faced in the back seat. Nanna, in between them, was leaning forward, staring straight ahead at the blizzard. It was so tense, I almost forgot my terrible nausea.

It wasn't long before we were down to just about zero visibility and our speed slowed to a crawl. When we came up behind a semitrailer, we used it as a guide by following its taillights, figuring that the trucker had greater visibility and at least would crash first if disaster lay around the next corner. Four grueling hours later, we had only made it to Placerville, a mere 60 miles from where we'd started. We soldiered on, white-knuckling it through the storm another hour or so until the truck in front of us suddenly turned off the freeway and we were left in complete darkness. That was it. "First sign of civilization we see," said my mother, "we're stopping." She didn't get any argument from us, and when we finally saw a coffee shop and motel, we cheered.

After checking in to our motel room, Nanna said to her sister, "A bottle of brandy would be good now."

Nanna took us kids and walked to the diner while Mom slipped into her ski pants and headed back out to the car. She saw a police officer and thought, "Well, he'll do."

"Can you tell me where to find the nearest liquor store?" she asked.

Without raising an eyebrow, he answered, "I'm headed in that direction — you can follow me," and led my mother through the dark, into town. I guess it would have been too much to ask him to escort her back as well, but, in any case, he left, and my mother had to remember her way back on her own. By the time she got back, we kids were already asleep. Nanna had brought back two cups of coffee from the restaurant, and the two of them went into the motel bathroom and proceeded to take the edge off.

In the morning when Steven asked, "What's that brown stuff dripping down the wall of the bathroom?" our mother and Nanna groaned. It seemed that pouring the brandy into the cups of coffee had gotten a little more difficult over time, especially after the coffee was gone, which hadn't taken long. But they managed — the evidence being an empty bottle leaning up against the tub. Although their heads were a bit foggy, it was a new day, the storm had cleared, and after a good breakfast and a reassuring call to Uncle Hermann, we drove home.

Chapter 3

~ Appendages and Bullies ~

I attended Adeline E. Kent Elementary School in Kentfield. Due to my surgery and treatment, I missed the last three months of fourth grade. When fall arrived, the fifth-grade class, too, met without me. After several months, though, I had regained enough strength to return to school. My mother had sewn me a beautiful set of clothes, custom-fit for my new body. Due to the chemotherapy, my shoulder-length, silky blond hair was all but gone, so she also sewed hats with soft linings that fitted securely over my bald head, with a little flair at the bottom.

I was looking forward to getting back to a regular routine — going to school, seeing my friends — that is, until I learned that Dr. Ablin had arranged an assembly at my school. The entire student body, staff, teachers, and the principal all filed into the multipurpose room, where Dr. Ablin stood waiting on the stage for all the kids to become situated and sit cross-legged on the floor. He explained that I had cancer, and the doctors had to amputate my right arm. So I would be returning to school with only one arm, and that I was also undergoing chemotherapy to cure the cancer. This had made me lose my hair, and I would be wearing a hat to keep my bald head warm. He concluded with a directive that if people wanted to be helpful, they should ask Sylvia first, and not assume that she would need help. He knew I had a very independent nature.

I couldn't help resenting this attention. I didn't feel I had changed, and I certainly didn't want to be in the spotlight. I just wanted to step back into my life as it had been before.

I was also reluctantly fitted with a prosthetic arm. The doctors all felt this would help me blend in more easily when I went back to school. "This is not who I am," I thought, but I felt pressured to give the prosthetic arm a chance. During one of our many ventures to the limb store in Vallejo, Uncle Jens met us there for moral support. Upon entering the establishment, he found himself surrounded by appendages, hanging from the ceiling, lying on shelves, leaning up against walls — fingers, hands, legs, arms, feet — all different sizes, shapes, and colors. Uncle Jens froze for a moment, uncertain how to react to this macabre environment. But without a moment's hesitation, I ran up to an enormous hairy arm, picked it up, and declared, "I'll take this one!"

Fitting me for my prosthetic arm turned out to be more difficult than anticipated. Because I had no upper arm or shoulder to attach the prosthetic to, a customized series of straps had to be made — two large ones that fastened diagonally across my body, and another that wrapped around my waist. It took many appointments to get it to fit properly, and even then it was very difficult to put on and heavy to wear. My main objection to the prosthetic was that it was strictly ornamental, incapable of moving on its own. I had to reach over with my left hand to operate it. Frankly, I didn't think I looked bad without it, so I didn't see the point of suffering through wearing it.

My first day back, I wore the cumbersome device to school, anticipating that it would deter attention, but instead, it drew it. I heard over and over, "We were told you lost your arm, so why is it still there?" As though I was trying to pull one over on them! By lunchtime I was completely discouraged. I went home, ripped the thing off, and never put it on again. It didn't bother me that I only had one arm, and I decided that if it bothered others, that was their problem.

I learned later that Dr. Ablin had hoped by speaking to my classmates they would admire my courage and refrain from teasing or bullying. It was a kind thing to do, and it worked for the most part, but kids are often tactless and cruel. It made Tess especially angry if anyone dared to tease me, particularly after Dr. Ablin's assembly.

There was this one boy, I will never forget his name, Greg Hanson, who had recently come with his family from England, and he was particularly nasty. He was a big doofus of a boy with no sensitivity or empathy for what I had been through. Making fun of me was great sport for him, and he never considered my feelings, instead seeing me as just an object to ridicule. I don't know if he went out of his way to find me, but when he did, he would walk past and pull off my hat. Embarrassed, I would be forced to go chasing after it. I got pretty good at catching it before it flew too far away.

I tried not to let him get to me, but Tess was not so forgiving. Things came to a head one day while we were in a covered hallway outside the classrooms. Greg ran by, slapped the back of my head, and, as usual, knocked off my hat.

That was the last straw.

Tess took off after him, chasing him down. When she got to him, she punched him in the face. She punched him again and again. She split his lip and bloodied his nose. It caused quite a commotion, and

Tess was sent to the principal's office. The principal told her that he understood why she had punched the boy but that she couldn't be beating up kids at school, and that in the future she should come to him and let him deal with it. Tess was still in a high temper and told him no, if anyone else picked on me she would beat them up, too. He shook his head and told her that the next time it happened, she would be suspended. Tess let him know she understood but said that would be fine with her.

Tess's mom later arrived and surely got an earful from the principal as well, but she told Tess that a suspension for defending me would be well worth it. As the days went on, I think the boy's embarrassment was greatly enhanced by the fact that he'd been beaten up by a girl. Tess and I thought it just made the whole incident funnier. No one ever messed with me again.

Having cancer didn't change the fiery dynamic between my brother and me, but possibly exacerbated it. We fought like cats and dogs. I had five years on him and, up until he reached middle school, I could wrestle him to the ground, where I would sit on him, pinning his arms behind his back. My mother, driven to the brink of insanity by our continual bouts, one day had had enough.

"Sit down and shut up!" she shouted. "I don't want to hear another word from either one of you." We flopped into our chairs, obeying her call for a cease-fire. My mother went on making our lunch: Danish-style open-faced sandwiches — leverpostej (liver pâté) on pumpernickel — which she placed in front of each of us on the table. Then giving me a stern look, she said, enunciating every word, "Do not provoke him."

Steven looked at me as if to say, "Ha ha, you can't get me now." It was just too easy. The minute she looked away, I made a face. To my great satisfaction, I could tell I had got him, but what I hadn't counted on was what came next. Steven picked up his sandwich and hurled it across the table, aiming directly at my face. I ducked. It missed and hit the side of the refrigerator with a smack. The room went silent for a moment as Steven and I stared at each other, then we burst into laughter. My mother turned, ready to read us the riot act, when she saw my dog Fefe standing at the base of the refrigerator, hardly able to contain her excitement as this tasty treat slowly slid down the refrigerator. Mom's face melted and she roared in laughter alongside us.

I cannot begin to imagine what my mother endured during those years. I'm sure there were people who called her a saint, and not because of her frequent use of the word Jesus, but because of her unrelenting, selfless fortitude. She laughed at any reference to sainthood because of the irony in that. She was tough — no-nonsense tough — and often cursed the situation at hand. If Steven or I spun a tale, she would listen with an interested "Oh yeah?" look on her face, allow us to finish, and then remark in her Danish-Argentinian accent, "Don't be a dumb-ass." She was quick-witted, always with a ready punch line followed by a wink in response to life's little jokes. She listened to Julio Iglesias, Herb Alpert and the Tijuana Brass Band, and Tony Orlando and Dawn (and still does). The song lyric "Tie a yellow ribbon 'round the ole oak tree," — ugh — is forever embedded in my brain.

After my amputation, my mother understood immediately that if I was ever going to fulfill any of my dreams, I would need to be self-sufficient. Fortunately for me, my remaining left hand was my dominant hand. Having this advantage was a big help, though it still took time and a multitude of struggles before I realized that to perform any task with one hand, I first needed to learn how to secure an object. For example, buttering a piece of toast: there are two ways to go about this. First, you could lay the bread on a cloth to semi-hold it in place, then gently spread the butter on the bread by applying just a light pressure. Or, without using a cloth, you could hold the knife with your fingers and, using your thumb to hold the bread in place, pull the knife across the toast toward your thumb.

Once I realized it was about the balance or pressure required to hold an object steady, this made things easier. I began thinking about performing different simple tasks and figuring out how to go about balancing things with one arm, or even using my body if I needed to create a sort of leverage. I already knew that without the counterweight of a second arm, maintaining my balance was very important to my posture. After discovering this technique for using one arm to do things, it didn't take long for me to relearn how to live my life one-handed.

I began tying my shoes again, buttoning my blouses, zipping my pants, erasing mistakes, making my own open-faced sandwiches, and riding my bike. It's not to say that I no longer struggled, but when I did and my aunt Nanna or my grandmother Mormor were watching, they wanted to jump in and help me, but my mother wisely wouldn't let them. I didn't want help, I wanted to be capable of doing things on my own, and my mother knew this.

The most challenging part of learning a new task was, unfortunately, the phantom pains. My body's normal impulse was still to use two arms to reach for objects, pull up my pants, or even just fill a glass of water. My brain didn't understand that one arm was missing, so when I would attempt a task, my brain sent the signal to use both hands. And when it reached my missing arm, a gut-wrenching pain would shoot out through the nonexistent arm with a pulse back to my brain like I was being stabbed with a knife over and over in the phantom limb. This caused me to drop things or even fall to my knees. The pain would come on so quickly, it literally took my breath away and rendered me completely useless.

That's when my mother would step in and hold me tight or massage my neck until the muscle finally loosened the grip on my nerves, and she would soothe me as I cried in agony.

Over time, I figured out that I could control the phantom pains. Not the actual pain, but my phantom hand. I could imagine it — feel it — opening and closing slowly. My entire arm and hand would have a tingling sensation, like when you've sat on your foot and it falls asleep. The sensation was not as bad if I could just anticipate the phantom pain coming on. It was as if I could direct its energy to operate my phantom hand, and this lessened the pain. Moving forward and accepting new challenges became much easier without having to deal with the crippling pain of my phantom arm.

Another person who was instrumental in my recovery was a wonderful nurse, Gail Perin, who began the idea of home visits. At that time there was no such thing as a pediatric oncology nurse. Children with cancer were typically kept in the hospital for the duration of their treatment. Dr. Ablin and nurse Gail understood that children would fare much better if allowed to return home and live life as normally as possible during treatment. Gail was a fierce advocate of no-nonsense communication with the primary caretaker. "This is no time for self-pity," she would tell my mother. "Your child is alive now and in the fight of her life, and she needs you to be strong." Gail believed mothers needed to be fully educated about cancer — how to read lab results, recognize warning signs, and pay attention to their own instincts regarding their child's status. Chemotherapy could wreak havoc with a child's immune system, and make the slightest infection potentially life threatening. Mothers had to be prepared to demand care from doctors and hospital emergency rooms that were likely to dismiss a fever as non-critical. Mothers could not afford to defer responsibility. They had to step up, and Gail trumpeted this message unapologetically.

Together, my mother and nurse Gail were a formidable team. I saw in them unwavering strength and tenacious perseverance. I drew on their strength during the tough times.

About a year into my treatment, Dr. Ablin and Nurse Gail realized that I was handling the loss of a limb and the chemotherapy regimen better than most children, and they commented on it. They saw that I had a strong sense of self and a positive outlook on my life going forward. And I was engaged at school.

It was true. I even went to all the school dances. I remember a blond boy with a bowl haircut who wore thick black-rimmed glasses. He was the only one who approached me to dance. It was typically toward the end of the evening, and he always chose a slow dance, so I knew he liked me rather than pitied me. He was very sweet, and I liked his shy, polite manners.

A psychiatrist who worked with Dr. Ablin and Gail thought my positive attitude might be infectious and contacted my mother to see if I would be willing to join his support group for children fighting cancer. My mother agreed to ask me about it, but said the decision was entirely up to me. I don't believe I was told the purpose of the invitation. I only knew they wanted me to sit around and talk about my cancer. So I declined. The psychiatrist continued asking my mother, though, and after being promised that I didn't have to talk about myself, I could just sit and listen, I agreed to go.

The support group meeting took place in a conference room on a dock in scenic Tiburon, with sweeping views of the San Francisco Bay. The scenery, however, did nothing to mask the depressing hour that followed. I hated it! It was one giant pity party. I understood the difficulties, the trauma, the mental and physical pain that each and every one of us was going through, but they weren't even the slightest bit happy to still be alive?

I blurted this out when I had the chance to speak. "You are all alive, isn't that better than the alternative...?" Everyone looked at me with tears running down their faces. One boy even responded with, "How could you even ask such a question?" I was so confused.

By the time it was over, I was so upset with everyone feeling sorry for themselves, I couldn't wait to get out of there. I felt the emotions welling up in me, so I bolted for the door the moment the psychiatrist said, "This has been..."

Making my way through the maze of boardwalks as quickly as I could, I reached the parking lot where my mother was waiting. She had the passenger window open and could see the look on my face.

"Let's get outta here. I am never going back there again, and you can't make me!" The words tumbled out of my mouth as I climbed into the car. The psychiatrist called us a few more times, but my mother fully backed my decision to not participate.

I later realized that what I had with my family and friends was therapy, and it filled the role of a support group. Support, whether from family, friends, a teacher, your doctor, or a formal support group, is very important. It doesn't matter — you just need to figure out which works best for you, and it can be all of them. The most important thing is to try, so you can know what feels truly supportive to you.

In retrospect, I also didn't understand very well what a support group was. It scared me. It scared me because I knew death was the alternative to what I was going through. I did not want to face that, it wasn't an option in my mind. In this group, the discussion for most of the other kids that day was about facing that option. Maybe if I had attended on another day, the topic might have been different. I realize now, I should have given it another chance. Maybe I could have even helped.

At the time, my therapy came in the form of water. I had always loved to swim, and my mother knew this exercise would be crucial to my physical and mental recovery. Several times a week, she made the 40-minute round-trip drive to Lucas Valley to visit one of her Argentinian friends who had a pool with a diving board. Steven and I would swim and play in the water while they sat under an umbrella, speaking in rapid Spanish and drinking maté, an herbal tea.

The experience was initially good for all of us, but, over time, my mother's work as a seamstress was increasing and it was getting more and more difficult for her to find the time to take us for a swim. She knew that it would be the best thing for everyone to sell the house at 48 Frances Avenue and move to a house with a pool. In addition, there were reminders of my father everywhere at our current home, and the large yard required constant care. It was time for a fresh start somewhere else.

An opportunity came through one of Mormor's salon clients who happened to casually mention, while Mormor was setting her hair, that she was going to be putting her house on the market. The house was located nearby in Larkspur, and it had a pool. Once my mother saw it, she declared it perfect. There she would be able to expand her seamstress business and, while sewing, watch me swim as often as I wanted. When I found out about this plan, I did not think it was perfect. I was furious. My father had built with his own hands so many of the features that made our house unique, and it would break my heart to lose touch with this part of him. In my sentimentality, I didn't understand my mother's decision. She was practical and saw that we needed to move forward as a family.

My mother bought the house in March of 1975, but it needed sprucing up so we didn't move in until June. This turned out to be a blessing, as it allowed us all to gradually make the move emotionally and physically. Since the new house was only a couple of blocks from our current home, Steven and I would often go over after school, bringing some of our belongings one trip at a time. Afterward we could swim and play. On one occasion, we decided to stay the night. We threw our sleeping bags down in the living room on top of some atrocious yellow-green shag carpeting and snuggled in. Within seconds we were back on our feet, slapping at our bodies. There, in the dim glow of a flashlight, we were horrified to see the rug hopping mad with hundreds of fleas frantically chomping at their first meal in weeks.

My mother and Nanna worked on the house nearly every day for months. That shag carpet was the first thing to go. They scrubbed, painted, and hung grass wallpaper throughout. Once our Danish modern furniture and belongings were in place, it looked and felt familiarly like home. Flowers were planted, and we brought over the large birdhouse my father had built and gave it a place of prominence in the backyard. The kidney-shaped pool had a Jacuzzi attached, and we were in the pool on a daily basis all that summer.

Chapter 4

~ A Promise Kept ~

Over the two-year course of my chemotherapy, I got monthly chest X-rays, both a front view and a side view to check for any possible spread of my cancer. The doctor would then compare the new X-rays with the old ones to make sure there was no sign of an emerging tumor.

Occasionally my mother brought Steven along, and Dr. Ablin inevitably had something up his sleeve to lighten the mood, not just for me, but the whole family. Steven was a towhead like I had been before losing my hair. One day when we came into the office, Dr. Ablin greeted us and remarked, "Steven! What a wonderful head of red hair you have."

Steven regarded him suspiciously and said, "My hair's not red."

To which Dr. Ablin continued the ruse saying, "Oh yes, it's a wonderful fiery head of red hair!"

I could hardly keep from busting up as my brother tried to convince the doctor otherwise. Steven, began to believe that he in fact had red hair, finally went over and checked himself in the mirror. We all had a good laugh.

After two years of treatment with no sign that the cancer had spread, I felt I had made it. I had one last treatment. Believe me, I was counting the days to the end. I was ecstatic. Soon there would be no more pricked fingers, no more IVs, no more nausea, shots, or chemo burns. And at long last my hair would have the opportunity to grow back. My desire for hair wasn't just vanity, it was also for comfort. I can attest that most of our body's heat is lost through our heads. It's amazing how cold you get being bald, and, with my immune system under attack from both the cancer and the chemo, I constantly felt chilled. Despite my gratitude for the hats my mother made, I was ready to never look at or wear another hat again. The anticipation of knowing I would soon have my own hair made me long for it all the more. Just around the corner I would have my old life back. I even proclaimed, "Maybe I'll join the swim team."

"Just one more treatment," said Dr. Ablin, finishing up my weekly chemo. I couldn't believe it. I had basically been given a clean bill of health.

All that final week felt like the last week of school. The anticipation and excitement built. When the day came, I had a big smile on my face as I went in for the final treatment. But Dr. Ablin was not smiling. A couple of days earlier, I had been in for my monthly X-rays and the radiologist had called to say they needed to retake them. I was not concerned; this had happened before because if I moved even a little bit, the X-rays would have to be redone. The new X-ray was examined carefully. Dr. Ablin explained that a small, unusual growth had been detected. Not knowing what it was, they wanted to do surgery because they couldn't take any chances that the cancer had returned.

I felt that this was all a horrible nightmare, a cruel joke, and that my suffering would never end. *How could I come this far only to die anyway?* Even Nurse Gail cried upon hearing the news.

"Well, let's take care of it," I said. Surgery was the only way to confirm if the growth was cancer. I was facing life with a grim determination and not a lot of hope at that moment.

Meantime, my bedstemor (my father's mother) and Anne-Grethe had flown out from Denmark to celebrate the end of my treatment. This would be the first time they would see me with just one arm. My mom told Uncle Jens that the company would have to stay with him until we had gotten through the surgery, and then they could come and stay with us, which I was excited about. It gave me something to look forward to. It had been years since I had seen them.

For this surgery, I checked into the pediatric ward at UCSF (currently known as the UCSF Benioff Children's Hospital). My mother and Uncle Hermann were by my side, each of us fearing the worst but hoping for the best. Doctor Ablin had recommended a surgeon who specializes in pediatric oncology. When he opened me up and located the growth, the doctors were all baffled. The growth didn't look like cancer, it appeared to be just bone. My chemotherapy treatment had been expected to stunt my growth, but this bone in my rib cage had continued to grow an eighth of an inch.

They cut off the small piece and sent it to the lab for testing. I was sewn back together, giving me an additional scar to add to my growing collection, and rolled to the ICU where my mother was anxiously awaiting my return. More X-rays were taken to ensure the bone now aligned with the original — the new image was overlaid on the old for comparison — but it still did not line up. It appeared there remained a suspicious growth. The doctors wanted to schedule yet another surgery, but that would have to wait because while in the hospital, I had caught a cold. I was sent home to recover and try to build up my immune system before I went back under the knife.

A week later, once again the three of us — Uncle Hermann, my mother, and I — arrived at the hospital for surgery. My little brother stayed at home with my aunt Nanna, and my cousin Bruce. Unlike our previous visit, we walked in silence, the gravity of the situation weighing heavily on us. This surgery was going to be more complicated. The surgeon would have to collapse my right lung to get an unobstructed view of the suspicious area. When they rolled me into the operating room, I remember counting backward from 100 as I drifted off. The surgery was long and involved, but they got their unobstructed view and were able to determine that the mass was a non-cancerous nerve growth. They removed it. They had never seen anything like this before, but I guess they didn't see too many twelve-year-olds with one arm either. Before they closed me up and re-inflated my lung, while still in surgery, X-rays were taken to ensure that all of the suspicious growth had been removed.

As I slowly came back to consciousness, I found myself in a large room with five others in the pediatric intensive care unit. There was one poor girl who had a pitiful, high-pitched moan that continued relentlessly all through the night. I could not sleep, and I was in more pain than I had ever been in. My phantom pains were relentless. I didn't want to be there. My immune system was in pretty bad shape, too, and I worried about catching something from the other patients. The girl's moaning did not stop. The other four patients and I were so relieved when the nurses finally rolled her out and said they were taking her to a different room.

In those days, UCSF was not equipped to accommodate the many parents who inevitably wanted to stay with their sick children. Parents like my mother would sleep anywhere they could, often on the hallway floors. Sometimes a room would open up and the nurses would set up cots. Regardless, my mother was constantly there through it all, and that's what mattered. I don't know what I would have done without her reassuring presence.

Now post surgery, having had my lung collapsed and my body cut open a second time within a two-week period, my torso felt like it had been sat on by a large cow. The pressure on my chest was unbearable. I was unable to swallow or cough effectively to dislodge the mucus that kept building up. Despite the drain tube coming out of my chest, the nurse had to come in every few hours and use a long tube to suction the fluid from my throat. I hated being suctioned; it made me gag but brought relief for a few hours. And although I couldn't clear my own throat, the urge to cough was automatic. Even a weak cough stimulated the nerve in my neck, causing stabbing phantom pains and aggravating the soreness in my chest.

Recovery from this latest surgery was not easy. I was in the hospital for days and then convalesced at home for a few weeks. Once I was settled back into our house, Bedstemor and Anne-Grethe were able to come and spend time with us. They helped my mother by cooking some of our Danish favorites. We played cards and other quiet games while I worked on my Danish with them.

Having made it past these scares, I experienced such a sense of relief when I got the green light from Dr. Ablin. Two years of chemotherapy, countless pills, and four surgeries later, it looked like I was finally able to celebrate my survival. I was twelve years old, and the best pronouncement I could hear coming from my doctor was "You're as healthy as anybody else now." These were Dr. Ablin's reassuring words. It was official. I was cancer free, and the first thing I wanted was for Dr. Ablin to make good on a promise. I had been waiting for years to get my ears pierced, but he had wanted me to wait to avoid any possibility of infection.

Dr. Ablin had promised me that if I hung in there, at the end of my treatment he himself would pierce my ears; he wasn't about to let some teenage hack in a jewelry store touch me after all I had been through. I don't think he had ever pierced anyone's ears before, but, as a doctor, surely it couldn't be that hard. On that special day, I was excited but nervous. By this time, I had enough of needles or anything poking me.

Dr. Ablin had me lie down on the same table where I had received my chemotherapy treatment. My heart thumped against my chest as he took his time setting up the earring gun. He was probably trying to figure out how it worked. I wonder now where he even got the earring gun. (Did he borrow one? Did he buy one just for the occasion? He probably did.)

Then this tall Santa Claus–like figure bent over me, squinted, and lingered for an eternity before finally pressing the trigger. Crrr-aaack! That thing exploded like a cannon in my ear. I heard the breaking of cartilage followed by the sensation that my lobe was on fire. My vision narrowed as the proverbial birds twittered around my head. I knew now why he'd had me lie down. After the first ear, I didn't know if I could go through with the second, but, after resting a bit, of course I did. I left that office wearing two gold posts and a smile from ear to ear.

PART TWO:

MY

~VIKING HERITAGE~

'Vikingr' (Vikings) are described as Scandinavian explorers, traders, and warriors who sailed in their longboats far and wide to raid, trade, and explore new lands in search of hope and new opportunities.

∾

Chapter 5

~ Don't Cry For Me, Argentina ~

L ife after treatment was good. It was the last few weeks before
school started in the summer of 1976. We headed out on what
would become our annual family trip, down to stay with the Bollisen's
in Southern California. My mother wanted to be on the road bright and
early. We couldn't figure this out, because it was the opposite of her
daily habit to sleep late. Maybe the idea was to beat the morning
commute into San Francisco. Either way, the drive was always
beautiful down Highway 101. Our first stop was Solvang, a little
Danish-American settlement in the Santa Ynez Valley.

Solvang is a quaint, picturesque town emulating the traditional look
of Denmark with its windmills and Tudor-style buildings with thatched
roofs, not to mention bakeries with delicious pastries. We knew two
families living there, and, unbelievably, they happened to live next door
to each other. One of the families was Danish Argentine, with whom
my mother had attended a Danish boarding school in Argentina.

The other, an older Danish couple along with the wife's sister, had
a large, beautifully manicured garden, just like back in the old country.
The inside of their house, too, was decorated in a way that made us feel

like we were in Denmark. I remember a wood-burning stove in the kitchen. Alfred, the husband, would tightly roll up newspapers, wet them, and hang them to dry. He would use these as a substitute for wooden logs. He would get up bright and early to get the fire started so the stove could both warm the kitchen and boil water for coffee. They also had a large box full of wooden three dimensional puzzles, which I loved. They were amazed at my puzzle-solving skills and said I was one of the only guests who could figure them out. The living room had an old foot-pump organ; my brother and I would play for hours. We would usually stay for several days, helping in the garden and playing games.

Our ties to Denmark have always been strong and, really, the defining characteristic of our family. I know that my ability to survive and thrive comes from my family and our strong connection to our cultural heritage. I'm a first-generation Danish American. My mother, Judith Vibeque Jensen, was born in 1939 on the island of Sjœlland (Zealand) in the town of Slagelse, just west of Copenhagen. Her early childhood was spent under Nazi occupation.

It was a time of intimidation and oppression by the invading force. Blackouts were imposed and evenings were mostly spent in the dark or underground. Although the family made it through the occupation safely, they all knew people who were killed by the Nazis. The Danish resistance movement was extensive, which left the country with a proud legacy after World War II.

Once the war ended, a thirst for a better life led many Danes to emigrate, in our family's case to Argentina. They left with a sense of adventure, enticed by the promise of cheap land and a warmer climate. Among those were my grandparents, Albert and Vibeque Jensen, along with their children John, Judith, and Nanna. Albert's brothers Axel and

Hans had emigrated to Argentina years before, and they told of great business and land opportunities.

Albert was a master pastry chef, certified in techniques from many countries. He felt certain he could find work if he emigrated, and he was able to pay the 1500 kroner required for his family of five to travel to Argentina. He booked passage on a large cargo ship that offered a limited number of cabins to passengers. With few ships going back and forth from Europe to South America, they were lucky to find passage.

The family left Denmark on August 15, 1949, traveling by train to Bordeaux, France, where they boarded the ship. Vibeque and her daughters Judith and Nanna were crowded into a shipboard cabin with fifteen other women, while Albert and John were in a cabin with the men. Rough seas caused many to experience terrible seasickness; unfortunately my Aunt Nanna, little at the time, was one of them and suffered horribly.

A much-needed respite from the rough seas came when they reached Casablanca in Northern Africa and were allowed to disembark. They visited the outdoor market — a riot of colorful fabrics and exotic items for sale — and found it teeming with African vendors hawking their wares. One, wearing a robe and a cylindrical hat, tried to sell them on the latest marvel, a pen that could write in four different colors!

"Keep on walking," said Vibeque in Danish. "It's just a bunch of shit."

Without hesitation, the man called after them in fluent, and heavily accented Danish. "It's not a bunch of shit. It's a very good pen!"

Vibeque and the girls were dumbstruck, mouths hanging open, while Albert roared with laughter. "I didn't think there was anything that could shut you up," he said.

Casablanca was the final destination for a good many passengers, so the family was upgraded to a room of their own. From there they sailed down along the coast of Africa and across to Brazil, where they enjoyed a brief stop in Rio de Janeiro. My mother will never forget her sense of awe when she saw the enormous statue of Christ the Redeemer on the hillside as they sailed into the bay.

They continued south, completing their journey after 29 days at sea, arriving in Buenos Aires. This was at the height of the Perón era, a vital and exciting time in Argentina. In later years my mother and her sister would break into a melodramatic, tongue-in-cheek version of "Don't Cry for Me, Argentina" whenever the old days were brought up.

Albert's older brother Axel had made the same trek a couple of years earlier, and he had convinced his younger brother he would prosper in such a large country, even persuading Albert to send money in advance for a parcel of land that they would develop together. Axel was waiting to meet them at the ship's port when they docked. He was driving a rickety old pickup truck. Judith and Nanna joined their mother and squeezed in up front, while John and his father rode in the back of the truck with the luggage.

The family of five bunked with Axel's family of four for a while. That is, until Albert realized that Axel had not bought land but seemed to be using the money to keep his own grocery business afloat. The dream of a partnership and of buying a home of their own was no longer possible, so there was a bitter parting of ways.

Not knowing Spanish, it was difficult for Albert to hold down a steady job. Through networking with other Danes, he was able to find odd jobs. Vibeque was upset that there was no Danish-language school available for the children and began homeschooling them. These were busy years, with three young children and many moves as they continued to try to find work.

Several years and a dozen moves later, Albert found a job in a bakery working for a pastry chef from the French region of Alsace-Lorraine. They settled in Moreno, a suburb of Buenos Aires, where they rented a small house and the kids were allowed to take in a stray kitten.

The creature seemed healthy at first, but it lost control of its hind legs until the poor thing could only drag itself along the ground. The vet diagnosed the kitten with polio, which would require constant care. My grandparents determined it would be best to simply put him out of his misery. So on their father's instruction, John and his sister Judith put the cat in a burlap sack with a large rock, tied it with rope, walked a few miles down to the river, and threw him in. It was heartbreaking, and the children were devastated.

A week later, a faint mewing brought Judith to the front door. There on the dusty walk, she found the kitten. Somehow he had escaped the sack, paddled to shore, and made his way home, dragging himself by his two front legs, leaving a trail in the dirt. Judith rushed out and picked him up, cradling him to her chest. "I'm so sorry. I'm so sorry," she sobbed. After making such a journey, there was no argument: this kitten deserved to live. Judith insisted she take on his care, and she devoted herself to the job. She cuddled and carried him everywhere, making sure he was comfortable and safe. Unfortunately, he only lived a week, then passed away in his sleep. My mother vowed she would never hurt another living creature again.

After years of homeschooling her children, Vibeque learned of a Danish boarding school a few hours to the north. Judith, twelve, and her brother John, thirteen, were sent there to further their education.

Judith was painfully homesick and unhappy. She met an equally miserable girl named Ursula, and together they plotted to run away. To earn money to finance their escape, Judith found that she could charge other students a small fee to eat their polenta. Students were required to clean their plates, and most despised the lumpy polenta that was served. Word spread quickly, and students would nonchalantly stop by to say hi while stealthily sliding their polenta onto my mother's plate. She was able to quickly save a stash of money.

When Judith and Ursula determined the time was right, they packed a few belongings and waited patiently until they were sure no one was awake. At around two in the morning, when the school was quiet, they gathered their things and tiptoed out. It was a moonless night; the darkness made it difficult to find their way. About halfway down the mile-long driveway, Ursula broke down in fear, turned around, and ran back. Left by herself, Judith continued on, eventually making it all the way down to the entry gate. That's when it dawned on her that the nearest town was miles away and she had no idea which way to turn to get there. Defeated, she realized she had no choice but to go back.

The next day, no one at the school had an inkling of what the girls had attempted to do. The two had succeeded in scaring themselves into a change of attitude. Going forward, they tried to fit in and find some enjoyment in their studies. Judith was especially talented in sewing class and excelled there. Her instructors noticed how advanced her skills were and taught her dressmaking techniques beyond the level of the class. Because of her love of sewing, she made it through the rest of that school year, but she did not return when the next term started.

Always in search of a better opportunity, the family moved again and again until landing a job on an estancia, a South American cattle ranch, where Vibeque became the cook.   By this time, they had all become proficient in Spanish, but they had absolutely no experience in rural living. The transition to life on the estancia was difficult.

Initially, the family lived in the main house until the caretaker's cottage was finished.   Vibeque was not amused to discover that "finished" meant most of the rooms had dirt floors requiring a frequent hosing down to keep the dust in check. To access the only toilet, one had to exit the house and enter the toilet room from the yard. This was common for the regional architecture in South America at the time. When it was cold, they would use copper bed warmers with hot stones from the fire to warm their beds before settling in.

While the family worked the estancia, Albert continued with his job at a bakery in Buenos Aires, commuting by train each day. Vibeque's main duty was to feed the crew of gauchos who lived and worked on the ranch.

The kids mounted horses for the first time in their lives and helped to move cattle.   Horses quickly became an integral part of their childhood, providing not just amusement, but their primary means of transportation. John and Judith now attended a local school a couple of miles away, and they rode horses to and from school; on days when the weather was inclement, they would hook a horse to a two-wheeled buggy and ride in style. The years they spent at the estancia were some of the happiest and most stable of their childhood.

After the unpleasant experience at the Danish boarding school, Vibeque was happy to see that all of her children enjoyed attending the local schools and that they made many friends. Judith continued with sewing classes, becoming an excellent seamstress and tailor at a young age. When she finished her formal schooling at age fourteen, she was able to get a job with a tailor who worked primarily for foreign diplomats. Here she perfected the skills that would serve her well in the future. She couldn't possibly know how these skills would someday keep her family afloat through unforeseeable circumstances.

As my mother grew into her later teen years, she began attending parties and social events. The local Scandinavian and Italian clubs held regular dances. Nanna wanted to go too, but Judith rarely agreed to take her — until Nanna learned that she could barter for the privilege. Around this time, a frog had begun showing up in the outhouse. No sooner had my mother sat down, pants around her ankles, when out would come a deep crrr-ooak. In a corner or behind the bowl she'd find it — blinking, bulbous eyes, greeting her with a grotesquely inflated throat. "Naaaaaanna!" she'd cry.

Her little sister would come skipping along wearing a broad grin. "Can I come with you to the dance?" she'd say.

"Yes, yes! Just get it out of here!"

Nanna would reach down and scoop up the frog, petting its head, allowing a leg or two to dangle from between her fingers. To this day, we all wonder if it wasn't Nanna who put the frogs in the outhouse to begin with.

The dances were an important part of Judith and Nanna's upbringing. Here they learned popular dances of the time such as the tango, waltz, samba, cha-cha, merengue, and paso doble. The girls were outgoing and fun loving, and the dances were well-attended community events — the glue that held the young people together in a way that we can't imagine today.

My mother's family stayed in Argentina for twelve adventure-filled years. My grandparents had what my mother called "a gypsy spirit," enthusiastically embracing new experiences and opportunities. When they received a letter from a friend living in the United States that included a job offer at a bakery for Albert, they jumped on it.

It was 1961, and the job entailed moving to Minnesota to work with a fellow baker who my grandfather had worked with back in Denmark. The children were not happy to be uprooted again, and John, who was 22 years old, decided to stay in Argentina. Vibeque was ill, so my mother also stayed behind with her in Argentina.

My Aunt Nanna, barely sixteen, accompanied Albert on the move to Minnesota. From Buenos Aires, they flew Aerolíneas Argentinas on a 1958 DC-4 — a four-engine, propeller-driven plane with an unpressurized cabin — via Santiago, Chile, over the Andes Mountains. My aunt remembers her ears getting so plugged, the flight attendant had to continually supply her with chewing gum. They stopped in Lima, Peru, with another stop in Panama before arriving an exhausting 24 hours later in Miami, Florida.

When they finally arrived, they were both famished and looked around for a place to eat. With neither able to speak a lick of English, they determined a nearby pizzeria would be their best bet, Italian being similar to Spanish.

When Albert ordered "Dos pizzas, por favor," the man behind the counter simply stared back at him and shrugged. Albert then raised two fingers. "Dos pizzas," he repeated. A light bulb went on in the man's eyes. He nodded, took their money, and after several minutes presented them with two full American-size, 16-inch pies. This was way too much food, but they ate heartily, as it would be another two-day bus ride before they reached their final destination.

The driver boarded the bus only after everyone had found a seat. He mumbled something over a microphone which they did not understand, he started the engine, and they were off.

They had bounced along route 95 for nearly two hours when the bus abruptly veered off the road and came to a rest in front of a small building. A neon light of a pint of beer with a frothy head blinked at them from its window. The driver opened the door, got up, and left the bus. "I think it's a rest stop," Albert told Nanna. "Stay here." Nanna watched as her father followed the driver into the bar.

Twenty minutes alone on the bus felt like hours to Nanna, and she was fuming by the time her father resurfaced. "How could you leave me here?" she demanded. "I had no money, no one to talk to, and no idea of when you were coming back!" Albert took the tongue-lashing, and, when the bus stopped again a few hours later, he handed Nanna a few dollars before disappearing again to have another beer.

Across the aisle, a Spanish-speaking gentleman noticed the abandoned look on my aunt's face and struck up a conversation. He was kind, but, more importantly, he understood English. He explained how much time she would have to stretch her legs, use the bathroom, or get something to eat before the bus left again. The nearly 2,000-mile bus trip to Minnesota would have been excruciating for my aunt without this man's generosity and kindness.

They found an apartment outside Minneapolis. Albert went to work at the bakery while Nanna set up the household. She couldn't wait to share with her sister the new experiences she was having. She especially knew her sister would like the Murphy bed that unfolded cleverly from the wall, and the fact that you could buy ice cream by the half gallon. Once things were in place, Vibeque and Judith were sent for. It was a painful journey for my grandmother who, shortly after arriving, had her gallbladder removed along with 67 gallstones — a wonder that she was forevermore linked to like a badge of honor. Ask anyone in our family, "How many gallstones did Mormor have removed?" and they would answer without hesitation, "Sixty-seven." Everyone loved to marvel over this accomplishment.

A new opportunity led them to leave Minnesota for Iowa, but after a time they realized that Iowa held little advantage. Life in the Midwest was proving to be unbearably cold, especially after living in Argentina for so many years. My mother said, "If we have to deal with this cold, we might as well be living back in Denmark." That's when the family decided to make their way west. Albert was able to find a job in sunny San Diego through the Danish-language newspaper called Bien.

Now they had sun, but Judith still missed the social life and cultural connection she had enjoyed in Argentina. The perfect place would offer both decent weather and a Scandinavian club. After some research, she found out there was a Scandinavian club in San Francisco. She was 23 now and able to drive. She had become her parents' driver and primary translator, as she had quickly picked up English. More than that, she had a can-do attitude and was determined to move. The family realized that they should move together, or she would be moving without them. Thankfully, once again the newspaper Bien came through with a job opportunity in the beautiful town of Sausalito, just north of San Francisco.

Chapter 6

~ Some Things Are Meant to Be ~

My father, Albert Rolighed Larsen, was born in 1938 at a place called Salgjerhøj, the highest point on a small island in the northern part of Denmark's Jutland peninsula.   Morsø is only 142 square miles and is surrounded by a shallow sound called the Limfjord. He was born to Laurits and Maren Larsen, the fourth of five children, the oldest being his only sister Anne-Grethe, then two brothers Karl and Søren, and a younger brother Jens.

At Salgjerhøj, my grandparents owned and ran a Danish kro, which was historically a stopover for the king's men.   A kro is a type of upscale inn, its origins dating back to the 13th century.   King Erik, looking for an easier way to feed and lodge his men during their travels, decreed that about every 30 kilometers, equivalent to a day's journey on horseback or via carriage, there should be built a decent inn for feeding and housing travelers.   As an incentive for local businessmen to build and run a kro, the king would grant them a special royal license that permitted them, free of tax, to brew beer, distill spirits, and bake bread, both for their own use and to sell to the public.

This was a powerful incentive, and up kros sprouted. They tended to be charming abodes with half-timbered walls and thatched roofs, beckoning with lanterns and the wafting smell of cooking food. A kro quickly became important to both travelers and the local community around it, as it provided a practical and festive location for gatherings and special occasions.

My father and his younger brother Jens were both born during the years the family lived and worked in the kro. Their kro was set in a beautiful location overlooking the fjord on a hill dotted with trees. It sat on the highest point of the island, 89 meters (or about 292 feet) above sea level. In many ways, they had a quiet and idyllic life before World War II and the Nazi invasion.

Due to its strategic location, the island was desirable to the Germans when they occupied Denmark. They commandeered the kro and used it as a command base for their local operations. My father's family was forced to give up their personal rooms on the second floor to the soldiers and provide them with meals, do their laundry, and clean up after them. As they waited on the Nazis, the parents, somewhat schooled in the German language and used to hearing German spoken by tourists, overheard information important to the Danish Resistance. Bravely, at great personal risk, they passed along the secret information.

In addition to providing information to the Resistance, my grandmother Maren found small ways to express her disapproval of the Nazis via subtle sabotage. One day while she was preparing a meal for them, a little white goat named Mr. Svensen jumped up onto the stove and began eating food from the pan, slobbering and chomping, bits falling out of his mouth. Maren shooed him away, but not before enjoying the disrespectful corruption of their dinner. She served that meal with particular satisfaction.

In 1945, the Allies bombed Salgjerhøj, destroying a portion of the kro and forcing everyone to evacuate. Fortunately, the family was forewarned (thanks to the Danish underground) and they packed up during the night and left before the bombing. They never did rebuild, but to this day a rectangular stone column stands as a landmark of our family's kro.

After leaving the kro, they settled on a small dairy and pig farm in a nearby town. It was a relief for the family to be out from under the yoke of the German occupation. The times were difficult financially, especially during the postwar years with so many children to care for, and so my father Albert was apprenticed to a mason and studied horticulture. This would shape his future endeavors as he found his natural ability while working with stone and landscaping.

Opportunities were limited in Denmark, especially for four sons from a small farm, and so my father, at the age of 21, came to the United States on a work visa. He went to work for a distant cousin, a devout farmer in Minnesota, who wouldn't let him milk the cows on Sundays due to religious observance. When my father one day took pity on a cow with an engorged udder and milked it, his employer erupted in fury, spewing out religious admonitions. My frustrated father shook his head and retorted, "Cows don't know it's Sunday!" As the two men couldn't come to an agreement on the morality of cow milking on Sundays, Albert visited a local job placement office where he found a temporary position in Ohio. After Ohio, he was happy to take a job in Woodland, California, where he enjoyed working for six months until his visa ran out and he returned to Denmark.

Under the requirements of his visa, Albert had to remain in Denmark for eight months before returning to the US. He came back via Ontario, Canada, where he met up with a friend, Eric, also from Morsø in Denmark. Eric had purchased a car, and together they drove to Edmonton, Alberta, to work on a dairy farm. Eric and Albert had been childhood friends whose siblings were married, Eric's brother to Albert's sister.

Five months later, Albert left the dairy farm and worked briefly at the Butchart Gardens in Vancouver before making his return to Woodland, California. One of the advantages to living in Woodland was that it wasn't too far from San Francisco and the Scandinavian Club Saturday Night Social.

This was where their lives intersected. Two nights after arriving in Sausalito, my mother and Nanna attended the Scandinavian Club Saturday Night Social. It must have been destiny that the girls showed up in their high heels and dancing dresses on that cool autumn evening. They were so happy to be back in their element, meeting other Danes, socializing together at long tables, dancing again — and were attracting a lot of attention.

"That guy keeps looking at you," said Nanna, leaning into her sister.

Judith glanced down the table in the direction of Nanna's tilted head. "Nah, you can have him. He's not my type." Then a gentleman's hand reached out, and she was off to the dance floor. Nanna watched her sister dance for a few moments before, turning, she found herself looking into the face of the same young man she had just been discussing.

He asked if she would take a turn on the dance floor; she accepted, and afterward he offered to buy her a drink. Nanna was only eighteen at the time, so she replied, "I don't drink, but you can ask my sister, she does." Nanna knew that this young man was really interested in her sister Judith, and she wanted to steer him back that way.

So, Nanna lured my mother back to the bar, where my father was waiting. He promptly bought her a drink, and they began to chat. Initially my mother was not sure about this farm boy from Morsø. But, by the end of the evening, he had convinced her to give him her phone number. He called her the next day to set up their first date.

My parents had begun their lives back in Denmark a mere 139 miles apart, but they traveled over 16,000 miles collectively to find each other at that dance. I think some things are just meant to be. They eloped eight months after the dance, marrying in a private ceremony in Reno. Her parents held a reception for family and friends in Sausalito upon their return. Of course her father made a spectacular wedding cake. And so, across the bay from San Francisco, they settled in to married life.

My mother worked as a seamstress in a small boutique in Tiburon near the bakery where her father was a baker. My father got a job working as a mason for another Dane he knew in the area, and they moved into a small apartment perched on the hillside in Mill Valley. There they were very happy, and soon after getting married they discovered that I was on the way.

Only a few months passed before another wedding took place, this one at the Lutheran Church in Novato. My future uncle Hermann waited anxiously for his bride-to-be — my dad was almost half an hour late delivering Nanna to the ceremony. My mother, a good seven months pregnant, was also full of anticipation for her sister's wedding.

Nanna was breaking from tradition by marrying outside the Danish community, but everyone forgave her because Hermann was such a great catch. Hermann was German and had immigrated to the United States in his early twenties to attend Cal Poly State University.

I wasn't due for another six weeks, but I guess News Year's Eve 1963 was when I was destined to enter this world. New Year's Eve would always be my night. According to the New York City Police Department, it was the drunkest Times Square New Year's Eve crowd ever on record. Across the nation, Americans threw off their sorrow from the recent death of President John F. Kennedy — assassinated just a month earlier — by partying hard. In California, my mother lay holding me swaddled in a hospital blanket as a new year was ushered in. It was a time when America was looking for its path forward with uncertain footsteps. It was a time of turmoil, when we sought to find our strength and resilience. It was into this generation I was born, and so I have always believed that you can't take the good without the bad.

Marin General Hospital is 6,000 miles from Denmark. Immediately following my birth, my father could not contain his excitement and ran down to Western Union to send a telegram home to the family overseas. I am not sure if it was the emotion of the moment or the realization that he had no name to write down, so he chose Anne-Grethe, his only sister's name. For a middle name, he tacked on Rolighed, the name of the original family farm on Morsø, a name that everyone on his side of the family carried. It means "tranquil" or "easygoing." Later in high school, my girlfriends would bring my middle name up at parties as an icebreaker, especially when meeting boys. Everyone would get a good laugh out of it.

When my mom found out that my dad had sent a telegram naming me, she was livid. It wasn't the name she objected to, but rather, not being consulted in the naming of her own child. So as a compromise, my mother chose Sylvia after a childhood friend from Argentina, and they agreed to keep Rolighed as my middle name. Unfortunately, no one told Aunt Anne-Grethe in time, and she rushed out to have a silver spoon made, forged in the shape of a grandfather clock and engraved in my honor:

Anne-Grethe Rolighed Larsen

December 31, 1963

Tuesday 4:30am

2.8 kg

48 cm

I still keep that spoon in a drawer.

My parents were loving and proud. I was a happy, chubby, towheaded baby, and my parents could not wait to share their joy with the family. When I was six months old, they brought me back to Denmark to introduce me to all the relatives. It was a month of parties and social gatherings, as the family connections were extensive in Copenhagen and on Morsø. This set the stage for a lifetime of close relationships with family far away. Separated, yet together. The bonds of blood and culture are indeed strong in our extended family.

Chapter 7

~ 48 Frances Avenue ~

Back in my very early childhood, approaching my first birthday, I teetered out onto the deck that hung suspended over the steep, wooded hillside of our Mill Valley apartment and climbed up on the railing. If my parents needed one last push to buy a home that would be safe for a baby, this was it. My mother, a resourceful woman, spoke to her previous employer at the boutique and was able to borrow $2,000 for a down payment for a home of their own. We moved to Larkspur, buying a two-bedroom, one-story house on Frances Avenue. My father was starting his own landscaping business, and Larkspur was centrally located in Marin County, which was an ideal location.

Marin had begun primarily as a weekend playground for wealthy San Franciscans. Many of the small "townships" were comprised of quaint little cottages and grand mansions. The railroad barons and captains of industry built large estates. Once the Golden Gate Bridge was constructed in the 1930s, the population expanded as it became possible to live in Marin and work in San Francisco. By the 1960s, Marin had become a much sought-after area to live in, with its natural beauty, majestic Mt Tamalpais, and proximity to San Francisco.

My mother, with her flair for style, decorated our new home with modern Danish furniture and kept it immaculate. Outside, our home was a reflection of my father's talents as a landscape designer and mason. He and my mom collected fieldstones in Sonoma that he used to build retaining walls and stairways throughout the property. He built walkways, a large brick patio with a giant built-in barbecue, a deck with built-in seating, a trellis, and terraces. A beautiful long curving Danish slat-style bench overlooked the fish pond and grass area below. To house all of his equipment and multiple trucks, he built a huge garage.

We were surrounded by a joyous group of family and friends made up mostly of our Danish Argentine community. If we weren't gathering at one of our homes for an evening of festivities, or simply playing cards, we would be holding picnics out in the redwoods.

I can remember many nights in which the children, who were supposed to be sleeping, instead spent the evening jumping on beds and peeking around corners to watch the festivities. With my cousins Bruce and Alan, I saw the adults dancing the tango, the paso doble, the merengue — usually as couples, but if the men were not obliging, that didn't stop the women. They would pair up and carry on without missing a beat. The crowd switched seamlessly between Danish and Spanish as they laughed and danced the night away. Our parents would eventually gather up our limp bodies and carry us off to cars, careful not to wake us as they took us home to be tucked into bed.

Several times a year, we headed up to Little Switzerland in Sonoma for live polka music. Little Switzerland was a European dance hall with live bands and accordion music. A grassy field out back featured rows of large picnic tables where traditional, European beer hall food was served.

After a hearty meal, the adults would let us kids join them on the dance floor, and they would attempt to teach us to dance. It was a family affair, with all generations enjoying a good time together.

Another favorite place was Samuel P. Taylor State Park, nestled among the giant redwoods on the western edge of Marin County along Lagunitas Creek. Our adventures began the moment we jumped out of our cars. The adults would begin the Argentine-style BBQ and heat water for their maté. The tables were decked with cloths and set for a sit-down meal. As the adults socialized around the fire, the children ran down to the enchanting babbling brook that ran through the park. There we scrambled over rocks imagining we were pirate explorers, searching for treasure. When the weather was really hot, our parents took us down to the swimming hole for a dip in the cool water. A log would become our boat for a journey into the deepest part of the pond.

The adults always gathered in a circle of folding chairs and passed the yerba maté, the tea that they brewed in the traditional Argentinian style. To make it, leaves were packed into a hollow gourd and covered with boiling water. A metal straw with a sieve was inserted, and the beverage was shared by passing the gourd around the circle of friends. Additional hot water was added as the gourd made its way around. This was a ritual that appeared to be very special, so when I eventually tried it, I was shocked to find the maté bitter and unpleasant, but in our family, the tradition continues.

A trip to Samuel P. Taylor State Park was always on the list when family came from Denmark. I loved it when relatives and friends visited because it was just another excuse to have a party or visit the museums and the Japanese Tea Garden in Golden Gate Park. If the weather wasn't cooperating for a picnic, we would bundle up and hike through Muir Woods and show off the hills of the Marin Headlands and the views of San Francisco.

In so many ways, my early childhood was a joyous and carefree one. Our neighborhood was filled with children to play with. Across the street from our house lived a large Italian family, the Nichelinis. There was Kimmy, whom I adored. She was several years older than me, but the youngest in her family. She had one older brother, Kevin, who teased us relentlessly, plus three older sisters. I was always impressed with the huge galley kitchen in their house. It had an island that divided the cooking area from the dining area, with a built-in, wood-fired grill constructed of red brick with an old keystone arched opening leading up into the chimney. On the other side sat a long table. Every so often they would invite me to dinner, and when I was very small they would sit me at the center of the table on a tall stool with a big cushion. I spoke primarily Danish, since that was what my family spoke at home, and at the end of the meal I would say, "Tak for mad" (Thank you for the food). At first they thought I was asking for more food, but when I declined all of their offerings, they finally realized that I was done and just needed help off my stool.

Eventually, Kimmy learned some Danish. When one day I showed up at her doorstep without any shoes saying "sko og strømper," she knew to run back to my mom and tell her that Sylvia needs her "sko og strømper." My mother, puzzled at why the neighbor girl was asking for my shoes and socks, finally went and got them for her, and Kimmy brought them back to me so we could go out and play.

Next to the Nichelinis lived the Freezes, with Jody, my age, and her older sister Dana. Midway down the block was an Irish family, the Murphys, with two boys and two girls who organized most of our block's games, and the Bakers who lived next door, with two older boys and one girl, Sally. Our games were joined by another dozen kids from around the neighborhood. Most evenings we would play capture the flag, hide-and-seek, or kick the can. Besides Danish, I had become fluent in Spanish because of my family's sojourn in Argentina and now our Danish-Argentine community in California, and I had to work on developing my English as I played with the neighborhood children.

My Aunt Nanna used to come over to visit her sister almost on a daily basis and let Bruce (my cousin who is a year younger) play with me in the yard. Once, we decided we would go fishing in the pond and eat our catch for lunch. Bruce attached a string to a stick and pretended to land a goldfish, which he actually just scooped out of the water. I collected sand from the sandbox and brought it over to my toy stove, where I proceeded to bread the fish and cook it up. When Mom and Nanna realized what we were up to, they offered us lunch. "Can we have hot dogs?" I asked. No, I have already made you sandwiches. Well, Bruce and I then announced, "When we grow up, we're going to get married and have hot dogs on our honeymoon!" My mother and aunt raised their eyebrows at that. I think we lost four fish that day.

Being the first girl, and for a while the only girl in our stateside family, I was doted on by all the women. My mother loved to dress me up in adorable outfits that she designed and sewed herself, while Nanna and Mormor were forever doing my hair. Strangely elaborate hairstyles are documented in photographs. The arrival of my baby brother, Steven Rolighed Larsen, did not exempt me from having my hair done, and the tradition extended to the new baby. Steven didn't have much hair, so, I would ask my mother for some red yarn from one of her many knitting projects, to create hairstyles on him. The pictures of this are even more amusing than the ones of me. Being a baby, he liked my attention and would laugh and smile as I styled his red hair.

The following year, not long before the start of kindergarten, Kimmy told me,

"I have a new friend for you."

"But, you're my friend," I protested.

"No, I mean someone your own age."

I was baffled as to why this was important. In reality, our age difference had never registered before, at least not with me. As Kimmy got older, though, I am sure the novelty of having an adoring preschool tagalong had begun to wear off.

"Come on," she said, taking my hand and walking me down to the end of the street and around the corner of a steep, curved road. When I looked up, I saw a huge, wood-shingled house that sat perched on the hill. A long winding staircase led up to it. As we climbed, a brown-eyed girl with a cute bowl haircut (similar to mine, except brunette), came running onto the deck and waved hello. This friendly girl was Tess, the middle child of three sisters. As time went on, we would become inseparable to the point of nearly belonging to each other's families. We were then, and remain today, the best of friends — like sisters.

One of our favorite games was pretending we were stranded on a deserted island and had to find ways to survive. We smashed berries and built forts. Sometimes we built imaginary rafts that would take us home to safety. Other times we had to live high up in the trees.

"Quick, it's coming!" I would shout, and the two of us scurried up a Liquidambar tree by jumping to grab the lowest branch and then swinging our legs over it like the monkey bars on the playground. From there we could pull ourselves up to sit on the smooth bark of the branch. We would get ourselves into a standing position, place one foot on a branch, then grab the next one to pull ourselves higher and higher, glancing back down to marvel at how we had just missed being swallowed by molten lava. The views from up there were beautiful. On a clear day if we climbed high enough, we could see the San Francisco Bay and even Alcatraz. We often climbed up to enjoy our afternoon snack. One day while climbing with a large dill pickle in one hand, Tess fell out of our leafy refuge and got a concussion. After that, her parents didn't want us climbing so high with snacks.

On the first day of kindergarten, our mothers walked with us, but after that we were on our own, or so we thought. We later learned they had followed us the first few times to make sure we didn't get distracted or wander off and get into trouble. Tess and I were both known to cause mischief. We had set up a meeting place at the end of my street, where it intersected with the bottom of her street, but when Tess was late, which was often, I would trudge up the hill to get her. I soon became tired of walking up the hill and all those stairs, so we worked out a system: I would stand at the bottom of her hill and holler out a Tarzan call — "Aahuaaa, uaaa, uaaaaaaaa!" If she heard me, she would come out on the deck and call back. If I didn't get a response, I would walk halfway up the hill and do it again. That usually worked, and Tess would come running down.

We were imaginative girls, always on the search for a new adventure. One day Tess and I struck gold at school when we found a couple of wooden pallets behind the gymnasium; they made perfect rafts. A few of our classmates saw us having so much fun, they wanted to be marooned along with us. For weeks those slats of wood kept us afloat on the ocean, withstanding giant waves, storms, and shark attacks. Every recess the group bolted out of class and raced over to the pallets like they were the best things on the playground. And they were.

Chapter 8

~ What's Cookin' in Denmark ~

It was 1971, my parents had been working hard to grow Dad's business, and by the end of my kindergarten year, it was really taking off. At last they were making a comfortable living and our family could afford several weeks off to visit relatives in Denmark.

Tickets were bought, preparations were made, and my mother finished sewing matching outfits for her and me to wear on the flight: perfectly tailored, sea-green polyester pantsuits with brass buttons. (It was 1971.) The night before our departure, we all gathered for a family meal with my Mormor and Morfar (Danish for maternal grandparents) at their home, a beautiful old Mediterranean Revival style house on a leafy street in Kentfield.

The main living quarters were on the second floor, with a garage and a second kitchen on the street level. A big backyard was full of fruit trees, including a giant fig and a pomegranate. We loved picking the fruit from those trees and eating pomegranates, staining our clothes as we picked apart the red seeds with juice dripping down our arms.

After dinner, we kids went outside to play a game of hide-and-seek. The ground-floor kitchen had a low, double-hung window that faced the backyard. This we designated as home base. Our players included my cousins Bruce and Alan, my little brother Steven, and the girl from next door; we circled to choose who was "it" with eeny, meeny, miny, moe. When Bruce lost, he turned and leaned over the low window, covered his eyes, and began counting. We all scattered and hid. I ducked behind a bush and crouched, being very quiet, and after a moment I heard my cousin shout, "Ready or not, here I come!"

He started immediately in my direction, walking slowly and methodically until he stopped next to my hiding place. I thought for sure he would see me, but to my surprise he continued past. That's when I saw my chance and bolted, but Bruce caught sight of me and tore after. At full speed I propelled myself forward while my cousin's long legs gained on me — until we arrived simultaneously at home base and collided into each other, me bouncing off of him and into the window, a crescendo of shattering glass and screams.

My right elbow entered first, engaging the jagged edges that dug in and ripped open my arm, leaving a V-shaped flap of flesh dangling and another long gash down my forearm. Blood was everywhere. Panic-stricken adults came running, a blanket materialized, and my father whisked me into Uncle Hermann's VW. We sped to the hospital, running every red light. Thankfully, the hospital was only a few minutes away.

I was immediately laid on a gurney, my right arm stretched out by the doctor on call. After a brief assessment of the situation, the doctor numbed both sides of the gash with numerous painful shots of Novocain, which actually only partially numbed the area. As he stitched, I could feel the tugging when he pulled the long black thread through my skin to close the wound. Periodically I glanced over to watch the progress of the stitching, which was crisscrossing back and forth the way my mother did her embroidery. When he was finished, I had 34 stitches in my arm that were then bound tightly with layers of gauze bandages that held my arm straight for the next few weeks. The next day we were still able to take our flight to Denmark, bandages and all.

When it came time to remove the stitches, we were on Morsø, the small island where my father's family lived. I was taken to the old family doctor, who was probably the only doctor on the island. To me he was ancient, and I don't think I was alone in believing he was senile. The old doctor stuffed me full of lollipops and candy and repeated himself a few too many times.

"It's okay. It's okay." I began to wonder whom he was trying to comfort — him or me?

His eyesight was obviously not very good because he wore glasses with Coke bottle lenses, and he also needed a magnifying glass to see what he was doing. I was terrified as he fumbled, yanking and pulling on the threads so hard it seemed he would rip the wound open, while my mother and father tried to keep me still. I was thankful when it came down to the last handful of stitches that had grown under the skin and my mom stepped in and said, "That's enough."

The old goat was probably just as relieved and said, "Okay, we'll just let the rest of the stitches work their way out." Actually, my father took care of them shortly after returning to his parents' farm.

My Bedstefar and Bedstemor (generic terms for Grandfather and Grandmother) lived in a one-story yellow brick house on an old farm. This is where my father and his younger brother Jens had begun their masonry apprenticeships, back when they were just teenagers. Here my dad showed us the first walls they had built, along with concrete steps and decking in the old barn.

My Bedstefar Laurits was your typical, jovial, round-bellied Dane, who wore black-rimmed glasses and suspenders, and chewed tobacco. Once, when he came to the United States to visit, Bedstefar thought the local pizzeria was a public bathroom because it sounded like "piss-area." For years afterward, we laughed every time we drove past the old Straw Hat Pizza parlor near our house. It was a fond memory that always made us smile.

My Bedstemor Maren was a strong, stocky woman with a sweet, gentle personality. She wore modest, below-the-knee house dresses topped with an apron (she never wore a pair of pants in her life). Her skin was as soft as the flour she used to make our bread. Before she married my grandfather and became, by marriage, a Larsen, she was already a Larsen. No relation, just a common Danish surname.

Back when the Vikings, who originally didn't have surnames, began to use them, it was a patronymic system in which a child's last name was derived from the father's first name. If your father's name was Lars, and you were his son, your surname became Larsen. If you were the daughter of Lars, your surname would be Larsdatter.

Bedstemor was a good cook, and her stove usually held big simmering pots with tempting smells that drew us in. I remember wandering into the kitchen one morning when the air was steamy and pungent. "Mmmm, What's Cookin?" I said in Danish.

To which my grandmother replied, "I'm boiling underwear."

I stretched up on my tippy-toes and peered into the giant cast-iron pot on the stove, and there indeed was everyone's underwear, floating around together, bubbling away! In the summer, clothes were hung out on the line to dry and were stiff as a board when you got them back. Everything here was done the old-fashioned way and required strength, patience, and resourcefulness. It would turn out to be the perfect place for me.

The barn at my grandparents' farm was a rustic, L-shaped, yellow brick building, covered about three-quarters of the way up with ivy. Although it was attached to their home, there was no direct entry into the house. Once one exited the barn, the door to the house was nearby and led to the bryggers, or scullery, the room for cleaning and storing dishes and cooking utensils. It served as a sort of mudroom with a large sink. Off of the scullery was a big bathroom — basically a tiled room with a drain in the middle of the floor. The showerhead projected from the back wall, and against the opposite wall was an old pull-handle toilet and a sink. Off the scullery was also a bedroom where my dad and his three brothers had slept when they were growing up. It was one big "bed" room, being mostly bed and no room. This is where Dad, Mom, and Steven slept when we visited. I slept in Aunt Anne-Grete's old room, best described as a shoebox.

Halfway through the galley-style kitchen on the right was the door to Bedstemor and Bedstefar's bedroom, and opposite that was a sink and workspace. At the far end of the kitchen sat a built-in bench and table, common in Danish farmhouses and usually situated near a large picture window. My favorite moments were spent staring out the window at the wheat fields that grew right up to the back of the house. I loved to sit and watch the wheat sway under the force of the wind and hear the sound that the wind made as it whistled through the young stalks. The wheat fields looked as if someone were running through them. It was mysterious and mesmerizing.

In the living room was the old Jydsk Aktieselskab Danish wall-hung telephone, with a double bell and hand crank. Their telephone number was 4 because they were the fourth home on the island to get a phone. My father said that while he was growing up, this phone provided an unlimited source of Saturday night entertainment for him and Jens. Since it was a party line, anyone could hear the latest gossip by simply picking up the receiver and listening in. This is probably why I've inherited the mischievous pastime of finding out what others are up to. We still have that Jydsk telephone hanging on our wall.

After several weeks with my father's family, Bedstefar loaned us his car to visit my mother's side of the family. My morfar (mother's father) had three sisters still living. First we visited the aunts we called faster (father's sister). There was Faster Johanne and Faster Gerda in Slagelse, then a drive to Copenhagen to visit Faster Ellen and her daughter Else who lived nearby with her children Henning and Merethe.

Faster Johanne and her husband Knud owned a local købmand (grocery store). The small store was stocked from floor to ceiling with the latest products. Behind the counters stood old apothecary-style cabinets with hundreds of little wooden drawers that held innumerable wares and the most extensive selection of gummy treats and candy imaginable to a child. Once a customer had made a choice, the candies were placed on a dish of an old mercantile scale, with brass weights used to counterbalance and denote the product's weight. Then the candy was slid into a small, colorful bag and rung up at the old register; this became my first job. For compensation, Uncle Knud would tell my brother and me, "Go help yourselves to whatever you want." It was a child's dream come true!

Outside the store stood two old-fashioned gas pumps supplied by Exxon. Exxon offered a promotion whereby customers who filled their tanks received a wild animal sticker with each fill-up. A hardcover book was for sale at a discount after ten fill-ups. Uncle Knud gave my brother and me each a copy of the Wild Animals of Africa book, along with a new sticker every day. It was very exciting; we were able to complete almost the whole book before we left (and gained a desire to go on safari!). In Denmark, stickers were used to promote businesses, similar to how we use business cards. Every shopkeeper, product, and festival had stickers to coincide with their campaign. I collected them, just like other Danes, and kept them in a cigar box I received from Faster Johanne once she had smoked all the cigars.

Faster Gerde (the oldest sister) lived over a famous Danish porcelain shop. Each time we visited, my mother would buy a figurine to add to her collection back home. Faster Gerde was a podiatrist, and her hospitality came in the form of the best pedicure ever. Her practice was set up in a room within her apartment. It reminded me of sitting in a reclining chair at the dentist's office, with foot pedals. She had a rolling cart laid out with sterile instruments that she used with expert facility. A soothing foot soak was followed by the ruthless removal of calluses — layer upon layer of dead skin sliced away with a sharp scalpel, then heels and toes buffed to a sheen before turning her attention to cuticles and nails. She finished off the job with a firm, stimulating rub. I'm not sure who enjoyed it more, my aunt or us. Faster Gerde brought her little black podiatrist's bag with her when she traveled, and as a result we received the same professional treatment every time she came to visit us.

My mother's family enjoyed going on en skovtur, which translates literally as "a forest tour" but in practical terms means to go on a picnic. Our destinations were rarely preplanned. Uncle Knud was the only one who could drive, so Johanne, Gerde, and my mom and dad took up the passenger seats while Steven and I sat on their laps. We drove along enjoying the conversation until someone would see a spot and declare "skovtur!" Abruptly we'd turn off the road and everyone would jump out. Up popped a table adorned with a lovely tablecloth. Cloth napkins and real utensils (never plastic) were laid out. Baskets of food appeared: sild (pickled herring), rødbeder (pickled beets), smørrebrød (open-faced sandwiches), with snaps (akvavit) and øl (beer) for the adults, sodavand (soda) for the kids. A smoking break was always taken after eating, and prior to dessert. This was when my great aunts would pull out their slender lady cigars for a relaxing puff prior to finishing with the traditional coffee, cookies, and cake. We would sit and enjoy delicious food and company for hours.

The castles around Copenhagen sometimes served as charming backdrops for a skovtur. We lounged on bright green lawns watching the gracefulness of the swans that for centuries have swum in the moats of the castles and in nearby lakes and, of course, at Tivoli Gardens. The swan is the national bird of Denmark. My brother, fascinated by the swan and her flock of cygnets, once got too close to the water's edge, and the protective momma bird rose up angrily, grabbed him by the pant leg, and began dragging him into the water. My mother sprang to her feet and ran down to the water's edge. A fierce tug-of-war ensued. My mother, who was also in protective mother mode, finally won and the swan released his pant leg and swam briskly away with her flock tucked in behind her large wings.

Chapter 9

~ Jultide ~

(Danish Holiday Traditions)

E very year as the yuletide holidays approached, packages wrapped in brown paper and tied with twine would begin to arrive in California from our relatives in Denmark. Bedstemor literally sent hundreds of småkager (small Danish Christmas cookies), consisting of brunkager (flat brown spiced cookies), pebernødder (hard "peppernut" cookies), and klejner (fried pastry twists) — all lovingly made just for us. Other packages contained bags of gummy bears, assorted hard candies, and presents for Steven and me from Anne-Grethe and Kristian. Additional goodies came from my father's brothers and cousins.

In Denmark, it's traditional to cut your tree and bring it home on Christmas Eve, when you decorate it with little white candles that clip onto the branches in special golden holders. In America, however, we would get our tree a couple of weeks before so we had time to enjoy it. We wouldn't light the candles until Christmas Eve, though. The tree provided a place to keep all the incoming gifts. We loved to watch the piles grow as presents arrived, landing under the tree on the hand-sewn tree skirt my mother had adorned with little Nissemænd (Santa-like gnomes). We would usually get a Silvertip fir, resembling the Danish trees my parents had grown up with. The layered branches left plenty of room for ornaments, garlands of miniature Danish flags, and handmade hjerter (heart-shaped baskets woven from paper or felt, which hung on the tree, filled with nuts or candies).

For us females, my mother sewed matching holiday clothes. This particular year as I was about to turn seven, she made us both red, modern-looking, A-line dresses with white lace collars and cuffs. Aunt Nanna would come and style our hair.

We always had a big group of relatives — mother's parents plus Nanna, Hermann, cousin Bruce, and my dad's brother Jens and his wife Joan with their son Mike and daughter Lanisa. Friends from our Danish Argentine community rounded out the immediate family — my "uncle" Knud had gone to school in Argentina with my mom, and he brought his wife, my "aunt" Sonia, and their son, Alan. It wasn't until I was older that I realized there was no actual blood connection; they have remained like family to me.

We had a traditional Danish Christmas feast of roast pork with crackling called flæskesteg. To accompany it was a warm, pickled red cabbage (rødkål) braised with apples, and a large spoonful of lingonberry jam cooked in red wine vinegar, plus cucumber salad (agurkesalat), and caramelized potatoes (brunede kartofler) covered in a brown gravy (brun sovs) that was my favorite. Special occasions were served on my mother's Royal Copenhagen porcelain dishes.

Plenty of beer, wine, and akvavit flowed throughout the evening. After our feast, we all held hands and sang as we "danced" around the Christmas tree. Once the kids became too big and rambunctious, my father switched the tree lights to colorful Christmas strands, with the real candles only as decoration for fear that one of us would topple the tree and start a fire. After singing and dancing, the kids were allowed to open presents first. The adults would give thankful toasts to a good year and a better one to come. Then came coffee and dessert.

Dessert on Christmas Eve is always Danish rice pudding (risalamande) with whipped cream and warm cherry sauce (kirsebœrsovs).   Hidden in the risalamande is a whole blanched almond. Whoever finds the almond wins a prize, usually a marzipan pig.   There were also plates of småkager (cookies sent from Bedstemor), and typically a kringle (pretzel-shaped pastry filled with almond paste custard) scattered across the table.

Thousands of years of hygge had bred into us Danes an appreciation for life and a strong desire to gather and revel in good company and excellent food. Through food, song, and tradition we felt connected as a family, and this reinforced the knowledge that life was good.

Christmas didn't always go smoothly, though. When I was five, I came down with a terrible flu and my mother, who didn't want me getting the others sick, sent me to bed, where I had to listen to the festivities from afar. This was when Mormor snuck into my room with an early delivery. She was so excited. She had sewn my "Sylvia doll" — a three-foot stuffed doll in my image. It had yellow yarn for my blond hair, blue yarn for the eyes, and little red lips. The doll was wearing a soft teal dress Mormor had made from an old bathrobe. It was perfect. It even kind of resembled me. I grabbed the doll and gave it a big hug, I was so excited.   And then Mormor got a big hug. Mormor was always full of life, and an extremely special person in my life. I still have that Sylvia doll.

On Christmas Day in the afternoon, we would usually be a larger group and gather at Mormor and Morfar's house for a traditional Danish smørrebrød. A true smørrebrød includes a variety of open-faced sandwiches and takes hours to enjoy. Fortunately for us kids, we were placed at one end of the table or sometimes at our own smaller kids' table, allowing us to run and play in their huge yard between courses.

Traditionally, the first course of the smørrebrød begins with fish options, including sild (pickled herring), made up in several forms — smoked eel, shrimp, smoked salmon — served with a bit of scrambled egg on top. The fish was primarily served on pumpernickel bread. The bread would be buttered on a smørebræt (a small wooden board), then placed on your plate where it was loaded with a fish topping and garnishes. Each topping has a specific garnish to accompany the food for the most enhanced flavor and visual appeal.

Once everyone had their first open-faced sandwich ready to eat, the toasts would begin in excess and carry on throughout the meal. We began each toast by raising our shot glasses filled with Danish akvavit (a clear liquid flavored with caraway seeds, known to Danes as "snaps"), with a few favorable or comedic words spoken, then a clink of glasses, where you must look each person in the eye as you clink, and finish with a Skål! Then the snaps are thrown back and followed with a beer chaser, preferably a Carlsberg.

Sometimes prior to beginning the second course, a bowl of suppe med boller (chicken broth with small dumplings) is served. The second course is known as the meat course, consisting of leverpostej (Danish pâté), roast beef, pork roast, or one of the non-meat open-faced options such as egg and tomato, potato, or beet — all complemented again with their specific condiments and garnishes. The third course is a variety of cheeses garnished with herbs, bell peppers and fruit, served on pumpernickel, knœkbrød (Danish crispbread crackers), or a nice French bread.

After all this eating and drinking, a small break would ensue before we indulged in dessert. Sonia made an excellent citronfromage (lemon chiffon mouse), which was served with coffee, tea, and any leftover Christmas cookies from the relatives in Denmark.

After Christmas, we enjoyed playing with all of our new toys, and the days passed quickly as my birthday on New Year's Eve approached. Because the holidays were already so festive and full of presents for the children, my mother started a tradition in which we would celebrate my birthday with my friends in the summer. She'd host my party out at Samuel P. Taylor State Park, where all my friends could attend. It was like having two birthdays each year!

My birthday would still be recognized on New Year's Eve with family and a few friends. Over the years, my memories of this festive evening included a house full of people, the liquor flowing, and everyone dancing. We would celebrate either at our house or at Uncle Jens and Aunt Joan's house. Since New Year's Eve was my birthday, it was always a grand night.

Chapter 10

~ Laughter Is the Best Medicine ~

When I find things funny (which is often; I'm easily amused) I cannot contain my laughter. It bursts out of me and usually causes heads to turn. This started early in life and quickly became known as my signature laugh. It probably should have come with a Surgeon General's Warning. It's been described as a sudden, extremely loud shriek followed by a cackle and has startled many a person into fright or flight, including my poor mother. In public over the years, people have turned and stared. Some smile back like they want to be in on the joke, while others look annoyed that anyone could be having that much fun. Ok, maybe they were a little annoyed that I scared the pants off of them. Sorry, but not sorry. My laugh is as much a part of me as my eye color or fingerprint, and my best friend Tess thought it was hysterical.

Life was good. Tess and I pretty much ran free in our neighborhood. When we were seven we attempted her steep driveway on our roller skates with no helmets or knee pads, just reckless abandon.

Off we went, screaming down the hill with our arms outstretched until we gained so much speed that we made the mistake of grasping hands and ended up knocking each other down — tumbling, skates over bodies, knees and elbows banging into pavement, leaving us sprawled on the ground with the breath knocked out of us — then a momentary pause to make sure we were okay followed by a burst of laughter. We removed our skates and limped back up the hill to Tess's house, where after washing our scrapes we covered them with Band-Aids. A year later we tried the same thing on our bikes, this time down Hippie Hill (a small hippie commune in our neighborhood), where we ran into the hedges below. We were always getting into scrapes. Literally and figuratively.

Somehow we managed to be in the same class each year. Looking back, we can't believe that the school didn't separate us. What were those teachers thinking? We both had a lot to say and couldn't contain ourselves. Why the teachers let us sit next to each other, we can't fathom, but our talking was legendary. Mrs. Hardy, our second-grade teacher, actually resorted to taping our mouths shut and tying us to our seats with jump ropes. The silly part was, she continued to let us sit next to each other, but separated us from all the other students. That did not stop Tess and me. We quickly figured out how to loosen the tape without it falling off our upper lips so we could continue our conversation under the tape and not be caught. Because we were tied, we could not lean into each other to talk, so we had to scoot our chairs toward each other when she turned her back. This was the same teacher who would smack our hands with a ruler, and who denied me my left-handedness and made me write with my right hand. Basically, the year with Mrs. Hardy was an ongoing battle and we were overjoyed when we survived.

Tess often came over to my house after school. To her, it was a striking contrast to most American homes, and she admired its simplicity. She loved my mom's Danish open-faced sandwiches made with ham and Italiensk salat, which was peas and carrots mixed with mayonnaise, to make the colors of the Italian flag. She often stayed the night and in the morning we were treated to Danish pancakes, and if we were lucky my dad would make us each en rør æg — a raw egg yolk whipped with sugar into a frothy treat.

By third grade, we were opting for Tess's house after school because her parents weren't home. We talked about boys, made crank phone calls, and ravaged her dad's stash of Tillamook cheese and beef sticks he always kept in the fridge. Primarily, our crank calls were to a girl named Jody, who once made us a trio, and whose only offense was drifting away from us and into her books. We didn't say anything malicious, just the usual, "Is your refrigerator running? Well, you'd better go and catch it!" followed by hysterical laughter and — click. Sometimes we just called and didn't say anything and she would shout into the receiver, "I know it's you guys!" and hang up. Come to think of it, we also toilet-papered her house — several times. She had to have known it was us, but we never got in trouble.

I ran into Jody years later at a high school reunion. I apologized for Tess and my behavior from when we were kids. We chatted. Now we are friends on Facebook.

Every year on May 1, Tess and I would make small paper baskets to fill with bouquets of flowers that we collected from our gardens. We would hang them on people's doors with an anonymous note, "Happy May Day." Then we would ring the doorbell and run as fast as we could to hide. Per tradition, we wanted people not to know who had left the flowers.

In our neighborhood, there were a few houses people feared. One was Old Lady Dunny, and the other was a house with three nasty boys who owned snakes and spiders as pets; one boy had lit a neighbor's bush on fire. We still felt these houses deserved a May basket, but for the boys' house, we decided to give them the smallest basket. It was our worst basket. There was a long staircase up to the front door, so our escape had to be planned very carefully.

Although we would usually take turns being the one to leave the basket while the other waited in our hiding place with the remaining baskets, in this case neither of us wanted to go. So, we decided to both ascend the narrow stairway. At the top, we practically dropped the basket and banged the doorbell, running away as fast as possible. But, we'd made it only to the bottom of the stairs and behind a small wall when the mother opened the door and saw the ugly bouquet.

"Who left these beautiful flowers?" she hollered. As she began to descend the stairs, Tess and I were panic-stricken. "What a sweet thing! Come out so I can thank you!"

We couldn't let her get all the way down and find our other, beautiful bouquets. We looked at each other and quickly popped up and went around the wall, leaving the other baskets on the ground. She grabbed us and hugged us, insisting we come in for refreshments. She exclaimed how she only had boys, and never received anything like this, and that the flowers were so beautiful.

We left with bellies full of lemonade, cookies, and candies, feeling badly that we had given her the worst bouquet. We vowed from that moment forward to always do our best and treat everyone equally.

PART THREE:

~MOVING ON~

I learned that courage was not the absence of fear, but the triumph over it. The brave person is not the one who does not feel afraid, but the one who conquers that fear.

Nelson Mandela

Chapter 11

~ No More Hats ~

Summers were great in the neighborhood, hanging out with Tess every day and playing hide-and-go-seek in the evenings with the whole gang. My life couldn't have been more idyllic — that is, up through the last trip to Southern California with my father. Luckily we had spent the time to find my father's relatives that day in Orange County.

Because after that, the next two years were spent surviving my father's sudden and unexpected death, along with my battle against cancer. Life was tough, but it could not make my family lose our ability to laugh hard and look forward with optimism. Once it looked like I had defeated the odds and was going to survive, we could really get back to living life.

Our annual family trip to Southern California was a highlight of the year. After staying in Solvang for several days, where we helped our friends with their gardens and played a lot of games, we would visit Santa Barbara. This was one of my mother's favorite parts of our adventure. Eventually we made it to the Bollisens', where we would stay a few weeks and swim, play cards, and make countless wonderful trips to Disneyland.

Their daughters Debbie and Randi were in college now but still had their summer jobs, leaving us in The Happiest Place on Earth. They lived only fifteen minutes from Disneyland, if you knew the way. Our mom seemed to find new and interesting routes each time we went. Sometimes it would take up to two hours to find our way back to Olive Tree Circle. After a few summers of this, my brother and I spotted a special license plate frame just for Mom. It read;

"Don't follow me; I'm lost." We thought it was hilarious and never really let her live it down.

I think my mother rather enjoyed making my clothes, and she was the best dressmaker around. She could make her own patterns, follow any design a customer might bring, or tailor the finest of men's suits. People would come from miles around to have her sew for them. But by my seventh-grade year, I wanted "real" clothes — what the other kids were wearing. Realizing that it was time, my mom gave in and took me to the Strawberry Shopping Center, where I bought a pair of dark blue pants in a soft fabric. They had a rainbow beginning at one hip and extending across to the other and down the length of one leg. I loved those pants, along with my corduroy bell-bottoms. I still wore a few of the things my mom had made, including a corduroy vest, and many favorite sweaters she had knitted for me. My mother was not only an incredibly talented seamstress, but knitted my brother and I, along with many others beautiful fisherman's sweaters and afghans. If she wasn't kitting, she would be working on one of her countless embroideries.

I also had quite a collection of homemade hats by now. I don't know what I would have done without these through my chemotherapy. My mom had sewn so many hats that fit snugly around my bald head, hats in a variety of colors and patterns that matched the outfits she had made. Just knowing the love she had put into them was like a security blanket — not only for my exposed scalp, but for my mental stability. She even bought me a white swim cap with multicolored rubber flowers affixed here and there, so I still had this feeling of comfort when I swam.

Not having hair was one of the worst aspects of my cancer ordeal. As if losing an arm and going through years of being violently ill wasn't enough, I also had to endure losing my beautiful blond hair. It makes you feel like you're holding up a big sign, "Yes, I have cancer" wherever you go when all you want to do is continue your life normally and blend in.

When I began sixth grade at Kent, it was the year the school converted from K–8 to middle school. So, many of the kids with whom I had attended kindergarten and who had transferred to another elementary school now returned to Kent for sixth grade. This was when I walked up to a girl I remembered from back in kindergarten and said, "We know each other."

It now seems like one of those simple things you understand when you are eleven. That is, when two kids know each other, it's just time to play and get on with the day. Sandy did not remember back to our kindergarten days, but later told me it didn't matter. She was just happy to have a new friend. That fateful day when I walked up to her started a friendship that is now over forty years old.

What Sandy did remember was looking at me as a girl with a pretty face framed by a cute mushroom cap (one my mother had made) and realizing that none of this mattered to her, we were friends. Eventually, the mushroom caps were replaced with my natural hair. The one thing that was not replaced was my arm. She noticed, though, that I never seemed to miss it, nor did anyone else. She said that my bravery and determination is something she has always admired, and she later used my story to teach her children that everyone has a cross to bear. What sets us apart is how we handle it, and she says Sylvia is the person who taught her this.

Needless to say, my hair finally, very gradually, began to grow back a few months after I had finished the chemo treatments. To my surprise, it wasn't blond initially — it was brown, a dark brown! — and it came back extremely slowly, or so it seemed to me. It was baby soft and billowy, and once it reached a few inches in length, I would brush it straight up into a poof atop my head to make my mom and brother laugh so hard, my mom nearly peed her pants. Although my hair was dark, at least I had hair again! I promptly threw each and every hat away.

"I never want to wear another hat again," I told my mom.

Meanwhile, Tess and I didn't cease our mischief. Tess had an aunt that she had begun visiting in San Francisco on her own. She would catch the bus at the end of Frances Avenue and ride across the Golden Gate Bridge, get off, catch a cable car as far as it could take her, then walk the rest of the way to her Aunt Diane's apartment in the Sunset District.

We pestered my mother relentlessly to let me go with her, but only after assurances from Tess's mother that she knew what she was doing and that we would be okay, did she finally agree. We were only eleven years old. The first time we jumped onto a cable car and hung off the sides holding tightly to the trolley's pole, a passenger wanted to know what had happened to my arm. We were polite and described my cancer and the need for amputation. Then another person asked, and another and another. By the end of the trip, it had become tiresome describing this horrific event over and over. We decided that in the future we would use our imaginations, as we always had growing up, to embellish the story a little.

"She lost it in a burning fire," Tess blurted out the next time we were asked.

"She was attacked by a shark at Stinson Beach." This version always made me laugh.

People's jaws dropped. We began concocting stories beforehand so as to make them sound as authentic as possible while maintaining a straight face, since I usually would start laughing, and they would know we were making it up.

"She was run over by a train," said Tess, looking as earnest as possible. "She's lucky to be alive."

Inevitably, they would turn to me with wide eyes and I would nod a sad yes. We could hardly keep from cracking up. We would have to jump off the cable car at the next corner so we could burst into laughter without the people seeing us. We could get a good chuckle out of this for hours afterwards.

Time after time, we rattled over the tracks hanging out over the edge, my hair and sleeve blowing, holding on tight to that pole with my one hand, exploring the city wherever the cable car would take us: Chinatown, Fisherman's Wharf, Ghirardelli Square. We liked to get huge hot fudge sundaes at Ghirardelli Square in the morning before taking the trolley out to Golden Gate Park, where we would visit the

Japanese Tea Garden, then eat piroshki's from a Russian deli for a late
lunch.

At home we were equally daring. It seems we had not learned our
lesson from our earlier roller-skating debacle. We skated everywhere
and zipped down Sir Francis Drake, a busy two-lane road, on our way
to get frozen yogurt. Just as we miraculously arrived safely at the shop,
I attempted the steep driveway. The 90-degree turn at the bottom came,
and I smacked into the back of a parked van — arm outstretched and
face firmly planted, just like in the cartoons. It's a wonder I wasn't
seriously injured.

Another hypothetically dangerous pastime was straddling the
windowsill in Tess's second-story living room. It was a large picture
window sandwiched between two casement windows that opened out.
We loved to sit there, talk, and eat ice cream. One day while dangling a
leg outside the open window and facing me, Tess cried out.
"Oh my God. You have two arms!"

"What are you talking about?" I replied.

"Look!" she said. Her eyes lit up as she pointed to my reflection in
the window.

I bent out the window as far as I could. I saw my reflection and
found myself staring at a ghost. It was an intriguing optical illusion
that gave me back my arm.

"Cool," I said. And it was cool, but I never actually wasted time
wishing it were true.

Losing my arm hadn't changed who I was. By this time, I was
already recognized as a happy-go-lucky girl with a kind heart, a
friendly smile, and a contagious laugh that everyone wanted to be a part
of. I continue to live my life just that way.

In 1976, the movie Rocky, starring Sylvester Stallone, came out on the big screen. It was hugely popular, and everyone, including Tess and I, went to see it. It struck a chord. I was mesmerized and inspired by the underdog story: how Rocky Balboa, with all the odds against him, worked and worked, never giving up; no matter what the obstacles were, he persevered. The message was embellished by the music, especially the theme song, "Gonna Fly Now" — nah-nah-nah, nah-nah-nah, nah-ne-nah-ne-nah-ne-nah as Rocky climbed those 72 stone stairs at the Philadelphia Museum of Art, sweat dripping off his face, and reached the top, triumphantly raising his arms and jumping in the air. It was my story, too, and by the end of the film, I was pumped. I was also quite smitten with Sylvester Stallone, or "Sly" as people started to call him. I even considered drinking raw eggs to emulate my new hero/heartthrob, but gave that idea up pretty quickly when I realized how slimy they would be going down. When I came across a Rocky poster, though, I just had to have it. My mother didn't object. She let me buy it and tack it up on the wall in my bedroom. She even took a picture of me standing in front of it — beaming.

Chapter 12

~ Danmark ~

(as the Danes call it)

By the end of seventh grade, I had been cleared for travel. I was feeling confident with a full head of hair, which was still very short and rather brown, but I was out of hats and ready to go. My mother kept her promise to my father's side of the family and flew with Steven and me back to Denmark for the summer. We landed at the small airport in Thisted just north of Morsø on Denmark's mainland. We disembarked the small plane out on the tarmac at the Thisted Lufthavn (airport), where Anne-Grethe and her husband, Kristian, were waiting to meet us. We all packed into his tiny Renault, the kind of car you would imagine in a circus, where clowns keep climbing out, and the audience wonders, "How did they all fit in there?"

We took the car ferry to reach Morsø. Once there, we drove the narrow, one-lane roads that wrapped around wheat fields swaying in the wind. The tranquil beauty and serenity of the land mesmerized us. Denmark is known to be as flat as a pancake with only the occasional mounds (not even deserving to be called hills) that we traversed so quickly, there wasn't even time for a "whee!" Despite the narrowness of these winding roads, people drove them like race car drivers. So did our uncle.

Occasionally, he would slow to go through a small village no more than a block long. Here you would typically see old, Tudor-style buildings with thatched roofs. The village had little more than a few buildings, a grocery store (købmand), post office (posthus), sometimes a cheese shop (osteforretning), and always a bakery (bageri) identifiable by its pretzel symbol. The pretzel shape, called kringle, represents the original symbol of the Danish bakers' guild. The villages were so quaint, and the people who were coming and going, carrying baskets and wearing traditional wooden clogs, added to the local color.

Upon reaching the end of each village, Kristian accelerated and off we zoomed. He was excited to get us back to the farm where he told us he had a surprise waiting for us.

"What, what?" Steven and I wanted to know.

He pretended to reluctantly give in. "We have a newborn colt — a pretty little chestnut with a white stripe down his nose. Suzy, his mare, just gave birth two days ago."

My eyes grew wide. "What's his name?"

"Pellé, after the neighbor boy who was there at his birth."

I couldn't wait. No sooner had we arrived at the farm, I bolted from the car with Steven close behind. We quietly slid the large barn door open and approached the stall where the newborn Pellé was curled in the straw near his mother's legs. The mare was not too pleased with strangers. I slowly reached my arm through the bars of the stall and began rubbing his face and his lovely mane. I was instantly infatuated with Pellé and promised to take care of him every day I was there.

Anne-Grethe and Uncle Kristian's farm lay on the south end of the island and was appropriately named Sønnegård (Southern Farm). It was considerably larger than my grandparents' farm had been and was still a working farm. They had 750 pigs, a half dozen Arabian horses, and approximately 90 hectares (222 acres) of wheat fields. This along with hedgehogs, a handful of feral cats, and a husmår (a stone marten, which is a type of wild rodent similar to a weasel) that lived in the attic and that my aunt would feed.

The approach to the farm was a majestic, half-mile, tree-lined gravel driveway. Just before the courtyard, a beautiful garden and lawn area featured a flagpole surrounded by flowers. It hosted a grand red flag with a white cross — the Dannebrog, or flag of the Danes. The Danes are proud of their flag, recognized to be the oldest continuously used flag in the world. The legend is that it fell from the heavens in 1219. All Danes fly the Dannebrog — it's both patriotic and an indicator of a special event. If someone has a celebration, the flag is flown at full mast. If someone dies or something sad happens, it will hang at half-mast. When nothing in particular is going on, Danes fly a vimpel flag that is similar to the Dannebrog but in the shape of a very long pennant that tapers into a swallow's tail. Driving around the country, one can see dot after dot of red cloth flapping in the wind announcing, "The baby is born!" or "Morfar has passed." I imagine this form of communication came in handy before the telephone was invented.

Both the barn and house were constructed of red brick, forming a big square with a large courtyard in the center. The barn comprised three sides of the compound with the residence occupying the fourth side and closing the square. The driveway passed through into the courtyard. The formal front door was on the right, but failed to announce itself as such. There was another door, very similar, near the left end of the house and it beckoned, "Enter here." This was the entry we used on a daily basis. Next to this door hung an old cast-iron bell. It was used to announce one's arrival to anyone out in the barn, or to announce that a meal was ready, as when Anne-Grethe gave it her signature "Clang, clang, clang!"

Upon entering, one was struck by the wonderful scent of baking bread and sounds of conversation emanating from the nearby kitchen. Coats and shoes were left in the vestibule and, as all good Danes wore træsko (wooden shoes, or clogs), they were easy to slide on and off. Shoes were not worn inside. My aunt and uncle's kitchen was the heart of the home. This was the place everyone wanted to be. Anne-Grethe was always bustling about, turning out wonderful treats and Danish specialties while my uncle had lively discussions with anyone willing to match wits — or in my mom's case, butt heads. Even when it rained, the flies seemed to seek refuge in the kitchen, buzzing in the tall windows like they usually were in the barn. We simply hung up long rolls of sticky fly tape and crowded onto the enormous built-in bench that took up half the room, and we carried on. My uncle was a boisterous and opinionated man, but once you got past his rough exterior, inside he was a bighearted softy.

I have so many fond memories of time at this table — eating, talking, and also sitting for countless hours of canasta with the neighbor kids who would come to help with the farm work, then stay to play. Beyond the table, this wonderful kitchen offered many exciting corners to explore. There was the pantry, lined with shelves covered in homemade jams, jellies, rødbeder (pickled beets), asier (Danish pickled cucumber), rødkål (red cabbage), leverpostej (liver pâté), and småkager (cookies). At the end of the pantry was a window my aunt would leave open a few inches to let her cakes cool. If we were lucky, one of them would be Anne-Grethe's famous kaffekåge med smørcreme (mocha cake with vanilla buttercream filling). Down a small, narrow staircase that required one to watch their head was the cellar where all the Carlsberg, Tuborg, Apollinaris (sparkling water), and soda pops in every color imaginable were kept.

The house was divided into three sections. If you could pull yourself from the kitchen, through the far door was what they called the daily living room. In this room was a very comfortable sofa, and chairs to sit and watch TV (which was limited to only a few hours a week) or to enjoy our evening coffee and cakes. Moving onto the third section of the house, there were two sets of doors to choose from, one on each side of the room. The one on the left brought you into a formal living room that had a beautiful leather sofa ensemble; from there a set of French doors would lead you out to the back patio, next to the huge lawn. The door on the right led to the entry room with the formal front door and a floating staircase up to the second floor.

The entry room was invitingly decorated with places to sit and filled with games, puzzles, and a chess set. This room was where my aunt taught my brother and me how to play chess and mancala, and how to solve countless wrought-iron and wooden-block puzzles. The floating staircase consisted of five-foot-long open treads supported by a central steel tube that rose up to the second floor. The second story ran the entire length of the house, where you would find five bedrooms. We were given the one nearest the floating staircase. It was a spacious room with several windows providing a view of the garden, Dannebrog, and anyone coming up the drive. My mother and I had two single beds pushed together and my brother a third smaller bed tucked into an alcove — each topped with a wonderfully thick and fluffy down comforter.

Straight out from our room was a long, usually dark, spooky hallway that ran under the steep pitch of the roof. The only natural light in the hall came from one of the bedrooms. Interestingly, all of the doors in the house had wrought-iron skeleton keys sticking out from the keyholes. My aunt and uncle's home had served as a bed and breakfast for many years, although there were no guests at this time, so not all upstairs rooms were used. Each room had two single beds and giant dormer windows that overlooked the courtyard. In each dormer was a teakwood table where we liked to sit and gossip or play cards with the neighbor children. After my first summer, my aunt gave me one of these rooms to stay in.

As you continued down the long hallway, you needed to stay close to the left side of the wall so as to not bump your head on the steep slant of the roof. A small single bedroom with a small bureau, nightstand, and no window came next on the left. When my cousin Laurids would visit, this was usually the room he stayed in. Next to Laurids' room was a small half bathroom, with a WC (toilet) and very small sink.

At this end of the house, a narrow staircase led back down to the vestibule off the kitchen. Just past that was another room that overlooked the fields out back. I believe that the room at the end of the hall was rarely used because it was next to the attic storage area where the husmår lived. Although the animal was rarely seen, it made quite a racket. My mother, Steven, and I were a little disturbed that we could hear it scurrying around at night while we lay in bed. Sometimes when I got up the nerve, I would open the attic door in the morning to see if the food my aunt had left was gone, before quickly jumping down the narrow staircase to get my tea and breakfast roll.

My father's family were a bunch of jokesters, and Anne-Grethe was no exception. She would appear on one side of you while tugging your ear from the other. She was always putting a smile on your face. Anne-Grethe got up every day at the crack of dawn to make fresh baked rolls that we ate with cheese and jam to go along with our cup of morning tea. This was just a quick snack, as breakfast followed morning chores in the barn. First stop was the mudroom to slip on our rubber boots and hat, called a kasket. All the farmhands sported these lightweight painter-style caps, and I always wore a special blue one I had received from my Uncle Kristian.

Once we had wrapped the bottoms of our pant legs tightly around our calves and slipped our feet into tall boots, Steven and I would head out with Uncle Kristian to begin our morning chores. It was a quick jaunt over to the barn, whereupon entering you would be hit with a wave of stench that burned your nose hairs, it was so awful. Thankfully, our olfactory senses adjusted rather quickly, and once in with the pigs themselves it never seemed all that bad.

The barn had a long center aisle with pigs occupying the pens on each side. Our first few summers helping on the farm, we had to push a food cart through all the aisles to feed the 750 plus pigs by hand, using a giant scoop to pour the grain into the troughs. We each had our own aisle to distribute the food to the pigs, but the pigs knew it was mealtime and screamed and squealed in anticipation so loudly, it was deafening. We would move as quickly as possible to get them their meal. The pigs would then press their snouts up against their nozzles to dispense their own water to wet the grain and begin chowing on their slop. It was a relief when Kristian installed automated food dispensers to supply the troughs with grain at the appointed times. He never did automate the manure process, though, and we still had to clean the pens.

Despite their smell, pigs are surprisingly clean animals and never soiled their own living space. Instead, they had access to a smaller stall through a gateway behind their main stall. This is where they went to do their business. Each morning, it was our job to close off the main stalls, creating a back alley, and go into every stall one by one and scoop out the old hay, shut the gate into the back, and take a wide shovel and push all the old hay and scheisse down into a trench with a conveyor belt that transported the waste up into a huge concrete holding tank. This gylletank, or slurry tank, open at the top, was where the waste sat until it was used to fertilize the wheat fields and my aunt's vegetable garden. Then we would give the pigs clean straw, and they would grunt with appreciation.

Farm life had its educational value; we also learned a lot about the birds and the bees, so to say. The sows — the female pigs in heat — were brought to the breeding pen, along with a prized stud. I'll never forget the first time I walked in and saw that stud in action. To my amazement, his privates looked like a giant corkscrew. I'm not kidding when I say giant. This was definitely more information than I wanted. It was especially embarrassing to watch when we were together with neighbor boys who came to help.

There was always plenty to be done at the farm, and fortunately we had extra hands. Most days, the Panduro boys — Thomas, Jasper, and Pellé — would ride their bikes over, ringing their bells to sound their arrival.   Torvill, a troll of a man whose twisted and missing teeth caused him to muffle his words, would arrive on an old Vespa called a kanalet, a Danish onomatopoeia that conveyed the click-clack motor sound that scooters made, "Ka-na-let, ka-na-let." Together we gave the pigs their shots, weighed them to see which ones qualified to go to market that week, and maneuvered some into a contraption where they were hung upside-down for castration. After two quick slices, Uncle Kristian pinched out the testicles, released the device, and each little pig fell with a thud before running off squealing.

We finished chores around nine o'clock in the morning. Then the Panduro boys, Torvill, and anyone else who happened to stop by would all come in for breakfast. The newspaper deliveryman and sometimes the mailman would conveniently show up just in time for breakfast. Anne-Grethe never minded, though; she was a gracious host and everyone was welcome. This second meal of the day consisted of a toasted slice of pumpernickel or Anne-Grethe's fresh rolls with butter, a slice of cheese and jam or a delish thin slice of special chocolate coldcut.

There was a satisfaction with rising early and getting a lot done in the morning, and its reward was to take a well-deserved break after breakfast. Uncle Kristian would sink into the comfy sofa and was soon snoring softly as the rest of us either played canasta in the kitchen or went in to play the numerous games and puzzles my aunt had collected from around the world, many of them gifts from her previous lodgers.

Anne-Grethe would eventually call us away from our games to help her begin preparations for our third meal of the day, our middag, which, literally translated, means midday meal, typically the hot meal of the day. The middag would be just our family. We all sat together at the built-in table in the kitchen and ate Danish pork meatballs, called frikadeller, with potatoes and gravy, and sometimes fried eel.

Good weather in the summer was celebrated with a picnic at the beach near their summerhouse. Anne-Grethe would pack us a big picnic basket filled with goodies, and off we would go on an adventure. One summer, the Panduro's bought a small motorboat for waterskiing. Although I could snow ski pretty well, I found that when launched on the water, it's really hard to hang on to the lead with only one arm. Yes, the water was cold — very cold — but we loved to get in and play.

There always seemed to be jellyfish in the fjords, and we learned quickly how to pick out the harmless ones from those that sting, and we would have jellyfish fights. We enjoyed the warmth of the sun until around three o'clock, when it was time to unpack the picnic basket and lay out our fourth meal of the day — afternoon coffee, cakes, and cookies.

After getting cleaned up from the beach romp, we would once again gather for a meal at around six o'clock. Our fifth meal of the day was a light dinner — usually smørrebrød, but sometimes Anne-Grethe would make us Danish pancakes, complete with fresh strawberries from her garden and whipped cream. I remember sometimes, when driving, she would swerve off the road and jump out to pick large flowers that honestly looked like weeds to me, and she would cook these flowers into the pancakes. I preferred the strawberries, but the flowers were good too.

In Denmark, the sun barely sets in the summer. It was wonderful for playing late-night games of fodbold (soccer). Nearly every farm had a soccer net set up, ready for play. If it wasn't soccer, we would play kick the can until around nine o'clock when, believe it or not, we had our sixth and final meal of the day, evening coffee. Which was, once again, a cup of coffee or tea served with cake and cookies. If us kids were too preoccupied running about playing games, we wouldn't stop, not even for a sodavand (soda).

Anne-Grethe had hired the local veterinarian's daughter, Henriette, to help with food prep, cooking, laundry, digging up potatoes from the garden, and general cleanup. Henriette usually arrived by the time I had finished my morning chores out in the barn, but sometimes I would sleep in a little and help her instead. Come rain or shine, we had to go out and collect as many little new potatoes that we could dig up with a pitchfork, bring them back and dump them into a seemingly magical device resembling a large metal blender. With the flick of a switch the potatoes were spun rapidly around, knocked into each other and, with nothing more than friction, peeled. I had never seen one of these machines before, nor have I since.

Henriette and I were the same age and quickly became fast friends. I began frequently staying the night at her house. She had two sisters and we all hung out together, often riding their beautiful Norwegian horses. We rode English style, which was tricky for me without a horn to hold on to. Other days, we would all jump on our bikes and ride down to Sillerslev havn (the beach at Sillerslev harbor). All harbors had an "Is Kiosk" (Ice Cream Kiosk). We would get an ice cream and search for seashells or flat pebbles that we could skip in the ocean, or just lie topless on the beach. On rainy days, we would stay out at the farm, sit up in my room and play cards, and chat about boys.

Another friend was Inge-Grethe, who lived on a neighboring dairy farm. They had the cutest little baby calves who would latch onto our fingers, hand, or anything they could get ahold of in the hopes of drawing out some milk. It was amusing until they cut their teeth. She also had a sweet pony, a brown Shetland with a cream-colored main. We took turns riding him bareback, as he was too small to ride double. Inge-Grethe would clasp her hands together, leaving an open space for my foot, and boost me up. I could only offer her one hand in return, but being a small horse he was not difficult to mount. He was fairly obstinate though, and we could never tell if a little kick would elicit a begrudging walk or a full gallop. Whichever he gave us, we took several turns around the field. When he'd had enough he simply stopped. For his trouble, we gave him a friendly pat and a fat slice of pumpernickel.

In Denmark, everyone on a farm learns to drive tractors. I was excited to learn as well. Uncle Kristian taught me on the little gray tractor. We started with the basics: how to start, stop, and shift the gears. Then he allowed me to take the tractor up and down the long, grassy runway behind the barn. It was a little risky, as I had to let go of the steering wheel at times when I shifted gears — the tall gear shaft was situated between my legs. It was a bumpy ride, and I had to make sure I was firmly seated so that I wouldn't bounce out. I spent most of the time in first gear, but on occasion I got up to second or third gear. I knew I wouldn't lose control of the tractor as long as I planned my moves carefully and made sure I was on smooth ground prior to changing gears. I had already realized that despite having just one arm, there was nothing I couldn't do. It usually took a little forethought in figuring out how, but I always found a way. Anyone who knows me, even strangers who see me in action, realize, I mean business.

I became adept at anticipating any interaction with the world — always thinking three or four steps in advance. For example, if I needed to carry a lot of things through a closed door, I would strategically plan how to balance and secure everything either under my arm or in my hand, so I would still have a few fingers free to grab and twist a doorknob. Doors with a handle (which at that time were the only type used in Denmark) were much easier, and you could use your elbow or one finger to grab it. Once it was opened a few inches, I could then slip my foot into the opening and swing the door open wider if it was spring-loaded. Thinking ahead about how to tackle situations was a process that increased my creative problem-solving skills. Learning to anticipate logistical challenges has served me well, going forward in life.

Many people have said to me over the years that they were surprised when they realized I have only one arm. Others have remarked on how easy I made it look. Children have even asked me if I was magic. My answer to them all has always been the same.

"I only need one arm, because I can do everything with just one."

Every year, on June 23, Denmark celebrates Sankt Hans Aften (St. John's Eve). The night of the summer solstice is the shortest night of the year, and legend has it that on this night, evil runs amok. To keep the wickedness at bay, people build bonfires and burn "witches" made of old clothes stuffed with hay. Over the years the tradition has come to focus less on averting evil forces and more on fun, songs, and wishing for a good harvest.

Like most of the island residents, we went down to the beach for this event. Families could be seen all along the shore stacking branches to build a conical bonfire topped with a witch tied at the stake. As nightfall set in, the fires began to glow, and burning embers floated into the air as groups held hands and danced around their fires singing. Once the witch was burnt and the evil vanquished, we would cuddle under blankets, drinking coffee or hot chocolate, sitting around the fire telling stories and singing more songs.

Midway through the summer, my mother, brother, and I took the train to her hometown of Slagelse. Since Denmark comprises approximately 400 islands, we would ride the train as far as it could go on land, then board the ferry along with all the cars, and sail on to the next island. Once the train was locked down in the ship's hull, the passengers were able to go out on the deck to enjoy the scenic beauty of Denmark's many coastal communities, with their boat-filled harbors and quaint fishing communities. Or passengers could sit inside and be mesmerized by the steel-gray water splashing up the sides of the ferry creating a cold misty spray, while enjoying a sodavand or a nice cold Tuborg. We went through this scenario several times before reaching our destination on the main island of Sjœlland. This train ride across the Danish islands was an amazing adventure.

After visiting my great aunts, Faster Gerde and Faster Johanne, for a few weeks, we headed on to Copenhagen to stay with my mother's cousin Else and her kids. They lived on the fifth floor of a historic yellow brick apartment building on one of Copenhagen's main canals. There was no elevator in the building, and although Else's apartment had its own toilet, many of the other apartments had to share a communal WC down the hall. Showers were installed at a later date up in the attic under the high pitch of the roof. Luckily for us, that was only one floor up. It was a wonderful apartment with fantastic views of the boats passing through the canal and close enough to see the nightly summer fireworks at Tivoli Gardens.

Often our mothers would take us down to Tivoli to watch the Danish soldiers marching in the parade and to ride the rickety wooden roller coaster from 1914. Live music usually played, and we could hear the concerts as we walked through the gardens. At dusk the magical gardens were lit by thousands of tiny lights accentuating the exotic and historic architecture that Tivoli is so well known for. These gardens have a fairy-tale quality that makes your imagination go wild.

Before leaving Tivoli, my cousins insisted on having a silly photo taken as our summer keepsake at the photo booth shop. There you get to choose a life-size painted character cutout and set your head in the hole for a hilarious photo. One summer we looked like a group of prisoners in our black and white stripes. Our mothers couldn't stop laughing.

Copenhagen is a city of many canals, and we enjoyed sightseeing on the local rundfart — a boat ride through the canals. We would sail past the Queen's palace, the Royal Opera House, the statue of the Little Mermaid from the Hans Christian Andersen tale (it's actually very small), and Nyhavn (the historic harbor area with the colorful boats all adorned with the Danish flag flying high). Danes love their flag! There is even a giant ship painted red and white to resemble Dannebrog. Nyhavn in the old days was where you found drunken sailors and ladies of the night. Now it is better known for upscale beer gardens and restaurants. If you travel a little farther down along the canal, you come to a house where Hans Christian Andersen lived.

The city is adorned with numerous towers that were built by King Christian IV in the early 1600s. He was responsible for most of the historic buildings that I admired around the city.

Once we disembarked, we headed off to Strøget (the main pedestrian walking street in Copenhagen) for shopping and a trip to the top of the Rundetårn (the famous round tower). The tower was designed for King Christian IV so he could ride in his horse-drawn carriage on a continuously curved ramp up to the top to admire the views of his beautiful city.

After several weeks in the big city, we returned to Morsø, where our summer travels culminated with my favorite event of the season — the wheat harvest. The wheat had been eight to ten inches tall when we arrived in Denmark. By summer's end it had grown to about 36 inches. My uncle spent countless hours walking through his fields, inspecting his crops for weeds, rodents, and proper growth. That August, there was a palpable unease as farmers followed the weather. They knew that if a rain came shortly after cutting the stocks, it would have a devastating effect on the harvesting of the hay.

When the tops of the wheat were golden brown and it looked as if a good stretch of weather could be relied upon, the farmers would dust off their harvesters. Large rotating cylinders cut the stalks, leaving them in rows on the ground, while simultaneously removing the wheat kernels, shooting them into a grain tank. Once the stalks were cut, there was no turning back. Daily walks of the fields were made to check on the stalks as they dried into the hay that would be used in the barn. Good weather was essential in the drying process because a rain could ruin the hay with mildew. It took several days before the baling could begin. When it was time, this task required all hands on deck, and that's when the fun began.

My cousin Laurids would travel from Aalborg, about an hour and a half northeast of us, to help. He, Steven, and I slid on thick work gloves to minimize blisters, and then we climbed into the back of our uncle's hay wagon. As Kristian drove, the baler miraculously gathered up the stalks into neat rectangular bundles, wrapping them with twine and hoisting them by way of a conveyor belt and pitching them into the wagon that followed. It took all three of us to keep up with the work, passing the bales to each other and stacking them in neat rows in order to collect as many as possible per run.

Once the wagon was full, we headed back to the barn where we unloaded the hay onto another conveyor belt that delivered them up to the hayloft. The bales were spilled into the hayloft, and if we had a couple of extra helpers we would be able to stack the bales neatly as they came up. Otherwise they tumbled all over the place and we kids would have to go back later and sort them out. Since the hayloft was one of our favorite hangouts, we didn't mind. We built many a fort up there over the summer. It was even where I received my first real kiss.

From morning to night traversing back and forth, up and down the fields, lifting and stacking hundreds of hay bales, climbing, jumping and falling off of haystacks, our only breaks came when we heard the clanging of Anne-Grethe's bell calling us in for our midday meal. It wasn't leisurely. There was no chitchat during harvest. We simply ate, then got back to work. Around seven o'clock, we returned to the house exhausted, sore, and shaking the hay out of our hair, ears, and boots. I was quick to call, "First in the shower!"

That hot water never felt so good. Anne-Grethe served a light meal those evenings. If we could manage to stay awake, we watched a little TV, then despite the sky still being light well into the night, we fell into a deep and sound sleep. This routine generally lasted three to four exhausting days.

I found the hard work motivating and exhilarating at the same time. It was a wonderful feeling to be part of a team effort, especially something that sustained my aunt and uncle. If we were not there to lend a hand, they would have had to hire outside help. They took such great care of us all summer. Helping with harvest was the least we could do, and it was a blast. Laurids would usually stay on a few extra days so we could hang out and enjoy each other's company until his older brother Ib and his longtime girlfriend would come and pick him up.

We usually scheduled our flights back to California after the harvest. Harvest was the best part of the summer, yet it always felt bittersweet as it signaled the end of our trip.

I was still struggling with the loss of my father, but when I was with his family it strengthened the feeling that I always had, of his presence watching over me.

Chapter 13

~ Don't Label Me ~

Although I missed my friends in California, Tess and my classmate Val from middle school both had my address at Sønnegård, and I would receive letters throughout the summer keeping me updated on the fun they were having back in California. In return, I would write and tell them about all my adventures in Denmark, and the boys I had met.

Upon our return, I asked my mother if I could take English riding lessons. In Denmark they rode only English, which was very awkward for me with the dressage, popping up and down with no horn to hold onto. The reins were also held differently. I could never quite get the hang of it. My mother and Nanna had taken Bruce, Tess, and me countless times to a local stable and taught us how to ride horses with western saddles. Since my mom and aunt were expert gauchos from their days growing up in Argentina, they taught us well. Throughout the years I had also been riding with Val on her horse. She enthusiastically supported my interest, even though she wanted to try and learn to ride English herself.

My mother contacted a stable that she had heard of located in Woodacre and explained to them how she had taught me western, but I was looking to learn to ride English style. They said to come on out; I could join their group class. The place was nothing fancy. It had some modest stables and a ring and a field with jumps for the English riders. It smelled wonderful, a mixture of bay leaves, oak trees, leather, and horse manure. I stood eagerly watching the other kids preparing to ride as they brushed and saddled their horses. I was feeling impatient to join the fun when something caught my ear, and I froze.

The program director was explaining to my mother in a loud whisper that as a "handicapped person," I would require more expensive private lessons.

"What?! "

I was... furious. Who was she to assume my potential? She didn't even know me. I turned around and burst out,

"I am not handicapped, and I do not need private lessons!"

Stomping away, I could hear my mother behind me giving that lady a piece of her mind. We got in our car, slammed our doors, and drove off. I decided then and there that I was never going to let people label me, let alone tell me what I was capable of.

When eighth grade started, I chose for my elective an Architectural Design class. I was the only girl in the class. I was also the only student with one arm. Neither issue fazed me or the other students or the teacher. We were all friends and had a wonderful teacher, Mr. Cadwalder.

Our culminating project was to design a building of our choice and build it to scale. Trying to figure out how I would build something, I spoke with my teacher and together we came up with an A-frame house.

I drew it up and measured out the thin strips of wood he recommended I buy for the project. He supplied the hammer and tiny nails in class. I used a miter box to cut the needed lengths and angles with a rectangular shaped miter saw. I would hold the wood in place with either my knee or a clamp as I sawed. Sometimes one of the guys in class would lend me a hand. Aligning the angles to form the top of my "A" frame, I used a thumbtack to start the hole and then press a small nail until the tip of my nail sat securely in the wood. I would hit that nail dead-on and sink it in one blow. It was a noisy class: thump, thump, bang, whack! Occasionally a boy would miss the nail and slam his thumb. An arm would fly up along with an "Ouch!" Not me — I never had that problem.

No one ever suggested I might choose a "more appropriate" class, and I never doubted I could do everything required to build my project. Architectural Design may have seemed like an impossible class for me, but the support of my family, teachers, and peers allowed me to believe that the only obstacle to a person's success was their own thinking. I loved the design aspect, and then to see the project come to life was very exciting. It was at this point I realized I wanted to go into architecture.

Tess and I had made a lot more friends in the past few years, and so we expanded the group that joined us in our numerous mischievous escapades. Val became another one of our closest friends; she was the youngest of five siblings, all free spirits. Her brother played the drums in a band, and her sisters all seemed to be groupies. We spent many Friday nights partying at her house as her brother's band played to a full house. If there weren't any parties going on, we would sneak out and go down to the fields at College of Marin, our local junior college, and jump on the large track mats, or roller skate through the tennis courts.

In the mornings we would take the bus out to Sleepy Hollow, where Val boarded her horse, for a weekend ride in the hills. We would ride double on Brie, her gray Arabian/Quarter Horse mare. Most people thought we were sisters, as we were both petite blond girls, so we began telling everyone that we were, embellishing the story with all sorts of adventures and places we had lived.

If we weren't out riding, we would hang out at each other's houses, a couple of miles apart. As we walked, two of us would tie our shoelaces together and walk in unison, similar to a three-legged sack race. We would take turns being tied together. Although we had practiced the three-legged walk many times, one day we decided to tie all three of ourselves together.

I guess we were an easy target with our clumsy attempts to get synchronized because a boy named Skip who attended the Developmental Center that shared the same campus with our middle school began to follow us. The faster we tri-walked to get away from him, the faster he pursued us until it became a chase. He wanted to be a part of our fun, but honestly, I was afraid of Skip and a few of the other children from the Developmental Center.

The Developmental Center shared the same administration office and drop-off zone as the main campus of Kent Middle School. A few times, I had by chance walked past the office when the bus was dropping off the children, and I was grabbed and attacked by them.

One time a student ripped my shirt. I'm not sure if they did that to everyone, or if they thought I was different and wanted to learn more about me. Either way, I did not appreciate this and would find myself going in another direction whenever I saw the bus pull up.

Tess knew this, and when we saw Skip chasing us, and we three were all tied together, she quickly untied herself so she could try to handle the situation. Val and I tried as well, but the knot had tightened, and so we scrambled frantically up a small embankment to get away. The harder we tried, the more we slid back down. Tess grabbed her hairbrush out of her back pocket, turned, and began waving her hairbrush and yelling.

"Back off! Back off!" she cried, until Skip slowly retreated.

We all dropped to the ground, laughing uncontrollably, realizing what had just happened. We asked Tess, "What were you going to do, brush his hair if he came any closer?"

I did feel sad for him at the moment he finally walked away. He had just wanted to join in. After that incident, we decided that tying our shoes together probably was not the best idea.

Since our school had been transitioned from a K–8 school to a middle school, we were the last class to begin kindergarten at A.E. Kent Elementary School and end in A.E. Kent Middle School. This was celebrated with a special end-of-year party, and both our original kindergarten class photos and our eighth-grade photos were in the yearbook. Most of us had been together for the full duration, and this made for a lot of sadness for the ones not continuing onto the same high school.

My mother sewed my formal graduation dress. All the girls had to wear an off-white, full-length dress, and the boys were required to wear suits. My Mom, in true Danish tradition, threw a big party for me, with all of our family and my friends. It felt like life was starting to fall into place once again.

Chapter 14

~ No Guts, No Glory ~

For my middle school graduation, Anne-Grethe and Kristian sent me a plane ticket with an invitation to spend another summer with them in Denmark. This time I would go on my own. I was both scared and very excited. I had suffered from homesickness as a small child, so I was concerned about how I would handle being away for three months.

When I was little, I couldn't even stay across the street without having to go home early. I had tried to sleep over at my cousin Bruce's many times, but by 2 o'clock in the morning either my dad would come and get me or Uncle Hermann would bring me home. Granted, I was much younger then and by now had mastered the art of the sleepover, but a whole summer on my own seemed like a challenge. I was determined to face my fears, though. When my mother gave me a suitcase to start packing, I asked,

"Can I have an extra one?"

"Why? What do you need that for?" she said.

"If I'm going to Denmark for three months, I'll need to take my own menstrual pads. I'm not about to use those giant duck pads that they have over there," I explained.

I knew I wouldn't last the summer if I had to use those Danish pads. My mother seemed to sympathize, so I also tried talking her into letting me take toilet paper. Anyone who has spent time in Europe in the 1970s knows why, but my mother drew the line on the toilet paper. She gave me a small, bright red suitcase, and I filled it neatly to the brim with pads; it was the perfect size.

Val came with us to the airport to see me off. We arrived early and had lunch at the airport restaurant. I chose the French Dip like I always did when we went to drop off or pick up relatives. As I said my goodbyes, I put on a brave face and managed to make it onto the plane without crying. Once I found my seat and sat down, I looked out the window and saw my family and friend waving at me from the terminal. My bottom lip began to quiver, and tears started rolling down my cheeks.

"Little girl, what's the matter?" said a deep male voice.

I turned to find a tall black man sitting next to me with a big, beautiful smile. I told him I was going to Denmark for the whole summer and was worried about being homesick.

"You haven't even left yet," he said. "How do you know it's going to be so bad? I leave home all the time."

"You do?" I asked.

"Sure. I'm in a band and we travel all around the world, going on tour."

"Really... What band are you in?"

"Tower of Power," he answered, pointing around to his other bandmates.

I didn't know who they were, but it didn't matter. He was super nice and introduced me to the other band members. I was so impressed. They told me about the places they had visited, and some of the funny escapades and adventures they had. By the time the plane took off, I was thoroughly entertained and excited about my adventure.

We landed in Copenhagen, where I changed planes to a small puddle jumper that would take me to Thisted. My luggage, unfortunately, was not so lucky in the transfer. I didn't care about the one containing my clothes; it was my pads I was worried about! Oh, the angst. I knew I should have taken them as carry-on. To add misery to the situation, I had to file a missing baggage report and disclose the contents. Right there in front of my aunt, my uncle, and complete strangers I had to disclose that one suitcase was completely full of sanitary pads. Ugh! Two long days later, a small delivery truck from the airport pulled up with my luggage. What a relief.

Kristian's youngest brother Eric lived in California along with his wife and daughter, whom I knew very well. I was happy to see that they had also come to visit. If you recall, my father had connected with Eric in Canada before he immigrated to the US. When Eric emigrated to California that following year, he initially stayed with my parents until he could get settled. It was great to see his daughter Diana again, we were like cousins, and I knew it would be fun to spend time with her in Denmark.

Uncharacteristically, Uncle Kristian thought we should all take a vacation to Germany in celebration of his brother's visit. Getting away was something he rarely was able to do. Kristian and I were constantly teasing and joking around, and Eric thought it would be humorous to join in; however, I never found his teasing funny. We spent many long days on the road as we traveled through Southern Jutland, with a brief stop in the historic town of Ribe, known to be the oldest town in Denmark with its cobblestone streets that date back to the 9th century. We crossed into the northernmost region of Germany and visited a Schleswig-Holstein castle, which until 1864 belonged to the Kingdom of Denmark.

The sites were fabulous, and I tried not to let Eric's teasing get under my skin. I had resorted to asking him directly to leave me alone on numerous occasions, but it continued. Squished into a small car with him and four others made it a difficult situation to get away from. When we finally arrived back at the farm, Sønnegård, I sat down at the teak table in my room next to the big window and wrote a letter home to my mother. I complained, "What an asshole" and if Eric didn't knock it off I was going to start yelling, and "tell him exactly what I think of him." Luckily, Eric and his family went to stay with another relative once we returned.

During my summer, I would also spend a few days with my father's brothers and their families. My cousin Mariane and I were the same age, and equally mischievous. We got along great. My Uncle Søren was a schoolteacher, and their house was on the school campus. We spent most of our time at the summer beach house they owned on the island. Søren would go eel fishing in the fjord, while Mariane and I would hang out on the beach. Earlier that summer, Mariane had been pictured in the local newspaper, topless on the beach. Her parents weren't very pleased.

My Uncle Karl and his wife Hannah lived in Aalborg with my cousins Laurids and Ib. Karl was my father's oldest brother and probably the biggest kidder in the family. He was a blacksmith down at the shipyards and made beautiful wrought-iron candleholders and gifts for the whole family. Hannah was the sweetest lady and, having only sons, she really enjoyed it when I stayed with them. We made pastries and cookies together, and each year she bought me a beautiful Danish porcelain figurine. She also sent me one every Christmas. Over the years, I have acquired quite a collection.

When staying on the farm with my aunt and uncle, I spent a lot of time with my friend Henriette, including weekends at her house. Friday night was the big night on Danish TV; there were only two channels, and one showed news while the other played reruns of old American TV series. I'll never forget the summer we watched Dallas on Friday evenings and then Henriette, her sister Kirstine, and I would get dressed for a night on the town. This meant going to Nykøbing's Pavilion, which was the local dance hall. The dimly lit Pavilion was always crowded with teenagers and played a mix of Danish and American songs. Abba was a favorite, as they were from nearby Sweden and were popular worldwide. We would squish into a booth with Henriette's friends. They usually sat at one of the big corner booths, with the boys perched on top of the booth, their backs against the wall, acting cool. The boys would supply the booths with plenty of Tuborg. It was exciting to me that teenagers could drink beer at a club in Denmark.

"Where are you from?" the boys would ask, because most people on the island knew each other.

I told them, "I am from California." They would give me a funny look.

"California, USA."

"We don't believe you," they responded. "Your Danish is too good, you can't be from the US."

"Yes, it's true, I was born in California," I said.

Then the next question. "Where do your parents come from?"

"My father is from Morsø, and my mother is from Sjælland."

Aha! That's why my accent was different — because my mother was from Sjælland. Their sudden satisfaction made me laugh.

Denmark has many dialects. Especially if you are from one of the small islands, your regional speech can be like its own language. I was well versed in what they called Morsenbo, which came up quite often. I could never figure out if it was just a pick-up line or they really didn't believe that I was from the United States. Usually the discussion of where I was from ended with a dance or two, and more Tuborg. About four in the morning, we would call a taxi for a ride home, which included a stop at a bakery, where the heavenly smells pulled us in. At that hour we would get the first batch of fresh rolls coming out of the oven.

Toward the end of summer when I was there by myself, my Aunt Nanna also came to Denmark to visit with our family in Copenhagen. She knew I was spending the summer on Morsø and called to check up on me, knowing I had a rough start with homesickness. To her surprise, I was only speaking Morsenbo and she could not understand me. She had to ask me to speak English, claiming that I needed to practice for when I got back to America.

I told her, "I don't want to go back."

I wanted to stay and go to school on Morsø! Aunt Nanna was furious, and she immediately called my mother to report my defection. A few weeks later, I was on my flight home as scheduled.

Once back in the States, I realized that I was excited to see all my old friends and looked forward to signing up for high school.

Registration back then was done the old-fashioned way: students crammed into the Redwood High School gymnasium where teachers were situated at tables around the perimeter, with boxes of index cards in front of them. We surveyed the room, then lined up in front of the classes we hoped to get. In every line I joined, there was a girl named Kim. Kim's younger brother and my brother Steven were best friends. That year we ended up having almost every class together, except for sixth period.

Kim had mapped out the route from class to class. She told me to meet her on the first day of school and I could accompany her to our classes. The design of Redwood High was in essence a giant square with a center courtyard. It's an unattractive two-story dirty yellow concrete structure with a repetitive sequence of square windows on all sides. If it had a taller fence with barbed wire around it, you might have mistaken it for a prison.

In hindsight, it was a simple design, but at the time it seemed like a maze. The first floor was numbered in the 100s, and the second in the 200s. This may seem straightforward enough, but every corridor resembled the next one, lined with lockers on each side and staircases equally spaced. Many of us found the layout confusing and would get lost. And there were no windows in the corridors, so it was difficult to figure out where exactly you were. It all looked the same.

It was not unusual for freshmen to lap the hallway several times before landing where they were supposed to be. At the start of the school year, I didn't realize any of this because I had Kim. We met near the front of the school on the first day, and I followed her to each of our classes from periods one through five. When it came time for us to part ways, she simply pointed me in the right direction so I could find my sixth period. Every day after that, we did the same thing. We would meet in our usual spot and I followed her from class to class, never paying attention to how we got there. We were chatting away, and I was always too busy saying hello to everyone I passed.

This went on for several weeks, until one day Kim was absent. I waited around for a while until I realized that she wasn't coming. Then it dawned on me that I had no idea where any of my classes were located. I walked around and around the tiled hallways struggling to find a familiar landmark until eventually I stumbled, late and embarrassed, into first period. Then I had to do this all over again for each subsequent class. I was sent to the office several times that day for being tardy. I would be told by the teacher to go get a late slip, which would then necessitate me having to find my way back to class again. Half the period was over by the time I returned. My first lesson of high school had been learned. Always get your bearings and know the lay of the land before navigating a new building.

My sixth-period Mechanical Drawing class was the only period of the day where my schedule diverged from Kim's. I was very excited to begin to learn drafting. The teacher was a stern Russian, Mr. Suzdaleff. He and the students who did not already know me gave me skeptical looks when I first walked into class. All eyes followed my entrance. I spied a familiar face and made my way across the room to a table by the window. The friend was Dario from my Architectural Design class at Kent Middle School.

The tall drafting tables were covered with a light green Borco. Borco is a thick vinyl material that provides a smooth, cushioned surface to draw upon. Mr. Suzdaleff instructed us all to go and pick out a T-square and triangle from the far wall where they hung on the pegboard, along with an engineering scale from the bin. An engineering scale is a three-sided ruler with different scaled numbering systems on each side. I was familiar with these from my architectural class, and I also possessed a cherished few of my own that I had inherited from my father.

The teacher began by explaining how to position the T-square along the left side of the table so it could easily be slid up and down while holding it with the left hand, enabling us to draw a straight horizontal line with our right hands. He added that if you were left-handed, the T-square should be placed on the opposite side of the table. I was left-handed, but I also needed to hold the T-square with my left hand. So, I opted to leave the T-square on the left as if I were right-handed. We practiced this a few times before he had us add the triangle for drawing vertical lines.

The triangle should be placed so that the vertical edge is on the right side for right-handers. This way, Mr. Suzdaleff explained, you could slide the T-square up and down and the triangle from left to right with your left hand while continuing to draw with your right. We were required to use mechanical pencils to achieve crisp, neat lines. Mr. Suzdaleff demonstrated how to twirl our pencils as we drew to help us maintain an even thickness.

I was so excited to get started; it never occurred to me that others were wondering how I was going to do the drafting. I could sense them watching, intrigued to see how I would manipulate the T-square, triangle, and pencil-twirling all at the same time. I continued with the right-handed setup, maintaining a light pressure on the T-square and triangle with the palm of my hand.

By managing the tools with my palm, I could hold the pencil with my fingers. This enabled me to slide the triangle while simultaneously drawing and twirling my pencil. The arrangement seemed to work to my advantage, as most left-handers holding the tools on the opposite side would find that sliding their palms along the paper from left to right as they drew caused the lead to smear.

Not only was I one-handed for this two-handed task, but I was also left-handed.   For the rest of the world at that time, including Mr. Suzdaleff, being left-handed was not acceptable.   Nor was being a girl in this type of work. He liked to make an example out of me whenever he spotted even a small error.   He would also come by my desk to inform me that while my work might be passable, I would never make it in architecture. I was determined to prove him wrong.

I had learned early on that proficiency in managing a task was about two things: foresight and balance.   The foresight part meant thinking ahead about how I might tackle any given situation before it occurred.   The balance part was distributing my weight evenly — whether I was holding multiple items while walking upstairs, or navigating a door without dropping everything or falling over.   And sometimes, like now, balance was about applying equal pressure to two objects simultaneously with my one hand.   Tackling tasks as if I were right-handed often created a better balance among the objects, like in the drafting table setup.

Knowing this, I was determined to show my teacher that I was better than just passable.   If the classroom was open at lunch, I would go in and practice my lettering.   This was not enough, though.   I convinced my mother that the teakwood drafting table I had been eyeing at the Scandinavian Designs store was on sale and I really needed it.   Then, setting up my very own drafting table that both tilted and height-adjusted, I grabbed one of the bar stools from the family room and began practicing my lettering every day after school until I felt comfortable enough for our weekly Friday presentations.

Our teacher would have us hang our assignments on the wall each Friday, with our names on the backs of our drawings. He would then pace along the wall, stopping to critique each piece before announcing which drawing he thought was the best that week. His main complaint was that people couldn't draw or visualize in 3D, and that these people should not choose architecture as their career. This day of reckoning was always stressful. We would cringe as he pointed out the mistakes. When he demanded to know, "Who drew this?" the culprit would have to step forward to receive their punishment. I was on the receiving end of many a sharp critique, as were all the others.

At the end of several months, we turned in a final architectural lettering assignment. It was time to hang these on the dreaded wall of shame. After having my lettering criticized many times, I had worked hard to improve and was proud of my assignment. I was still nervous, though, because Mr. Suzdaleff had been coming by my desk almost daily to offer negative comments about my lettering. Others had noticed how he was extra critical of my work, and even Dario said to me, "Boy, he seems to have it in for you, why doesn't he leave you alone?"

On this day, Mr. Suzdaleff started with the worst lettering in class.

"Whose is this? Is it yours, Sylvia?" Now he was actually singling me out, and I could feel my face growing red.

"No," I said. "It's not mine." I sure felt bad for the person who it did belong to, though.

He continued until there were only three left on the board. Mine was one of them.

"These are the top three," he announced. I was ready to jump out of my skin. I couldn't believe it. Surely he must have realized mine was still up there.

"This one stands out as the best. Can you tell me why?" he said, as he looked around the room trying to see his students' expressions.

"Ok, who wants to own up to it?"

"It's mine," I said confidently, jumping off my stool like I was receiving an award. Everyone began cheering for me. They knew how hard I had worked on my lettering.

I would like to think that Mr. Suzdaleff was hard on me because he knew I was capable, and this was his way of pushing me to be my best. Maybe, though, he was just the first in a long line of assholes that I've had to prove myself to. The most important thing was, I needed to prove to myself that I could do it, that I had what it takes. It was a good feeling of accomplishment to know that my hard work did pay off, and it was moments like this that motivated me.

My mother booked our annual trip to Denmark, leaving in May. I had to make arrangements to take my final exams early. I gave Val strict instructions to pick up my yearbook and have everyone who signed her book sign mine. We exchanged addresses so we could write to each other; she was going to spend most of her summer in Indiana where her family had roots.

When we arrived in Denmark, we first visited Bedstemor, my grandmother on my father's side, who had recently moved into town. The winters on their farm had become too long and isolating for her since my Bedstefar had passed away several years earlier. Now she lived in a quaint little retirement community where she had an apartment. She still managed to make wonderful meals for us in her little kitchen when we came to visit.

In the back of each unit, a little covered patio opened to a large communal grassy area overlooking the fjord. Supposedly, this fiord was the very one that my father walked into one night in his teens when he had been drinking and almost drowned. Or so the story was told by Bedstemor.

She was happy in her little retirement community where she had decorated her apartment hyggelig (a uniquely Danish word for cozy), and she could enjoy all of her friends and neighbors. They liked to meet up a few times a day for coffee and the local gossip. For a small island, there was an amazing amount of gossip. Now I realized why my father and his younger brother Jens used to love to listen in on the party line when they were kids. There was no lack of drama on the island of Mors.

Bedstemor was the sweetest, kindest, most soft-spoken person, and I always enjoyed spending time with her. I knew she had moved into a smaller place and needed to scale down her belongings. I understood this but was surprised when she began to return items that we had previously given her — little things, including the photo album I had made with pictures of my brother and me when we were younger. I told her that I had made the album for her and I wanted her to keep it. She continued to insist. I didn't want to argue with her, so I finally accepted it. I was quite bewildered as to why she didn't want our photos anymore.

On this visit, I went to Norway with Henriette and her sisters' marching band, instead of our usual tradition of joining the family on the beach for Sankt Hans Aften. I went by bus with a group of about fifty students and a few chaperones to a Norwegian town where Norwegian families hosted us. I didn't have much to compare this marching band to, but "we" must have been pretty good otherwise

Norway wouldn't have transported us all the way from Denmark to march in their big state celebration.

Our band members, with the exception of the drum majorette, wore white button-down shirts, blue neckties and blazers, short white skirts, white patent leather boots, and blue berets. The leader wore a red blazer and tall white hat and carried a large baton. Once assembled in their rows, marching in unison and carrying their instruments, they looked just as impressive as they sounded. I was allowed to march alongside the band, and I enthusiastically cheered them on the entire way.

Following the parade, arrangements had been made for us all to attend the traditional witch burning for Sankt Hans Aften. We boarded various small boats and motored out into the fjord beneath the majestic cliffs with hundreds of other dinghies, vessels, and crafts. We gathered around an old barge stacked high with giant branches and topped with its straw witch. At least one boat had live music; most had plenty of beer flowing and people singing the Hurrah song.

The bonfire was lit to great applause, and before long there was an enormous blaze against the night sky, reflecting across the water. The fjord remained full of boats until the wee hours of the morning, with people drinking and cheering whenever the bonfire shifted and sent sparks soaring up into the night air. Once the bonfire had burned down, the barge itself burnt slowly. It was an all-night affair. This was my first time in Norway, and I was impressed by the spectacular scenery and welcoming nature of the people.

Upon returning to the farm, I learned that Henriette's father, Dyrlœge (Veterinarian) Dr. Bay, would be arriving mid-morning. He was my aunt and uncle's veterinarian, and it was time for my favorite colt, Pelle, to get castrated. They wanted to perform the procedure early, prior to the heat of the day.   Dr. Bay was wearing his blue surgical coat and carrying his black medical bag as he walked toward us with my uncle Kristian and Steve. I was already in the field holding Pelle and trying to comfort him.

This was before I discovered architecture, and my love of animals had me believing that someday I would like to be a veterinarian. Thoughts of continuing that ambition dissolved quickly as they proceeded with the gelding of poor Pelle.   I thought I knew what to expect, since I had already witnessed pigs being castrated many times, but I was wrong.   Pelle seemed to know something was up and was very skittish.   He was two years old now, and he had a bit of wild stallion running through his veins. As they approached, he pulled away from my grasp and galloped to the far side of the field. We had to lure him back with a nice fat piece of pumpernickel.

My uncle held him firmly by his lead as the vet reached into his black bag, removing a large syringe the size of a small soda bottle. He inserted the tip of the needle into a vial, slowly pulling on the plunger to draw up the medicine. My uncle, probably reading the expression on my face, looked at me and said, "This will numb any pain."   After disengaging the syringe, the vet held it upright and used his thumb to press the plunger, expressing a spray of fluid out the top.   Turning, he stepped toward the horse, my uncle holding the creature tightly, and injected the anesthetic into his neck.   As the horse fell to the ground, the needle was left dangling, with droplets of blood dripping out the back end. My stomach churned.

My uncle handed Dr. Bay the scalpel from his bag, and with two quick flicks of his wrist the veterinarian sliced open the sacs and squeezed out a pair of testicles the size of grapefruits. He flung them through the air as my eyes followed with amazement at the size of these things, watching as they landed with a bounce in the field. It was done, and so was I. My knees went weak. I felt dizzy and nauseous. Before I realized what I was doing, I was running back to the farmhouse, barely making it through the back doors before throwing myself onto the sofa. I nearly passed out. As the fog began to lift, I could hear Kristian calling out for my mother.

"Judith, Steven passed out in the field!" He was carrying my little brother in his arms.

I later told my mother,

"I don't want to be a vet anymore. After everything I went through with my cancer, I could never cause anyone pain, not even an animal."

It was horrible to watch, and I've never forgotten it. The word "gelding" still evokes the memory.

As summer on the farm continued, I enjoyed hanging out with our friends and spending the warm afternoons down at the summer beach house, and weekends going to dances at the Pavilion. We had so much fun. By mid July, we took the train to visit my mother's family on the big island of Sjœlland, where we primarily stayed with her Uncle Knud and Faster (Aunt) Johanne. Their house was attached to the grocery store they owned. This was where our great aunt and uncle allowed us to help ourselves to all the candy we could eat. It was a child's dream come true.

To keep us out of trouble, Steven and I were allowed to ride the old delivery bicycle, also known as a Danish cargo bike. It was a tall bicycle compared with the ones we had at home. It featured a 2-foot by 2-foot metal basket about eight inches off the ground, in front of the handlebars. It had a single small wheel in front of the basket for steering. We tried putting each other inside the large basket, quickly learning that the weight made it impossible for us to steer. Instead, we loaded it up with empty crates and pretended we were making deliveries to customers up and down the street. This kept us entertained for hours. I really enjoyed our visits in the cities and towns with my mother's family, as we were always laughing and enjoying ourselves. And after the bustle of our city visits, it was nice to get back to the farm, where country life was simple and carefree.

Cousin Laurids had again come to help with the harvest, signaling that another fabulous summer on the farm with Anne-Grethe and Kristian was coming to an end. At least, we thought we would be going home soon. My mother had instructed me to start saying my goodbyes to all my friends. She knew, with the harvest underway, that it would be busy and I always took a long time saying my farewells, since I had to do it personally to everyone I knew. My mother had booked our tickets and begun packing. It always seemed we went home with a lot more than we came with; I guess that's what happens when you visit family in another country. Fortunately, someone always had an extra suitcase, and the suitcase seemed to travel back and forth more frequently than the rest of us.

Once the harvest began, we were in the fields all day. It was mid-morning on the second day when Anne-Grethe started clanging her bell uncontrollably. We were way out in the fields collecting hay bales.

"Something is wrong," Kristian said when he heard the nonstop ringing. "We need to head back immediately."

News had come. My Bedstemor (Anne-Grethe's mother), who had been out on a field trip with her neighbors, had a heart attack and died immediately, just like my father had.

We were all shocked. My mother didn't know what to do. The family was insisting we stay; however, school was about to start back in the States. I hadn't even registered for my classes. Needless to say, we stayed in Denmark for another few weeks. I was glad we did, as it brought the family together even more. The only contention was amongst a few of the grown-ups who couldn't agree who should inherit the Bing & Grøndahl dishes or the Royal Copenhagen figurines. As I heard them argue, I had a déjà vu moment that maybe Bedstemor had been trying to distribute her figurines fairly while she was alive — like when she had insisted on returning items I had given her. It was like she knew something was going to happen to her.

The Rolighed Larsen family has been buried in the Sønder Dråby town cemetery for centuries and, as is typical in Denmark, the cemetery surrounds the local church. I was familiar with the whitewashed stone church with the tall steeple that housed the bell tower, not because we attended church, but because as part of our visits we would pay our respects to our departed. In Denmark, the maintenance of individual gravesites is left up to the family. The living relatives take turns planting and caring for the immediately surrounding areas. Once a plot goes unattended and begins looking uncared for, it is sold off to another family.

We always took our time visiting each gravesite and listening to the adults share stories and wonderful memories about the Larsen family ancestors. It was on these outings that I learned most of my father's family history. And of course, I heard the old joke about Danes only visiting church three times in their lives: first, when they are baptized; second, when they marry; and third, when they die. It seemed like I had heard this a hundred times. And now, here we were.

Another interesting thing about the Danes is how they bury the dead — nothing fancy; just plain, white, wooden coffins. They also do not embalm the deceased; therefore, the funeral service usually needs to be rather soon after the death, especially when the weather is warm.

I had not been in Denmark at the time of my Bedstefar's passing, but during the packed church service for Bedstemor, my cousins Lars Christian, Ib, and Laurids were all telling me that they hoped the coffin didn't start bleeding!

"What are you talking about?" I asked.

Well, as the story goes, at Bestefar's funeral the weather was unusually hot that day, and by the time the Lutheran priest and guests had finished their speeches in the church and the pallbearers began carrying the coffin out to be buried, it was dripping blood from its corners. I was mortified. I didn't hear another word from the speakers because I was filled with dread. I focused only on Bedstemor's coffin, praying it would not start bleeding!

We all followed the (thankfully not dripping) coffin out to the family plot, where Bedstemor would be buried next to her husband, my Bedstefar.   Once the coffin was lowered into the ground, three shovelfuls of dirt were scooped up and thrown down upon her as the words spoken from the priest rang true:

> All go to the same place
> All came from dirt and
> All shall return to the dirt

Silence surrounded us as the somber group turned and headed toward Bedstemor's place, where we then gathered to celebrate her life. As the drinking began, and the toasting picked up, and discussions of who-was-taking-what continued, my little brother picked up a framed picture of himself and started to wave it around.

"Who wants this picture of the cutest baby on earth?" he shouted.

Everyone burst into laughter, and we once again raised our glasses to skål (toast) in honor of Maren Larsen, my beloved Bedstemor.

Chapter 15

~ Time to Drive ~

By the time we were able to rebook a flight home after staying for Bedstemor's funeral, school had started. It had been almost two weeks, and my mother hadn't even notified the office at Redwood. I was so worried. How was I going to make up the time? Worse, I wondered if I was even still enrolled. I would be sixteen this year and really wanted to get my driver's license. It wouldn't be possible if I didn't take the school's Drivers Ed course.

Fortunately, I was able to register for all my classes, and if willing to take the Drivers Ed lecture session first, I would get my license after completing the driving portion. Most students wanted the semester of hands-on training in the simulator or car first, and then the classroom semester — that way you could get your permit and drive with your parents. I was just glad to not have to wait another year. I showed up to third period for my first Drivers Ed class and noticed an open seat next to an old friend.

"I know you," I said. Sandy, right?"

Sandy's resemblance to Betty Boop was incredible. She had big brown eyes and a cute round face framed by a stylish coiffure. As I took my seat, she responded, "Wow, I haven't seen you for a long time. We used to play when you lived around the corner from me in Kentfield."

"That was my aunt and uncle's home," I replied. "But, we need to get together and play again, like the good ol' days." We both laughed, until the teacher told us to settle down.

I adjusted nicely to school, as if I had never been away from my old friends. The semester went by quickly, and when the holidays approached we headed out on our annual Silvertip tree hunt. We looked for the evenly spaced branches that would best allow us to hang our Danish flag garlands and red-and-white, heart-shaped hjerter. It always gave us a good, cozy, and cheerful feeling of hygge when we entered our house and saw the tree. We would keep the tree up until after New Year's because that was my birthday!

This birthday turned out to be extra special. My Uncle Jens and Aunt Joan threw me a New Year's sweet-sixteen party. It was a wild night, with dancing and drinking. Many Rum & Cokes were enjoyed — until my stomach rebelled and I puked it all up. Lesson learned.

When spring semester rolled around, I was so excited to be enrolled in my final Drivers Ed class. I was going to learn to drive. Most students started with time in the simulator, which reminded them of video games at the pizza parlor. The school had a trailer with eight driving simulators in it for practicing driving. I was excited to get some simulator time but instead was given only time in the school's big blue station wagon. The instructor would sit on the passenger side of the long bench seat with one of us kids in the driver's seat; the remaining four students would all sit in a row on the back seat, without seat belts. This probably sounds crazy now, but that was how things were back in 1980.

We would take turns driving the car out onto Highway 101 or around town for the 42-minute class. I always wanted to try one of the simulators in the trailer, but I guess that wasn't in the cards for me. The instructor felt that I should get the hands-on training in the car due to my having only one arm. I consoled myself by thinking I was getting extra-special treatment.

I will never forget our first outing in the blue wagon. A curly-haired redhead named Tim was first up. The remaining four of us sat in the back, holding on tightly while the car jerked back and forth and Tim figured out how to use the gas and brake pedals as he navigated the parking lot exit. I thought, How does this teacher sit there so calmly when the four of us in the back are terrified we're going to crash? Our fears were heightened when he instructed Tim to turn on the blinker and merge onto the freeway.

"Watch out for the speeding cars as you merge."

We knew that the teacher had a brake pedal on the floor, but Tim was the only one steering, and the four of us in the back seat were ready to push our feet through the floor of the old wagon like it was Fred Flintstone's Foot-mobile. As we white-knuckled it, the teacher stayed amazingly calm.

We bounced along in the big back seat, traveling north on Highway 101. Just as we were beginning to catch our breaths, the teacher instructed Tim to pull into a bus stop at the next exit.

"Who wants to go next?" he asked.

The girl in the middle started waving her hand. "I'll go, I'll go," she volunteered.

"Okay, Julie, you can go next," he replied. We had only gone a short distance on the highway with Julie at the wheel when the instructor again gave the instruction to pull over at the next bus stop.

"Sylvia, why don't you go next," the instructor announced as we pulled off the highway.

Okay, I thought, let's go. I was nervous as I climbed into the driver's seat. But I figured I couldn't be any worse than Tim, and we had all survived his driving.

The instructor reached into the glove compartment and pulled out a gadget and handed it to me. "Here, it's a knob, I bought it for you to use," he said, attaching it at the ten o'clock position on the steering wheel. This was the largest steering wheel I had ever seen. It must have been two feet in diameter. The gadget was a free-spinning knob that I could use to help turn the steering wheel. As soon as it was secured into position, he said, "Are you ready, then go ahead, put your blinker on and pull back out onto the highway. Then take the next exit."

I eased the car into traffic and surprised myself. This wasn't so difficult.

After a bit, we turned around and began making our way back toward campus. I remember driving over the hill in San Rafael and past the famous Marin County Civic Center designed by Frank Lloyd Wright. I thought, this really is kind of fun, and not that much more difficult than driving the old gray tractor back in Denmark.

"Time to start slowing down, put your blinker on," he instructed.

Tick, tick, tick, tick went the blinker as I took the exit to get back to campus. I maneuvered through the crowded parking lot behind our high school, pulled up near the simulator trailer, put the old wagon into park, and just sat there for a minute. The other four students quickly jumped out and ran off, since the bell had already rung for morning break. But I had to take this in for a moment. I couldn't believe it; I had just driven that big old tank out on the freeway.

Six weeks later, I passed my driving test with a 94% and received my license. I was elated! Although it was nice of my teacher to buy me that steering wheel knob, I have to admit I never used it again. As usual, I wanted to do things on my own terms.

In spite of missing a limb, I really had a normal high school experience, and because I wasn't self-conscious about having one arm, others weren't bothered by it either. I don't remember teenage angst or a longing to be something I wasn't. I was very well-liked and had many close friends and even more students I was friendly with. Tess and I remained devoted friends even though she was now part of the "Organics," the hippie students who hung out on the front lawn. Sandy and I had reconnected through our Drivers Ed class and were pretty fast friends.

Tess was a hippie and I was a preppy. Yes, in the '80s there were such things. Look it up. There were other cliques at our school — the Jocks, the Popular kids (cheerleaders), the Stoners who hung out at the back fence, and the super fun kids from the projects in Marin City who had me in stitches. I had friends in all groups and ranged widely. Being a preppie, I wore a lot of Levi's 501 button-up jeans, Sperry Top-Siders, and my favorite, Ralph Lauren polo shirts. We bought our Levi's 501 jeans at an old Quonset hut, an army surplus store in San Rafael.

My core group of friends in high school included my old friend Val from middle school and two new friends, Cat and Staci. The four of us were thick as thieves. Val was a petite, pretty blonde who was full of spirit.   She was the youngest of five siblings and had the resourcefulness that came with it, along with a heart of gold. Val and I liked to make the rounds at school, visiting with people in the different groups. Each group had its area, and we would stop and visit all of them, including the Jocks (one of Val's favorites) and the Populars. Staci and Cat claimed that it was hard to track us down during break as we were free-ranging. The best way to find us was to listen for my laugh ringing out.

Cat moved to the area when we were in middle school, but we became fast friends in high school. One of my first memories of her was in the empty hallway at school one morning. I was on my way to the bathroom and saw her sitting there. She was really distraught. Her locker mate had kicked her out of "his" locker. I told her she could move in with me and share a locker. That was the beginning of a beautiful friendship. Cat was a very stylish girl of Chinese ancestry with a sunny personality.

Staci was the most loyal of friends. She was a sweet, wholesome girl who lived with her grandmother. Where they dined nightly under the original crystal chandelier from her grandfather's time, and read the classics together by the roaring fire. Her grandmother's estate was a beautiful mansion in the exclusive neighborhood of Ross. The house was amazing, and we would take the secret "servants" staircase up the back of the house to her room when we snuck in late, and her grandmother was none the wiser.

Val introduced Staci and me to each other. There was an instant connection between Staci and me that created an unbreakable bond. I can only hope everyone is as fortunate as I have been to have had this instant connection with several people throughout my life. It's made for the best lasting friendships.

My core group of friends had an interesting trait in common. None of us had our fathers in our lives. Maybe because of this we bonded more tightly, creating our own support system. We were all good students, but we also knew how to have a good time. We were fun and that is what we did.

We went to dances, parties, and all the rugby and football games, where we cheered loudly for our teams. A favorite pastime in class was to pass notes; we wrote our first names paired with the last names of our crushes and folded them into cootie catchers. We would have died if anyone else had gotten hold of them and read them.

Once we were all sixteen and driving, and the weekend hit and the sun was shining, we would head straight to Stinson Beach. Val was the first one with a car, and she and Staci met Cat and me at my house. With our bikinis on, we would grab cold pizza, beach towels, and a bottle of Bain De Soleil No. 2 suntan oil and head out. We would stop only to get just enough gas to get us there and back. It was a forty-minute drive over Mt. Tamalpais on the winding road through giant redwoods — the windows down, our arms stretched out, and our voices singing along with Casey Kasem's Top 40, which blasted from the radio. Luckily, no one else could hear, as none of us could carry a tune.

Stinson Beach, although a beautiful stretch of white sand, was usually windy. Sudden prickly gusts of sand could pelt you. Fortunately, we knew all the good spots where we could lie in the sun and be protected from the wind. We would bake under the hot sun until we couldn't stand it anymore, then go running and laughing into the 55-degree waters of the Pacific Ocean. The icy waters made us shriek as we dove into the waves, catching a few and body surfing. The rough waves often tossed us all the way back into the shallows, giving us the "washing machine" treatment which would require a cautious

rearrangement of our bikinis before standing up. Once we were numb
and freezing, we would run back to our towels and flop down with our
skin tingling under the warmth of the sun.

One bright, hot day when Cat flopped down on her towel beside the
rest of us, she rolled over, looked up toward the sky, and said, "Hey, the
sun is right over me today." We all replied, "Cat, it's over all of us."
To which she said, again, "No, I mean it's directly over me." The rest
of us laughed hysterically and have never let her live that down. We
were always in stitches, laughing and having fun when we were
together.

Unfortunately, my little brother Steven was not having quite the
same positive experience at middle school. I was five years older, and
five grades ahead of my brother, and I was the one who had lost a limb,
yet he was the one who was bullied. He never mentioned it or
complained to our mother or me about it. One story that he eventually
shared with me was about two Korean sisters who started taunting him
in seventh grade because he didn't have a father, and his sister had only
one arm. These two girls found ways to twist those facts into
humiliating remarks directed at my brother day after day for several
weeks. Steven finally had enough. During lunch one day, the two
sisters started with the nasty comments again.

"Leave me alone!" Steven shouted at the sisters, warning them, "Or
I'm going to kick your asses!" Even though Steven had been taught to
never hit a girl, he had reached his limit. He was so mad, you could
almost see the smoke coming out of his ears. The sisters began
chanting about his one-armed sister and dead father as they ran off
giggling, feeling full of themselves. Sadness, pain, frustration, and rage
overwhelmed my little brother. Automatic pilot took over, and he
pulled back his arm and pitched the apple he was holding about thirty

feet through the air, straight for the girls, nailing the younger sister in the head and dropping her like a sack of potatoes. It was an awesome throw.

An hour later Steven, our mother, and the two Korean sisters with their mother were all gathered together in Principal Warren's office. Our mother was furious, while the other mother had a smug look on her face. Principal Warren listened to the sisters' fabricated story, then asked Steven for his perspective. Steven was incredulous that they could have lied so blatantly.

He turned to the girls and repeated, "Tell them the truth, tell them what you really said. Tell them the truth. Tell them!" over and over until he was yelling uncontrollably.

The sisters finally broke, admitting to taunting Steven relentlessly over the past several weeks. Punishment was handed down and the two girls were sent home, having been told to apologize to Steven. When they did, Steven told them he did not accept their lame-ass attempt at getting out of trouble and went on to lay down the new rules.

"If you ever say another cruel thing about my sister or anybody that I know, I'm going to unleash my anger on you and I won't care what happens to me."

Rightfully, this resulted in another meeting with the principal. Steven owned up, as he is probably the most honest person you may ever meet. Principal Warren was sympathetic to Steven and talked with him about his struggles and thanked him for his honesty.

"For that, you can thank my mother," Steven replied.

Steven, thankfully, never saw those two sisters again. They might have moved or transferred to another school. Unfortunately, these two were not the only ones who harassed my poor little brother, and I found out later that our cousin Bruce had also been receiving flack from other kids. My brother was so persistently bullied that he realized he could not handle this himself. Bruce is a few years older than Steven and told him he was not going to allow him to be bothered again. Bruce and his buddy Eric then became Steven's wingmen. If Steven had troubles with anyone, these two would show up, and if Steven couldn't handle the situation they would threaten the bullies by telling them to leave Steven alone or they would come looking for them. I am glad we had the family and support behind us.

A few years after losing our father, my mother realized that Steven was going to need some extra support, and so she contacted the organization Big Brothers of America. It was a mentoring program for children who didn't have fathers, or at least fathers who were around for them. Steven's first big brother was Pat, a young married guy originally from Michigan. Steven absolutely worshipped Pat. Unfortunately for Steven, after a few years Pat and his wife wanted to start a family of their own and decided to move back to Michigan. California's cost of living was just too high for them. My brother was devastated after first losing his father and then losing his Big Brother. My mother went back to the organization to try to find Steven another mentor. They went through interview after interview for a new big brother, but Pat was a hard act to follow.

Finally, when Steven was about to give up, we met Sam Button. Sam was a bit older, a well-traveled man who had been in the military and told stories of his adventures around the world. We all later joked, when he wasn't around, that he was probably a spy and who knows? Retired from public service, he had become a successful insurance broker for Lloyds of London and had the time and means to devote to mentoring Steven. He quickly became part of our family, and Steven blossomed under his wing.

Meanwhile, I was fortunate to get my first job at Bucher's Patisserie in Novato. Paul Bucher and his wife Theresa had owned the bakery in Argentina where my grandfather worked during the time my mother's family lived there. Since Paul Bucher originally came from the Alsace-Lorraine, a province of France, and was a renowned master chocolatier and pastry chef, I enjoyed watching his work and learning from him. Plus, he reminded me of my grandfather. I typically worked weekends and holidays. When summer came, I was able to work more hours and make a little extra cash.

I was excited that we were staying home for the summer instead of going to Denmark. I was at the age where I wanted to be able to hang out with my friends by our pool. We had spent the last three summers in Denmark. My mother had put in a traditional barrel wood hot tub with a small deck in the backyard, and our backyard was now the perfect retreat. It was the beginning of a new tradition: Kahlua coffee liqueur and milk while lounging in the Larsens' Hot Tub. Hot tubs were the new fad, and our neighbors, friends, and many visitors from Denmark that summer all enjoyed it with us.

My Uncle Jens (my father's younger brother) and his wife Joan invited us to join them on a houseboat trip up the California Delta. Prior to our summers in Denmark, we used to join them for weeklong cruises in the delta. My uncle was an avid fisherman and still loved being on the water, like in the days he and my father had spent fishing out on the rocks in Bodega Bay while the rest of us ran and played on the beach. Jens is a fun, jovial fellow like the rest of the Larsens, and the only other member of my father's family who immigrated to the US. He missed having his brother around, and he took us in and helped my mother through some difficult times.

Jens had bought a yacht in order to spend more time out in the ocean fishing. Perhaps it also made him feel closer to his brother and reminded him of Denmark. We all were able to enjoy many outings on the ocean together.

I especially remember one Halloween party at the boat club where Jens docked his boat. At this party, I met a boy who gave me my first real kiss. Uncle Jens was so upset when he discovered us making out, he sent us back to the clubhouse and told me he would deal with me the next day. I hoped that the next day he wouldn't remember, as most of the adults were having a really good time and way too much to drink. Once back in the clubhouse, I suggested a game of pool. The boy was rather hesitant, stating he was the club champion. He probably doubted my ability to play pool with one arm. Sensing his hesitation, I didn't suggest that we bet money on the game. But maybe I should have.

I had played pool many times with my uncle, and learned a few tricks on my own. The look of surprise on that boy's face when my first shot landed in the corner pocket just as I called was quite amusing. This only made me more determined to win. The poor guy never really had a chance once I put my mind to it. As the game progressed, the other kids began gathering around watching, warning me that I would never beat Tim, since he was the club champ. The pressure was on. The look on people's faces was priceless when I kicked his ass, winning two out of three. My uncle forgave me after that, giving himself credit for teaching me everything I knew.

The houseboat trip that summer was a long, lazy drift up the delta. We would sun ourselves on the upper deck and then cool off in the murky water with a quick dip. Uncle Jens taught anyone who would participate how to fish, and a lot of fish were caught. Aunt Joan would fry them up, and then meals were made all the more exciting by the plates and condiments sliding back and forth across the table as the boat rocked on the waves. We all found this particularly hilarious.

Summers in California were great, although my Danish family and friends remained in my thoughts. I did miss them and spending time on the farm. Checking the mailbox was a part of my daily routine, as my friends in Denmark would write frequently. Missing Denmark was mitigated by the consistent California sunshine. The long, carefree days were spent hanging by the pool, swimming, playing backgammon and cards, getting a tan, and talking about boys. When summer neared its end, it was time for my mother, brother, and me to take our annual road trip to Solvang, then Disneyland and our stay with the Bollisens. As the three of us headed out, we felt an uplifting feeling of family unity. We knew that as long as we had each other, everything would be all right. Those trips are some of my best childhood memories.

Junior year of high school was notable because I was finally able to enroll in the Architectural Drawing class. Fortunately for me, Mr. Suzdaleff, who had been so discouraging when I had him for mechanical drafting classes, did not teach it. Mr. Bolt shared a classroom with Mr. Suzdaleff and therefore was somewhat familiar with my work. I was excited to learn more about architecture, and to not have to draw another 3D nut-and-bolt axonometric.

Over the summer, my mother had let me drive her car to my job at the bakery a few days a week, but when school started she was not about to let me take it to school. I needed a car. After my Bedstemor had passed in Denmark, there was a small inheritance divided amongst her five children. Since my father had already passed, his portion was divided equally between my brother and me. It wasn't a large sum, and my mother didn't really want me to use it all on a car, but it was enough for me to buy myself a used car with a bit left over.

Uncle Hermann owned a German automotive shop, and he recommended I look for a Volkswagen. I searched the newspapers and Auto Trader pages for weeks and came up with a VW Scirocco. It would be the cool, sporty car that I could afford. Deciding on the type of car then made looking much easier. I quickly found one; it was a black 1979 VW Scirocco for only $3,000 with low miles. The seller agreed to meet at the San Francisco Ferry Building, where I took the Scirocco for a test drive up and down the Embarcadero and checked all the items my uncle had told me to look for. Upon returning, I exclaimed to my mother in Danish, "I've got to have this car. It's perfect for me!"

I know my little VW didn't compare to some of the other vehicles in our school parking lot, because Marin County is extremely wealthy and many of the cars were Porsches, Mercedes, and BMWs — occasionally a Ferrari would even show up at school — but in my mind, my Scirocco was by far the coolest. The best part of owning my own wheels was escaping the embarrassment of having my mother drive me to school with her hair up in curlers, wearing a robe on rainy days.

Now that I had a car, I quickly realized that this opened new opportunities for me. The part-time job at the bakery was not going to be enough. I needed to get serious about finding a job in architecture. I pulled out our copy of the Marin County phone book that my mother kept in the drawer under the old wall-hung dial-up phone and began cold-calling names listed in the yellow pages under Architects, one by one, beginning with "A."

Eventually, Fredric C. Divine Architects in San Rafael responded with, "Come on by, and show me your portfolio." This caused me a lot of anxiety because of course I did not have much of an actual portfolio of work at that point. I decided to make up for this lack by bringing an enthusiastic attitude.

Two days later, with my drawings in hand, I drove down Lincoln Avenue in San Rafael peering at the numbers on the buildings. I was looking for an office building, and I drove right past my destination. The office was actually in a turn-of-the-century dark gray shingle house with a small front porch, a steep gable façade, and a narrow single-car driveway that flanked the left side of the house with several parked cars. That couldn't be his office, I thought. Nervously, I approached the front door and rang the old clock doorbell. A man answered the door.

"I'm here to see Fred Divine," I stated.

"Hello, I'm Rich. Why don't you come on in and have a seat in the kitchen. I'll get him." When Rich returned, he sat down at a drafting table — also located in the kitchen — and began drawing. "He'll be right with you," he said. A few moments later, a tall, slender man entered the room and extended his hand.

"Hi, I'm Fred Divine. Take a seat and show me what you've got," he said.

I sat down beside him and proceeded to present my mechanical drawing sheets and sketches. I figured he was wondering what a girl with one arm was doing pursuing a career in architecture.

As the silence stretched uncomfortably, I blurted out, "What do you think?"

"You did all these drawings?" he asked.

"Yes, I did," I replied confidently.

"Let me give you a tour of the place and explain what you would be doing here if you want to start," Fred said, standing.

I jumped up and followed. He circled first into the butler's pantry, where we found Rich running blueprints. I looked on in amazement, as I had never seen such a machine.

"Do you think you can run blueprints? Because you will be running a lot of them if you work here."

"Sure." I answered, thinking to myself, I can do anything, and I'm sure I'll be able to figure that out.

Back in the kitchen, Fred pointed out which desk would be mine and told me I would also be answering the phones.

"You can use Rich's drafting table when he's not here, until we get a permanent one set up for you."

"You seem very ambitious," he continued. "I'll give you a try, if you think you can handle it?"

"Oh yes, I can definitely handle it!" I replied. "Thank you very much for the opportunity." I shook his hand.

"See you on Monday after school!" I left feeling like I was floating on a cloud. I was so excited, I just wanted to scream for the whole world to hear,

"I got my first architectural job!"

I started out three days a week, which soon grew to five days. I also continued helping out at the bakery on Saturdays.

I was on my way!

Chapter 16

~ "Why . . . Is This Happening?" ~

As Thanksgiving approached, our anxiety level rose. This was always a difficult holiday for us, especially for my mother. It conjured up memories of the Thanksgiving weekend when my father suddenly passed away.

This year, Steven became ill, which only added to our unease. At first it seemed that he just had the flu, but his health worsened. He was drinking a lot of 7-Up (we thought it would keep him hydrated), but nothing seemed to help. By the time the weekend rolled around, he had worsened to the point that he was barely getting out of bed. Not only was he extremely lethargic, but he was also urinating a lot more than usual.

My mother realized that these were signs of possible diabetes and telephoned the pediatrician. Because it was a holiday weekend, she could not get our pediatrician on the phone right away. As we waited for a call back from the on-call doctor, Steven's condition worsened to the point where we were considering calling 911. Before we resorted to that, the doctor responded and recommended we bring Steven in right away to be evaluated.

This was out of the question because my mother was still recovering from the back surgery she'd had a few months prior, and there was no way she and I could lift Steven's dead weight into a car. Although he was only twelve years old, he was already a tall young man. My mother insisted that the doctor come to us. He arrived shortly, as my mother had impressed upon him how serious the situation was. As soon as he saw my little brother lying on the bed, he dialed 911, explaining to the paramedics that the patient was unresponsive. Within minutes, we heard sirens approaching, and the paramedics quickly loaded Steven into the back of the ambulance. My mother went with Steven to the hospital and I was left behind not knowing if he was going to live or die.

Steven had slipped into a coma by the time he reached the hospital. The doctors ordered a full blood panel, but Steven was so dehydrated that the nurse struggled to draw any blood. When they were finally able to get a sample and test his blood, his glucose levels were over 900 mg/dl. (Normal blood sugar levels are less than 140 mg/dl.) The doctors told my mother that yes, it was diabetes and that if Steven's numbers were to reach 1000, he probably would not recover from this. The nurses were frantic to get an IV started but due to his severe dehydration, his veins were not accessible. They explained to my mother that they would have to cut his arm open to access a vein and get the fluids started. She was also advised that she should contact any family members who would want to see him in case Steven was not able to pull out of this.

After performing the "cut down," they managed to get Steven set up with an IV and began pumping him with insulin and fluids to rehydrate him. I had been driven to the hospital by my aunt and uncle, and as the family stood by Steven's bedside, we endured a very tense half hour, watching him closely as he lay deathly still. When at last his eyelids fluttered, it was a moment of instant relief that I will never forget. It was miraculous — one minute it had seemed that we had lost him, and then he was back. Tears of joy immediately began streaming down my face. By the next day, he was essentially his old self. We couldn't have been happier.

The doctors kept him in the hospital for the next week. He would be allowed to go home only once he had mastered giving himself his own injections of insulin. The poor kid was only twelve years old and initially refused to inject himself. The patient nurses gave him an orange to practice on. My mother haggled with Steven over the insulin injections without making headway. His Big Brother Sam Button was there and witnessed the struggle and frustration and thankfully proposed a deal. If Steven injected his own insulin, Sam would take him to see the San Francisco Giants play. Steven was a huge baseball fan, and this turned out to be just the motivation that was needed. Steven reluctantly said he would be willing to give himself the injections.

Once Steven agreed, the doctors insisted that we all support him taking his shots. It was important for Steven that injecting himself around others become normalized. Everyone had been showing up to watch, and then eventually I was the last one. I had been there playing cards and keeping him company, but after all my years of needles from my chemo and all the blood tests, I just had a really hard time being stuck or watching anyone else being stuck by a needle.

I gathered my courage, as I had no choice, and agreed to watch him inject himself. I knew I couldn't let him see how much it was hurting me to watch what he was going through. I was determined to be there for him, but I knew that Steven was strong and would find the courage within himself. As he proceeded with his injection routine, I discreetly wiped away my tears and he successfully injected himself with the beginning of a lifetime of injections. It was a very stressful moment for me, and thankfully Sam lightened the mood, as he was there cheering Steven on with the pair of Giants tickets.

Having my little brother at the brink of death was so traumatic for me, it took months before I could move on. I was angry at the world, and at fate for continuing to put these immense challenges in front of us. I was so upset that I even began to pull away from my family. A single thought kept running through my mind. We have been through so much already.

That this had happened to Steven was especially hard for me to accept. But as the weeks passed and we got into a routine, I realized that he had not changed and that he would be okay, that we would be okay.

Chapter 17

~ The Sun Comes Out Again ~

During the holidays, my mother received an international call from Jørgen Panduro. He was an old family friend from our summers spent on Morsø in Denmark, when his three boys would come help with the morning chores on my aunt and uncle's farm. Jørgen was hoping his oldest son, Thomas, could live with us while he attended the English language program at College of Marin. Thomas had passed his "student exams" and taken a semester off to be a ski instructor in Austria, and now before he attended the university in Sweden, his father wanted him to improve his English language skills. My mother told Jørgen that he was welcome to come, if he didn't mind sleeping on the bottom bunk in my brother's room.

We were all elated to have Thomas come and stay with us. My brother and I had spent many hours together with Thomas and his brothers back in Denmark, helping on the farm, playing canasta, and hanging out at the beach. He was always a lot of fun.

Having Thomas stay with us was like having another brother, and a big brother at that. The days when Thomas did not have classes, he would come with me to high school, where he was forced to speak

English. I loved bringing him to high school with me because he was very tall, charming, and handsome. The girls flocked around him, complimenting him and flirting. He was a true chick magnet with his accent and good looks. When weekends rolled around, the girls would ask if Thomas was coming to the parties with me? They all had giant crushes on him, and he loved every moment of it.

Thomas, my brother, and I joked around all the time. We taught him how to play backgammon, and we also played a lot of cards. We usually were able to beat him because my mother would serve him a gin and tonic, which he loved. Thomas was a breath of fresh air and brought laughter and smiles to our house after all of the tragedies we had been through over the last five years. He seemed to have come at just the right moment, as we were realizing that life goes on and we needed to move forward to enjoy it. Having a special, positive kind of person around made us realize this very quickly.

I had begun looking into colleges with architecture programs, and Cal Poly San Luis Obispo was at the top of my list. They hosted an annual spring open house called Poly Royal. I wanted to tour the campus and see the Architecture Department in action. Now that I had my own car, I asked my mother if I could drive down to San Luis Obispo for Poly Royal. I knew she wouldn't let me go by myself, so I threw in that Thomas could come with me. The plan was, we would stay in Solvang with our old family friends, the Shernfields, who oddly enough had also attended the Danish boarding school in Argentina with my mother. Amazingly, my mother agreed and gave Martin and Edel a call to see if Thomas and I could stay a few nights with them. I was so excited. This was going to be the first college campus I had ever seen. I had driven past San Luis Obispo many times on our way to Southern California but never stopped.

Solvang is an hour south of San Luis Obispo. I knew it would be fun for Thomas to see our little version of Denmark in the US. Martin got us up early so he could take us down to the local bakery for pastries and coffee prior to driving back up for Poly Royal. We had a great time with them because Martin knew everybody in town and was quite the jokester as well. He seemed to think something was going on between Thomas and me and wouldn't stop teasing us about it.

After a delicious breakfast of rundstykker (the best Danish rolls ever), and saying thank you to Martin, we headed back up to SLO. Driving up Grand Avenue toward the entrance of Cal Poly for the first time, I couldn't believe I was there. I was actually going on my first college tour to walk the entire campus. When we finally reached the Architecture Department at the far end of campus, I entered the design studios and saw the elaborate projects, artistic drawings, and models the students were creating, and I had no doubt in my mind that this was the place I had to go.

When we got home, I told my family it was the best trip ever. I proclaimed, "That is where I'm going to go to college." My uncle Hermann was happy because he had attended Cal Poly as an exchange student from Germany, and it was also the town that Fefe my dachshund came from.

I really enjoyed spending time with Thomas on our trip, so when junior prom came around it only seemed fitting that I take him with me. I knew I had to save him from some of the more aggressive girls who were pursuing him. Sandy and a couple of her friends, Eileen and Randi, asked us to join them and their dates. The prom was going to be at the San Geronimo Golf Club in West Marin. Eileen invited us to stay the night at her family's beach house out in Inverness, just another twenty minutes west, so it would be closer than driving back home.

Randi's family lived in a mansion in Ross, with servants and a professional chef on staff. She invited us to have dinner at her place first. My mother had made me a beautiful prom dress, and Thomas rented a tuxedo for the event. We had a blast at the prom, dancing the night away, and then we headed out to stay at the beach house for the night.

When the end of the school year came, Thomas passed his exams with flying colors. My mother invited him to stay longer and join us on our annual trip to Southern California to visit the Bollisens and go to Disneyland. He was excited to accompany us, and we all piled into my mother's Audi for our road trip.

Thomas's English had improved significantly, but there were still a few things he said that gave us a laugh. Since no trip to Southern California was complete without a day at Newport Beach, we were there getting battered by the waves and trying to teach Thomas to bodysurf. Thomas had taken quite a tumble diving through the surf gallantly trying to recover my mother's bikini top, which had fallen off. My mother's modesty was saved, but Thomas was a little worse for wear. He flopped onto the sand next to Steven and me, panting as he caught his breath, and proclaimed loudly, "I have sand up my asshole." We laughed so hard, we didn't even notice the waves coming in and knocking us all over again.

The trip was a huge success. Thomas was amazed and really enjoyed our visits to Disneyland, Universal Studios, and Knott's Berry Farm. On the way back up the coast, we visited the beautiful town of Santa Barbara before making our way home.

As those lazy, crazy days of summer continued on, Staci and I hung out at my house, lying around the pool in our bikinis, playing backgammon or sometimes canasta if Sandy joined us. Sometimes we didn't wear swimsuits, or at least tops, which my little brother enjoyed immensely. In the evenings we soaked in the hot tub, and when we got too hot we dove into the cool water of the pool. Our cocktail of choice was a White Russian.

Near the end of summer, when Sigmund Stern Grove in San Francisco hosted a series of free concerts, my friend Val and her family invited me to join them. We spread out our picnic blankets on the sunny slope of the grassy hillside, high enough to have a clear view of the Preservation Hall Jazz Band setting up on the stage. Once the music began, everyone including Val and me started to dance. As anyone who knows the two of us can testify, we wouldn't be happy until we were positioned in the center of the action, right in front of the band. That's where we caught the attention of a trio of cute guys. They worked their way close enough to introduce themselves.

Mike, John, and Joey told us they attended St. Ignatius, an all-boys parochial high school in San Francisco. They danced with us the whole afternoon. Mike asked me for my number and invited us back to the city to party with them the following weekend. For the next few months, Val, Cat, Staci, and I were in San Francisco partying with the boys nearly every weekend.

One weekend, we decided to stay in Marin. It was a Saturday night, we hadn't been around for our own high school parties in a while, and it was great seeing everyone again. When the party scene began to dwindle, Cat and I wanted to leave but Val wasn't ready to go, and said she would get another ride home. Cat and I took off in my Scirocco.

As we headed out, "Urgent," a song by Foreigner, came on the radio:

"You're not shy, you get around

You wanna fly, don't want your feet on the ground…………

Urgent, urgent, emergency………..
Urgent, urgent, emergency"

We cranked up the volume, looked at each other, and decided on a whim that we should go to San Francisco to toilet-paper Mike's house.

"Let's do it!" we shouted simultaneously.

I swung the car around and, spurred by the insistent beat and taunting lyrics, drove onto the southbound Hwy 101 on-ramp. We were singing as loud as we could, heading toward San Francisco, when Cat asked,

"Where are we going to get the toilet paper? It's 12:30 a.m."

"I'm sure something will be open along the way," I replied.

We approached the Sunset District on 19th Avenue. We still hadn't found a place to buy the TP. We were getting pretty desperate. Sitting in the car, waiting for the stoplight to change, I noticed a Zim's on the corner. Zim's was a famous San Franciscan diner.

"I really have to take a pee, and we can just take a roll to go," I said, I pulling over to the curb outside the diner.

We couldn't believe all the red vinyl booths were occupied at 1:00 a.m., and not even a stool at the counter was available. We headed straight to the back where the restrooms were, and along the way we passed two police officers at the register getting coffees.

"What are we going to do now? There are cops standing right there," Cat whispered to me from the bathroom stall next to mine. She sounded like she was panicking.

"You have a big coat on," I replied. "Just take one of the rolls off the dispenser, I'll do the same."

"Damn it, it won't come off!" Cat exclaimed.

"I know, and you can't even unroll it. This stupid dispenser only rolls half a turn at a time," I said. "I'm going to try and get one of the rolls off the dispenser. This is ridiculous."

"Quiet! You're making a lot of noise. The cops are going to hear us," Cat said.

"I know, I know. I'm trying." Crash, bang! The whole two-roll dispenser came off the wall and I fell back into the stall partition.

"SSShhhh, SSShhhh," I could faintly hear as I burst into my loud, cackling, uncontrollable laughter.

"Here you go," I said, as I handed Cat the entire dispenser.

"What do you want me to do with this?" she said.

"Well, I got it off the wall. You can put it under your jacket," I replied.

"If I get caught, I'm blaming it all on you," she said.

"OK," I said. "If they haven't already figured out that we are up to something with all that noise you were making...."

I was still laughing. Trying to be as inconspicuous as two laughing teenagers could be at 1:00 a.m., we quickly made our way out the door and to the car with our toilet-paper dispenser.

Mike lived near the end of a dead-end street. We drove past his house and down to the end of the street to scope out the situation and decided it would be best to go back and park facing away at the open end of the block. As we walked down the moonlit street, the sounds of our cowboy boots sounded alarmingly loud in the night's silence. About 100 feet from his house we finally just left our boots standing along the curbside, and we crept along in our bare feet.

The house was a two-story San Franciscan style with a distressed red brick façade that had two archways leading to the entry. The front yard was mainly concrete, without much landscape. We set the toilet paper dispenser in a central location so that both of us would have easy access, forgetting that we had to unroll the paper from the dispenser manually because it wouldn't spin freely, making the task take much longer than expected. At one point we were frustrated almost to the point of quitting, but we figured we had come so far and gone through so much to get the TP that we should just get it done.

As we worked to decorate Mike's trees, occasionally a car would come down the street and we would run and hide behind the neighbor's parked car until the coast was clear. Trouble came in the form of an old Buick, which parked in front of Mike's driveway. Two large guys got out of the car and began screaming and yelling.

"Who did this? Come out and show yourselves!" said an angry voice. "We are going to find you and make you pay!"

"I think that's one of Mike's older brothers," I whispered to Cat. "He has nine brothers!"

We were terrified. We would have been shaking in our boots if they weren't halfway down the block. We really had no options but to hide. There was no way we could outrun them barefoot, so we stayed crouched behind a car in the neighbor's driveway. We scooted around the car to the back of the vehicle as the two men came closer, looking around to try and find us.

"Look, over here, we can hide behind that trash can in the corner," I whispered.

"It's really dark over there," Cat replied.

"Hopefully they won't be able to see us. Come on," I said.

We quickly made our move. We held in a silent scream as we slipped behind the trash can and our bare feet sunk into what we hoped was just mud. The icy ooze squished up between our toes as we shuddered with revulsion.

"Eeeewwww, this is disgusting," we quietly screamed simultaneously.

The torment extended for several hours because the two guys remained out front cussing us out as they speculated who could have been TPing their house. And they talked about girls. After an interminable length of time, they finally gave up and went into the house. Thank God!

Cat and I were stiff with cold and from crouching for so long as we straightened ourselves out to peek over the trash can. We weren't sure if they really had gone in or if they were pulling a "fake out." When we felt somewhat confident that the coast was clear, we ran straight for my car.

"Our boots!" I said.

"Forget them," Cat replied.

"No, my mother will ask what happened to them! She can't know this," I said.

It was almost 4:30 in the morning when we finally made it home and tiptoed into my house. "We need to wash our feet. They smell so bad," Cat said.

"I know, but I'm afraid we'll wake my mother," I replied. We washed as quietly as we could in the bathtub and then crawled into bed.

Sleep didn't last for long. "Get up, you two sleepy heads. You're wasting the day," my mother sang out, jolting us from our sound sleep.

"What time is it?" Cat asked.

"It's 8:30 a.m.," my mother bellowed back.

"She must have heard us come in," I said, as we both threw the covers back over our heads.

My love of a good party or prank did not detract from my focus on architecture. I was even more focused since my trip to Poly Royal at Cal Poly with Thomas. The projects by the students were so inspiring. I wondered if I should study landscape architecture because of my father's landscape design business, but I was undecided. I had learned a lot about plants and design layout from him, and I thought it would really be something if I could follow in his footsteps to help keep his memory alive. Now, I needed to figure out which path I would follow.

I was going to be a high school senior, which meant I could enroll at our local junior college, College of Marin. I signed up for a horticulture class to see if I felt the same way about landscape architecture as I was feeling about building design. It was a night class in a large auditorium with about a hundred students, and it met every Thursday, 7-10 p.m. During this class, I realized that as much as I loved my father, I did not want to go into landscape architecture. I would always keep him in my heart and would make him proud of me through architecture. I had found my direction.

The class had other perks. I met a lot of guys in the class who didn't realize I was still in high school. I ended up dating about three of them at one time until it became too difficult to keep straight, so I dumped them all. That seemed like the easiest solution before any of them found out about the others. There were two other guys from Drake High School in the class trying to figure out their direction as well. They happened to be at the beach parties I went to with Sandy and her boyfriend Todd. The local kids from Drake High usually partied at the beach on Friday nights by a bonfire. This reminded me of summer back on Morsø.

Halloween was approaching, and Staci and I had been invited to a costume party. As we worked out the details for our costumes, we headed down to the local fabric store, which I knew well from the countless hours spent there as a child with my mother picking out patterns and fabric. Staci was going to be a magician's white rabbit with pink ears, and I was going to be a Playboy Bunny. We needed accessories to make tails and chokers, and material to make wrist cuffs. We picked out fabric, ribbons, and buttons and brought them to the cutting counter. Staci passed her cloth to the lady requesting she cut out enough for two wrist cuffs. I then passed my material to the lady, asking for only enough for one cuff, and Staci blurted out,

"What about the other one?"

I just looked at her, smirked, and replied, "Think about it, Staci."
She stood there for a moment, confused, until it dawned on her, and we began cracking up. The fabric lady looked at us, bewildered.

This was one of the best things about my friends; no one ever thought of me as only having one arm. I always felt it was because I never let that define me or stop me from doing anything.

Thankfully, my mother helped us sew the cuffs for our costumes. Staci looked great, between the two of us, our costumes really caught everyone's attention at the party. I was not dating anyone at the time, so I made the most of flirting with all of the cute guys at the party.

Typically the first snow hit Lake Tahoe sometime in November. When the snow report was good, my cousin Bruce and I headed straight for the slopes at Squaw Valley. He would drive his father's (my uncle

Hermann's) cream-colored VW Squareback with our skis in the back. We would leave early in the morning, drive three hours, ski all day, and then drive home. I would be exhausted and sleep in the car on the way home, but Bruce had the stamina and loved to drive. I love to ski and would occasionally take day trips with Uncle Jens up to the slopes. He was a dynamo on the slopes. His specialty was going straight down at breakneck speed — no turning for him, he just went shooting down the mountain. I found it too terrifying to even watch.

Once I had my own car, I could drive up and stay with Kimmy, an old neighbor from Frances Avenue, who had moved up to Truckee and was now an instructor at Northstar. She gave me a few skiing lessons and improved my technique. After advancing my skills with experience and lessons from Kimmy, I had Special Olympics approach me with an offer to compete with their ski team. I didn't know much about their organization at the time, but because I only had one arm they wanted me to ski on their team. They said, I was really showing some potential. I was honored to have been asked, but I ended up not taking them up on their offer because it would have required a big training commitment. I was a senior now and I didn't feel I had time for that.

School dances were held in the gymnasium, and we were lucky enough to always get live bands. The anticipation for an upcoming dance was mounting because it was a local band who had hit the big time — Huey Lewis and the News had a new album out, and it was climbing the charts. For us girls, it was just another excuse to have a party. The gang met at my house for dinner, and we partied as we put on our makeup and styled our hair. I loaded my Scirocco with as many of us as could possibly fit, and off we went.

Once at the dance, it appeared that the punch had been spiked with alcohol. This was not really too surprising, knowing the boys in our class of '82. However, Sandy didn't seem to realize it in time and had quite a bit of it. I began to notice that she was unsteady on her feet and slurring her words, especially when the boys were asking her to dance. I decided it would be best if I took her back to my house to sober up.

I gave her a can of 7-Up to get her away from the punch and assisted her to my car. She set the can on the dashboard as I helped her into the passenger seat but as soon as I pulled out, that can came flying at her. Amazingly, she caught it between her legs, never spilling a drop. We started laughing so hard that she let go of her hold, and the can fell anyway. This made us laugh all the harder.

When we got back to my house, she hung on my shoulder as we unsteadily navigated the hallway going down to my room, bouncing off the walls. I was trying to hold her up as best I could as she swayed dangerously down the hall. We were both weak and still giggling from the car ride. Steven heard the commotion and popped out from his room.

"What are you doing?" he asked.

"It's a new dance," I told him. By then, my mother had come to see what was going on and just started laughing at us.

"A new dance, my foot," she said.

"I'm going to put Sandy in my bed, and go back to the dance for a while. I'm also Staci's ride so I have to go back," I told my mother.

Later that night, back home and sleeping, we were jarred awake by the phone ringing multiple times. It was Sandy's mother calling, saying she wanted her daughter home. My mother explained that we were all sleeping and she hoped that Sandy could just come home in the morning because it was so late. Ten minutes later, the doorbell rang and it was Sandy's mother at the door wanting to take her home. I guess she didn't trust that Sandy wasn't up to something. She noticed that she was drunk and Sandy got grounded for that.

Sandy's family was from Switzerland, and they were avid skiers. They had a rustic little cabin up at Donner Lake in the Sierra Nevada. The cabin was like a small Swiss chalet with dark wood, Swiss emblems, and cowbells hanging on the walls. It had one bedroom downstairs with a tiny bath and a very small kitchen and living room. A narrow wooden staircase took you to the second story with three additional rooms and a tiny bathroom. Sandy and I usually stayed in the first bedroom at the top of the stairs. In the summer we would have barbecues and swim in the icy water and take rafting excursions down the Truckee River. And in the winter we went skiing.

The cabin sat about a quarter-mile from the lake, and in the winter it would have an abundance of snow. Bright and early one February morning, we headed over to Squaw Valley USA to ski because it was her father's favorite resort. It was mid-afternoon and the shadows were getting long on the slopes. Maybe I was rushing a bit as I tried to catch up with Sandy and her father, and I slipped on a patch of ice and took a pretty bad tumble. My right leg twisted around and was just out of reach so I couldn't unclip my ski. Sandy's father sidestepped back up the mountain to my location to help me. He picked up my ski and flipped it around to untwist my leg and I heard a loud popping sound. I knew right then that something bad had happened in my knee.

Somehow I was able to ski down the hill, but by the time we got back to the cabin, the knee had swollen up like a giant balloon and I could barely walk on it. The next day when they dropped me off at my house, I was in pretty bad shape. My mother brought me to see an orthopedic surgeon who found that my ligament had been severely stretched and most of my cartilage was torn. Fortunately, I only needed to have arthroscopic surgery to clean up the rough edges of the cartilage. After outpatient surgery at Ross General Hospital, I was released with a leg brace, a few stitches (which turned out to my horror to be staples), and a pair of crutches. It seemed funny to me that they gave a one-armed girl a pair of crutches, but at least I had a spare, and one crutch did help support me.

After a few weeks of recovery, I was able to return to school. The attention I got was great because the football and rugby players would help me up the stairs and carry my books. Val, Cat, Staci, and I, along with several others, were almost like groupies of the rugby team, and we would go see all their matches. Getting around with my knee brace was difficult because the campus was huge, but thankfully, I got a lot of help.

When I began my six weeks of needed physical therapy, the therapist explained to me that he was going to teach me to walk. I found this funny, as I had been walking since I was a toddler. The therapist sat me up on the exam bench, released all the straps on my brace, and instructed me to stand. "Now, go ahead and take a few steps," he said. I stood up and took a first tentative step with my left foot. When I went to move my right leg, it was strangely stiff and I just kind of swung it around. I was quite surprised at how difficult it was.

"Let me try that again," I said.

The therapist proceeded to explain how to lift my leg first, then swing it forward, put my heel down, and roll my weight toward my toe. "Heel to toe, heel to toe," he chanted. This sounded easy, but my right leg sure didn't agree. After being in a splint for the last four weeks, the leg was strangely stiff and uncooperative. It made me realize how much we take the simple things in life for granted.

My employer at the architectural firm had been gracious, telling me that I would have a job waiting for me when I recovered. Once I was nearly recovered, though, I decided I wanted an even better job, so again I hit the pavement. I was immediately offered a position with another architectural firm in Mill Valley. The office was built out over a creek with a very woodsy feel.

There were rows of drafting tables and flat files with bumwad (sketch paper) lying on top of all the drawings. I was excited to be working in a real office instead of a home, but the allure wore off within a few days when I noticed a distinct aroma. I didn't initially attribute it to the office itself, and instead I figured it was the smell of pot smoking from some stoners hanging around the creek. Then I realized it was the bosses smoking in their offices. I knew I was in Mill Valley, but I still felt this was very unprofessional. I left after my shift and never returned.

On the day of my final physical therapy appointment, my mother reluctantly let me skip it because I was walking pretty well on my own again and I didn't want to miss the big game. It was the final game for our school's rugby team at Golden Gate Park against our biggest rival. Val picked me up in her VW Bug, along with Staci and Cat. I still hadn't been cleared to drive. Once we reached the polo fields in San Francisco, we sat down on the sidelines on the grass and began cheering. It was an exciting match. With only ten minutes left and the game tied, a bad pass was made, and the ball headed in our direction.

Both teams began running toward us, causing everyone on the sidelines to jump up. Suddenly there were people all around me screaming and running. The ball bounced, and I tried to get up and run with the crowd. But my injured leg just wouldn't move as fast as I needed it to, and before I knew it, the players were all around me tackling each other, and I was under the pile.

"Oh shit!" Staci screamed. "Sylvia's in there!"

The rugby players picked me up off the grass and sat me on the bench. Grass-stained and shaken, I think I was in shock because I wasn't in any pain, but I could not stand up and walk. I knew I was in trouble again and just wanted to go home.

When we pulled up in front of my house, all my friends were afraid to get out of the car. They knew what kind of reaction my mother was going to have. And sure enough, after her immediate shock, the lecture came. She had me sit on the sofa with an ice pack on my knee while once again calling the orthopedic surgeon. He said he would meet us in the emergency room at the Ross hospital, again.

The surgeon instructed me to sit up on the examination table with my legs hanging over the side and asked me to straighten them in the air. Only my left leg went up. My right leg continued to dangle helplessly.

"Is it paralyzed?" I asked. He took his hand and gently lifted my leg and straightened it out manually.

"Does it hurt when I do this?" the surgeon asked.

"No, nothing hurts," I replied.

He gently put my leg back down where it dangled pathetically and once again asked me to try and lift it. Nothing happened. I was sure my leg was paralyzed, and was starting to get a little freaked out.

"Don't worry," he said. "I can fix this." He explained that my quad muscle had been ripped off from my knee. The quad muscle lifts and controls the leg, and unfortunately it was detached and my meniscus was also torn again.

"Here we go again!" my mother said, as the nurse helped her fill out admission papers at Ross General Hospital while they prepared me for surgery. This time I was required to stay a few nights; the surgery was a little more involved than my first injury from skiing. The following day, the surgeon checked in on me. He was excited to let me know that he had a video of the procedure. He said I could watch it, if I liked. Just then, the rugby team stopped by the hospital and heard the doctor mentioning the video.

"Let's see it!" they said. The surgeon was happy to put it on the television in my hospital room for us all to watch. I couldn't bear to look, but the guys were fascinated.

Now I was faced with another six weeks of physical therapy, which came with a stern lecture from a very upset therapist. He made it clear that I was not allowed to miss or even be late for one appointment! At least I knew the routine, and believe me, I did not miss a day after that.

It was depressing to be back at square one with my knee recovery, and it didn't help that I had to miss my senior prom because I couldn't dance or get around very well. Instead of attending the prom, Staci said she would be my date and hang out with me that evening. After helping Val get ready, we went back to my place, took our normal spots on the long bench seat beside the pool, and played backgammon for hours while enjoying our Kahlua and milk. Regardless of the situation, we always made the best of it — and we probably had more fun anyway.

As senior year drew to a close, it was time to submit our architectural projects in a statewide competition. The goal was to design a houseboat and build a scale model. We had spent the entire term designing and building our models.   This was my first presentation model, and I had built it out of white foam core. I was proud of how it turned out.

The judging was held at the American Institute of Architects' office in San Francisco.   When my mother and I walked in and saw the number of models on display, we realized how many students had entered the competition.   Everyone gathered as the judges made their announcements.   I didn't win, but after the announcements I was approached by one of the judges who saw me standing next to my houseboat model. He informed me that I was a serious contender due to my open concept, which kept the small space from feeling crowded while meeting all the needs of a home's various functions.   I was thrilled. To me, it felt like I had won!

Graduation commencement for the Class of '82 was finally happening after all of our years of hard work. Redwood High School held its graduation ceremonies at the Mountain Theatre in Mount Tamalpais State Park. Better known to us as Mt. Tam, this mountain had been the giant backdrop to our growing up, on whose slopes mountain biking had been invented, with hiking trails, scenic vistas, and the curvy one-lane road we'd driven over countless times to get to Stinson Beach.

In early June we could never know for sure if the weather would be nice, but Mt. Tam also served as our daily weather forecaster — if you couldn't see the top of the mountain, it was sure to rain. Luckily for the Class of '82, not a cloud was in the sky on the day of our graduation. We were a class of over 500 graduates, and the only way to the amphitheater was via a curvy two-lane road up the mountain, so I knew it was going to take some time to get to the top, and parking would be difficult. We needed to leave early so my family could get a good seat.

Many of the graduates seemed to have started the party early and had lost their inhibitions. As the rest of us drove up the hill, they could be seen along the side of the road in their red caps and gowns, facing away from passing cars and peeing in communal relief into the woods. Occasionally one would "moon" us, showing his bare cheeks. People passing in their cars would laugh or roll their eyes in disgust as they tried to find parking. It was mostly boys, but every once in a while a girl would be squatting on the side of the road, too.

Once all of us graduates were seated neatly in our rows at the base of the amphitheater, with our relatives sitting in the elevated perimeter seats overlooking the sea of red satin caps and gowns, dignity was restored to the day. It was a spectacular setting and wonderful to be on top of a mountain on such a beautiful day. I appreciated the beauty of the surroundings and the occasion as I waited in a procession that moved toward the stage.

One by one, we walked up the steps to receive our congratulatory remarks and our diplomas. As they flipped our tassels from one side of our caps to the other, I heard a commotion. I was standing alongside Sandy, with Cat not too far behind, and we turned around to see what was going on.

A boy seated in the front row had jumped up and acted on something he apparently had been longing to do, and he pulled Cat toward him, leaned her back, and kissed her hard. When he released her, Cat attempted to collect herself. She straightened her cap, and with an enormous grin she continued on up to the stage where she accepted her certificate and took a beaming photo.

Commencement speeches were made, and it was official: We were the Class of '82. We threw our red tasseled hats — cheering, screaming, and laughing with the greatest enthusiasm — as they went spiraling everywhere. All I could think was, the world was ours, and I couldn't wait for the adventures yet to come.

Unfortunately for future classes graduating from Redwood High School, our rabble-rousing, partying class of 1982 was the last one allowed to have graduation on top of Mt. Tam. I guess we did not set the best example, but we sure knew how to enjoy life.

Back down the mountain, my mother had planned another wild and crazy party at our house for my graduation. I was the first to graduate high school in our family. She invited all our Danish friends and family. I was so happy to see the Bollisens had come up from Southern California, and I was lucky that many of my girlfriends were there as well. The bar was flowing, and Julio Iglesias was singing as my mother and her sister Nanna danced the tango. Some things never changed; and as I remembered my life growing up, I couldn't be happier to be a part of this wonderful family.

PART FOUR:

~ MAKING IT HAPPEN ~

Happiness is not a destination, it's the journey.

...Anonymous

∽

Chapter 18

~ Opportunity Knocks ~

The summer of '82, following my high school graduation, I was given an extraordinary opportunity to travel. As a graduation present, Sam (Steven's Big Brother) had graciously asked me to join him on a two-week, all-expenses-paid, guided trip to Europe with a few other girls he was taking on a reward trip.

Sam had an old college classmate who he had promised his daughter, Chris, years ago that when she graduated from high school, he would take her to Europe. Sam was a frequent guest at their home, and Chris had heard of the many wonderful places that Sam had seen. When the time for the trip grew near, Sam realized it would make for a better experience if he invited a few other girls to come along. Sam then invited his business partner's daughter, Bridget, and me. We had only met once prior to our trip — at Sam's house for a briefing dinner on where we were going — but it was clear that we were all going to get along. Chris and I felt that a two-week trip would not be long enough, so we purchased Eurail passes for an additional month.

Anticipation mounted when we met at San Francisco International Airport for our departure. I arrived at the airport wearing my button-fly 501 jeans, a maroon Ralph Lauren polo, a white Cal Poly hooded sweatshirt tied around my neck, and carrying my new Minolta 35mm camera my mother had just given me for a graduation present.   I thought I was looking pretty cool as I prepared to jet off on my adventure.

Twelve hours later, we were all a little worn around the edges as we arrived at Germany's Frankfurt airport. We rented a car and drove to the historic city of Heidelberg, a picturesque old town of red brick and stone with steeply pitched roofs on the banks of the Neckar River. We checked into a quaint little hotel, where we three girls shared a room and Sam had his own accommodation across the corridor.

Once settled in, Sam wanted to bring us to one of his old haunts from his military days. We stepped down into a dimly lit pub with carved wooden tables. One side of the pub had opened its shutters to the beautiful evening weather, and we marveled at the sight of the sparkling lights on the old bridge spanning the Neckar River.

Sam ordered us all our first stein of beer, along with the famous bratwurst and the best Pommes frites (french fries) I would ever have. As we ate our delicious meal, Sam chronicled for us the incredible history of Heidelberg, including the many battles that had left their mark upon the city. Heidelberg boasts Germany's oldest university, which remains one of Europe's most prestigious institutions.

The next morning we trekked up the 300-foot hill to the old castle, a magnificent blend of Renaissance and Gothic architecture. While listening to Sam's guided tour, we received more information than we could possibly absorb.   My mind kept drifting off, my thoughts overflowing with enthusiasm and excitement for what I would do next with my life.

Having graduated from high school, and then experiencing this amazing trip, I felt such a sense of freedom and anticipation — a certainty that I was about to embark on a great and successful life. It was just up to me to make the right choices to make it all happen.

From Heidelberg, we drove southeast to Munich and came upon a Bavarian celebration of the founding of the city. The men were dressed in traditional lederhosen and olive-green Alpine hats with a feather. The women were in traditional dirndl dresses with aprons. Their giant steins of beer clinked often as they sang together in celebration. We, of course, joined right in, and a local young man even gave me his hat to wear as we posed for pictures.

We enjoyed Munich, touring the Olympic stadium from the 1972 games and walking the Old Town and central Marienplatz square, where the Neo-Gothic Rathaus (town hall) housed the chiming glockenspiel clock tower. We were up early the next day to drive out to the Dachau Concentration Camp, which was an extremely sobering experience. The silence, from the moment we opened the car doors, until we exited the long gravel drive, was unbearable. There were many visitors, but all walked in complete silence in remembrance and respect for the victims. From standing in the shower room where they gassed thousands of innocent Jewish citizens, to looking into the death ovens, you could sense the terror that ran through the veins of the victims who had to endure this horror. This gave me a better appreciation for the gift of life even in the face of great adversity.

Sam knew that few words were needed and just observed our reactions. Afterward in the car on our way to Switzerland, it was hours before any of us spoke. We picked up a picnic lunch and ate at the park in Zurich en route to Lucerne. The weather changed drastically once we reached the Alps. Luckily, Sam had instructed us to bring warm clothes. I put on the fisherman-style sweater my mother had knitted me. Once we were settled in Lucerne, we rode a gondola up into the snow-capped mountains. The views were breathtaking, and at the crest of the mountain, it felt like we were at the top of the world.

The next day we continued on to Interlaken, where we overnighted at the Alp Lodge. From our rooms we could hear the rushing blue glacier water racing through the locks and see the old mill wheels turning in the Aare River connecting Lake Brienz and Lake Thun. Old stone and timber homes, called chalets, dotted the hillsides. Cows traversed narrow trails in the green grass, and we heard the clanging of their cowbells as we passed by. It was so beautiful, I half-expected someone to break out in a song from The Sound of Music.

Once we left Switzerland we drove through the French countryside, visiting an old chateau with a traditional wine cellar. On our private tour, the winemaker took us down into the dimly lit cellar where we could feel the temperature drop. Dug deep into the hillside, the man-made cave kept the wine cool as it aged. There he provided us with tastings directly from the aged oak barrels using an apparatus similar to a turkey baster. We compared the wines that were at different stages of fermentation, from the early fruity flavors to the more developed wine. It was fabulous.

The food in France was incredible, and Sam spared no expense introducing us to new experiences. At most of these places, Sam had previously visited or even knew the owners. He was a wonderful guide.

Knowing Danish and some German, I had been able to get by in Germany and Switzerland, but I had to buy a French phrase book for the later part of our trip. My attempt to speak a little French was not well received, to say the least.

Not easily discouraged, I continued to try. France was the first place during our trip that I experienced a cultural barrier. It seemed to me that to the French, Americans are just annoying tourists to be barely tolerated. The attitude was a bit of a letdown, but I wasn't going to allow this to take the "ooh la la" out of Paris for me.

Paris was our final destination with Sam and Bridget. I found Paris to be enchanting with its amazing historical sites, museums, monuments, and gardens. We toured them all — the Eiffel Tower, the Arc de Triomphe, Notre Dame Cathedral, the Louvre. In the museum, we saw many artists painting replicas of the great works of art to learn from the masters.

Each day was a trek around Paris, with good food at wonderful cafés along the way. I was even asked on several occasions if I was the granddaughter of the French film actress Simone Signoret. I had no idea who she was, but needless to say, my resemblance earned me "gratis" drinks. Although we were having fun, Chris and I were secretly dying to experience the city's nightlife. Every evening we were tempted by the sounds of music playing, people dancing, and the clink of glasses that wafted up to us as we sat in our hotel room. The temptation was just too much for us, so we waited patiently until we could hear Sam's signature snoring begin across the hall, then we slowly tiptoed past his room, down the stairs, and out of the hotel to the local celebration. Bridget was better behaved and stayed put, but never tattled on us.

After properly thanking Sam for his incredible generosity, we waved farewell to him and Bridget as they climbed into a taxi for the airport. Chris and I knew we couldn't afford the expense of Paris hotels on our own, so we headed to the train station with our Eurail passes. Standing at the station reading the schedule boards, we looked at each other and decisively agreed to get on the southbound train, toward the French Riviera.

I had brought the latest copy of Let's Go Europe, and with that and our suitcases in hand we boarded the train. Our first decision was where to get off. We figured we would pore over the travel guide for ideas once we got settled on the train. We knew we wanted a few days to relax after such an incredible yet exhausting journey so far.

On the train we found an empty eight-passenger cabin. We put our luggage in the nets above and took the window seats. Two other American tourists came in and asked if there were any seats available in our cabin? They were from Seattle. Annette was our age, had also just graduated, and was traveling with a chaperone who was only about ten years older, named Linda. They joined us, and we began chatting. They were headed to Nice, in the French Riviera and mentioned they would be staying at an inexpensive hotel on the main promenade directly across from the beach. That was all Chris and I needed to hear.

"Do you think they have any more rooms available?"

This sounded like a fantastic plan to us. I asked if they minded us tagging along, and they were more than happy to have the company. Seven hours later, we arrived in Nice and set off with our new friends, fingers crossed in hopes that their hotel still had rooms.

Hotel Flots D'Azur on the Promenade des Anglais was directly across from the beautiful blue waters of the Mediterranean Sea. The coral-pink stucco, three-story hotel had quaint scalloped awnings, French doors opening onto balconies, and a pair of palm trees flanking the entrance. I couldn't believe our luck when we nabbed not only the last available room, but the cheapest one as well. It was on the lower level, around back with its own entrance. It had two single beds and a private bath. It was a steal for only $30 a night, including breakfast.

Each morning we walked up to the large terrace that overlooked the ocean and had a fantastic breakfast of croissants, jam, cheese, and the best hot cocoa I have ever tasted. Daily we strolled with our new friends along the promenade that paralleled the Mediterranean Sea. We shopped on the main street, which was like an open-air market because cars were not allowed. I would insist we stop for a soft ice cream cone. The vendor had only a small portable cart, but he managed to serve every flavor imaginable. In the United States I had never seen more than just chocolate and vanilla in soft serve, but here I ordered a double, with mocha piled on top of strawberry. It was exceptional. I couldn't get enough soft ice cream, and sometimes I would walk back in the afternoon for a second cone.

After shopping and lunch, we would return to the hotel to put on our bikinis and head to the beach with its warm, crystal-clear, aqua-colored water. Embracing the old saying of "when in Rome," we abandoned our bikini tops in favor of a strapless tan. Annette and Linda were a bit hesitant at first, but I led the way because I was used to going topless during my summers in Denmark. Women without tops were not the only surprising sight on these beaches; it was also a bit shocking to see men (of all ages and weights) in tight Speedos.

At night we would stroll the main street, popping into clubs that overflowed with people dancing, music thumping, lights bright, and liquor always flowing. The French Riviera is known for its nightlife. One night, fireworks erupted over the glistening waters of the sea, and thousands of people were in the streets cheering "Viva Italia! Hurrah! Hurrah!" A parade of convertibles packed with Italians drove up and down the promenade, yelling and waving Italian flags. We finally found out what the hoopla was about. Italy had just defeated Brazil in the World Cup. The firecrackers and cheering went on all throughout the night. It was crazy! The excitement of winning the World Cup is huge in Europe, as soccer is the most popular sport.

One day, walking along the promenade, we noticed a US Navy carrier anchored offshore, and Nice was filled with US servicemen running around in their dixie-cup white sailor hats and uniforms. They reminded me of Popeye the Sailor. As we strolled the promenade eating our daily soft serve, showing off our tans (which had developed into a golden glow by this time) and long blond hair, we were getting a lot of notice from the sailors. That evening as we headed to the clubs, we were approached numerous times, and followed into clubs by sailors who wanted to get to know us. We all danced and partied until the wee hours of the morning, before wandering down to the beach to cool off from the hot and sweaty dance clubs. A dip in the sea provided a cool relief after a long evening of fun.

A sailor from New Jersey named Doug had attached himself to me, and we had a lot of fun dancing, laughing, and swimming. Over the next few days we partied with the sailors quite a bit. When it was time for him to ship out, he asked if it would be okay if he wrote to me once I got back to the States. Sure, I thought. It might be nice to have a pen pal. And I gave him my address in California.

I was later to regret giving him my address because once I was home, I received letters professing his undying admiration and love. He even sent me a Polaroid picture of himself, along with a marriage proposal! I was totally shocked and didn't know how to respond, so I didn't. I was only nineteen, and just starting my life.

Chris and I stayed in Nice for almost three wonderful and relaxing weeks. Then we decided we should probably see a few other cities before our Eurail passes expired. So we took the train to Amsterdam.

When we arrived in Amsterdam, we once again had no place to stay, so we headed in the direction of the main walking street looking for the youth hostel listed in Let's Go Europe. As we walked, a man with an Australian accent approached and asked if we had a place to stay. We explained that we were looking for the youth hostel.

"Oh no, come with me; I am from the Hotel California," he said. Chris and I were a little leery of the invitation but decided we could at least check it out.

It seemed like a decent place, and we definitely liked the name. We were given a room up on the sixth floor. On the third floor of this narrow, typical Dutch-style building was the bar where our new Aussie friend worked as the bartender and played his guitar singing the Eagles' "Hotel California."

In Holland, historically the buildings were taxed by the width of their street front. The Dutch, being very creative, developed a unique style of architecture, which is narrow yet charming and prevalent throughout the country.

We spent a week in Amsterdam. We toured the Van Gogh Museum, and we sailed through the canals under all the magnificent drawbridges. We opted to not visit the Anne Frank House after seeing Dachau. We didn't think we could handle the sadness of realizing how horrible the circumstances became for many during WWII. I was able to tour the Anne Frank house on a later trip to Holland.

The hotel owner and the bartender both took a liking to Chris and me. They brought us out to Zandvoort to see the white sandy Dutch beaches along the Atlantic. They were beautiful, but the waters were freezing cold. The Dutch didn't seem to mind, and thousands flocked there to sit in the sun. A wooden promenade built on the sand was dotted with beer gardens and cafes as far as the eye could see. We ended up spending quite a bit of time with these two, as they were quite interested in us.

No visit to Holland would be complete without a trip to see the Tulip Gardens and their miniature replica of Amsterdam. "Picturesque" was my word to describe this landscape, with its botanical array of colors. It was a magical ending to a wonderful trip.

The Eurail passes were about to expire, so Chris and I took our last train from Central Station in Amsterdam to Frankfurt, Germany, for our flight home.

Chapter 19

~ Chicken, Chicken & More Chicken ~

(An Unexpected Trip)

Rosie was an admissions counselor for the school of architecture at Cal Poly; we spoke several times so that I could understand the process and requirements for acceptance. She explained the challenges and strenuousness of the architecture program and recommended I attend a junior college for a year to take prerequisite classes. She advised me to take a foreign language (other than Danish) and to take calculus. I needed the credits for these courses to be admitted the following fall. So, I enrolled at College of Marin and signed up to take German, calculus, and a logic class because I thought that sounded fun. I was surprised at the increased difficulty and workload at the junior college, compared to high school, but I rose to the challenge.

My cousin Alan, who was a year younger, had heard me chatting endlessly about going to Cal Poly for Architecture, and he was also interested in building and wanted to attend Cal Poly for Construction Management. We agreed that we would meet and fill out our applications together. The forms were long and somewhat confusing, but somehow we got them filled out and submitted.

The junior college provided me with a good transition, and it was inexpensive for my mother as I was able to live at home. Because I was living at home and could watch my brother, my mother took the opportunity for a much-needed vacation to visit her brother John for a month in Venezuela. He had surprised her by sending her a plane ticket, and she decided to accept. This came as a shock to Steven and me. She had never left us before, and I felt a bit unprepared to take care of Steven as he needed three meals a day at specific times due to his diabetes.

My mother is a fantastic cook. Along with all the traditional Danish dishes and Argentine-style barbecued meats, she could whip up gourmet meals from very little. She never had a knack for baking, and had always left the pastry making to her father. Although I had learned to bake from my grandfather and from my years of working at Bucher's Patisserie, I would not say I was comfortable in the kitchen, because the kitchen at our house was my mother's domain. She disapproved of anyone attempting to use her kitchen, particularly if she thought you would make a mess. Needless to say, even though I was not allowed to cook, I had observed her on many occasions.

With her impending departure to Venezuela, I was now in charge of my little brother. My mother typically cooked him eggs every morning before school, packed his lunch, and cooked a healthy dinner.

"I've never cooked a meal in my life," I said. "What am I supposed to make?"

"You'll figure something out," my mother replied. "I'll leave you money for groceries."

Chicken, I thought, mm. My mother makes the best fried chicken, but I was intimidated by the thought of frying in spitting oil. I figured I could just cook chicken some other way. So I baked, sautéed, and barbecued chicken for the next month. Steven got fed up.

"Not chicken again. Can't you cook anything else?"

"No, that's it," I said with a giant smirk on my face. I didn't really mind the repetition, and was quite amused that it was annoying the crap out of Steven.

Our aunt Nanna had called to invite us for dinner the following week, and Steven was ecstatic.

"Now we'll get a steak! Nanna barbecues a lot," he said. When we arrived at her house, a wonderful aroma greeted us.

"What are you making?" Steven asked, the second he stepped foot into the house.

"Chicken," our aunt replied.

Cries of "No!" erupted from my brother as I explained, laughing hysterically, how we had been eating chicken every night since our mother left for Venezuela. Driving home later that evening, I consoled my brother with the thought that he still had another chance at a different meal. We were going to our Mormor's house for dinner next week. Mormor was living in San Francisco at the time. When we arrived, to Steven's dismay a chicken was roasting in the oven. I simply laughed while my little brother crumbled to the floor.

I have never been able to live down the fact that I made chicken in every shape and form for the entire month that our mother was away. To this day, my family continues to tease me about the great month of the Chicken.

Other than exercising my newly acquired culinary skills, I was spending a considerable amount of time in the math tutoring center.

One afternoon, while attempting to do my calculus homework, I noticed another student. It seemed that he was continually glancing my way. It took a few weeks until this boy, named Ben, asked me out. He later told me that he had to really work up his nerve to ask me out and was encouraged by his buddies.

"Are you talking about asking out the beautiful blonde with one arm?" they asked him.

"She's blond, but she has two arms," he responded.

"Are you talking about the one from the tutoring center you're always looking at? She only has one arm," his friends insisted, but he still didn't believe them.

After a few dates, he confessed all of this to me and explained that with the way I held myself, he had never noticed that I didn't have a right arm — and that it didn't make any difference anyway. We dated for a while in anticipation of our acceptance into Cal Poly, as Ben was also hoping to study architecture there.

In late March, I began checking the mailbox daily. This continued into May. I anxiously looked for my letter from Cal Poly. When it finally arrived, I stared at it for the longest time. I was terrified to open the envelope. What if I wasn't accepted? Finally, I ripped it open to find... that I had been accepted! I was moving to SLO town! I was ecstatic.

I couldn't wait to experience college life, and this seemed like the quintessential college town — small, quaint, and located only a short drive from the warm, sandy beaches of the Central Coast. I would be living on my own, meeting new people and partying (which I planned to do my fair share of), and, oh yes, becoming an architect.

Unfortunately, Ben was not accepted into Cal Poly and was quite disappointed. I could feel that he was envious, and our relationship slowly fizzled. He did not completely detach from me, though, because after I had left town, he began visiting my mother to ask how I was doing. Ben was an extremely talented and detailed fine arts illustrator; his talents eventually led him down a different, and successful path.

Chapter 20

~ The Dream Becomes a Reality ~

Cal Poly, SLO

I was accepted into California Polytechnic State University, San Luis Obispo (Cal Poly, SLO), a bit later than the first group of placements, so I was not initially given campus housing. Rosie (the placement counselor) had advised me not to worry, saying I could apply for the dorms when I came down for WOW week. Week of Welcome is scheduled the week prior to the start of classes. My mother suggested that we drive down a day early to try and sort out the housing situation. This turned out to be a good idea because although we came into town without much worry, our concern escalated when we arrived on campus and noticed the very long line outside a small shack located partway up the hill behind the Red Brick Dorms. A zigzagging path led up to it, with over a hundred anxious students awaiting their turn.

"What's going on?" we asked a girl we saw walking on the sidewalk.

"That's the line to apply for campus housing," she answered as she went to join the queue. I couldn't believe that it was the housing office.

I immediately jumped out of the car, telling my mother to find parking while I joined the line. After crawling along the hillside for about an hour and a half in line, I finally realized why the line was so long. It was because there were only two housing clerks helping hundreds of worried students waiting impatiently outside! After waiting so long, I was put on a wait list. I was encouraged that I was at least near the top of the list, being only third in line for the next available bed.

They asked where I was staying and informed me that they would call to notify me when a bed came available. As a backup plan, they gave us a list of other off-campus housing options. My mother felt it would be best for us to check out a few of these other options.

We checked into a small hotel downtown on Monterey Street, and Mom said she would stay with me until we found a place for me to live. The next morning she dropped me off on campus. I needed to sign in for WOW and meet my assigned group. Once our group was assembled, Stella and Brad, our WOW counselors, had us sit in a circle on the grass to get to know each other. They then led the group on a tour of the University Union, the main gathering spot with the bookstore, a student activities office, and a cafe with outdoor seating. We toured the dorms and the different dining halls before heading to downtown San Luis Obispo. There we explored the downtown, with its paths along the beautiful creek near the Mission San Luis Obispo, and we had to add our chewed gum to the walls of Bubble Gum Alley, which still exists.

Later that evening our group met at our WOW counselor Stella's apartment for a spaghetti feed, where I learned about throwing spaghetti noodles at the wall to see if they stick, and this told us if the noodles were done. Having been raised by my fastidious mother, I thought this was hilarious. I could imagine her horror if she saw us throwing wet noodles on the wall.

After dinner, Stella told the group that we would be going on a mystery tour that night. We loaded into cars and were instructed to put on blindfolds. Once blindfolded, we were driven to an unknown location. Everyone was apprehensive as to what was going to happen next. Was this some type of hazing? As we exited the cars, they instructed us to line up, single file, and hold onto the person in front of us. We began down a small incline; people were slipping and sliding as we entered this mysterious place.

"Where are we going? What's going on?" we asked.

"You can remove the blindfolds now," they said.

We all stood knee-deep in water. It was pitch-black, and we could not figure out where we were. "Is this safe?" someone shouted.

"This is the SLO sewer tour," Stella replied. "And there is no turning back!"

We proceeded slowly, stumbling over rocks and broken pavement as we tried to stay close to the walls while holding onto the person in front of us. We could hear screams coming from up ahead, and sounds of splashing. We realized that we weren't the only group in the sewer. Suddenly there was a loud shriek from the front of the line, followed by a plunk as the person leading our group blindly fell neck-deep into the cold water. The screams increased as several others also fell in. It was nerve-wracking and exhilarating at the same time. I had noticed that there really wasn't any sewer smell, so I didn't actually think we were walking in the sewer, but I had no idea where we were, and I definitely didn't want to fall into the water.

Finally, we could see some light emerging ahead of us, and after walking in cold water for blocks we reached the mouth of the tunnel. We realized that we had been walking through the creek in downtown San Luis Obispo, underneath the streets and buildings! When we came out by the old mission, a large group of frat boys, anticipating the arrival of the groups, stood up on the bridge above, throwing bags of flour over the edge and covering us like we were being tarred and feathered.

Now wet, cold, and covered in flour, Stella gave me a ride back to the motel and walked me to our room. The expression on my mother's face was priceless when she answered the door. Judging by the state I was in, she thought I had been assaulted. We all had a pretty good laugh, but I think my mother was a little concerned about the college scene.

The next day, a phone call finally came from the university. They had a bed for me on campus. It wasn't exactly a dorm room, but more of an apartment, something usually used as quarters for RAs (resident advisors). They assigned three of us to bunk together until a regular dorm room came available. My mother helped me unload my belongings into my new room and then took me out to lunch before beginning her drive home.

The week brought new adventures as I continued the WOW activities. We rafted down the Salinas River in inner tubes and concluded the week's festivities with a dance in the main gym where we danced to the music of Big Country, a popular band at the time.

My new home away from home was in the Yosemite dorms, which were situated the farthest away from the Architecture Department. I went back and forth several times a day. This made quite a trek for me, but I didn't mind. I was just happy to have a place on campus, and it was good exercise.

Before I left for Cal Poly, my mother had bought me a North Face backpack. It was dark blue with a rectangular leather base, several large pockets in front, and a cushioned strap that fit my body perfectly. I would load it to maximum capacity with all my folders, my sketchbook, and my architectural toolbox. The toolbox was like a fisherman's tackle box, a place where I kept my triangles, mechanical pencils, sharpener, sandpaper, Exacto blades, erasers, vellum paper, and so on. The backpack weighed about 18 pounds. I also carried my drafting board, which was a 24" by 30" hollow wooden board covered with green Barco material; I had fastened a leather strap to the top to use as a handle. I was five foot, six inches tall and weighed only 105 pounds, but I would march up and down the hill to the Architecture building several times a day lugging my drafting board and wearing my heavy backpack with my T-square sticking out of the top. I guess I made quite an impression — to this day people still comment on how they remember me that way.

Environmental Design (EDES 110) was my first architectural drawing class at Cal Poly. I showed up with my backpack bulging with my toolkit, vellum drawing paper, 3-sided architectural scale that was once my father's, triangles, and my drafting board ready to go. I settled in at a nice tall drafting table in the back row near the window and pulled up a stool. I thought it was a good spot to both work and watch the students passing by on the promenade outside. A very energetic and excited redheaded boy named Eric took the table next to mine. We quickly became the best of friends along with Geoff, another student in the class. The three of us would pull "all nighters" to finish our projects. We spent so much time together, we soon became known as "The three musketeers."

Our professor was a talented Japanese fellow named Ikenoyama. I would watch him in utter amazement as he drew on the chalkboard using multiple colors, producing drawings at lightning speed to demonstrate how to create perspective and how to add shade and shadows, reflections, and mirror images in every geometric shape imaginable. Every stroke of every line he drew on the chalkboard was straight and exact, and he did it all freehand. It was mesmerizing, but you couldn't just sit back and marvel at his skill because you needed to be taking notes. If you missed a step, you could easily become completely lost when you attempted this on your own time. So, I was grateful to have my other two musketeers to work with and thankful that I had turned in my old T-square for a parallel rule. A parallel rule is a long straightedge attached by guide wires to your drafting table. It can slide up and down without your having to hold it to secure its position. This enabled me to draft more quickly and keep up with Professor Ikenoyama.

Ikenoyama was our professor for the first two quarters. Then George Hasslein, the original dean of Cal Poly's College of Architecture and Environmental Design, was our third-quarter teacher. Hasslein had recently been asked to step down as dean and teach the first-year students. Mr. Hasslein did not believe that women belonged in architecture, and so he made the assumption that I was in the architectural engineering program.

Once again I was faced with the barrier of being a woman in architecture. He was much more critical of the work of the few girls in the class, mine included, no matter how good it was. When he criticized my work, he claimed it wasn't bad for an Architectural Engineering (ArcE) student. I couldn't seem to convince this man that I was actually in the Architecture program. My registration stated clearly that I was an Architecture Major, but he claimed it must have been a mistake by the administration. He explained that he gave me a "B" in the class because no matter how good my work was, only Architecture students could receive an "A" and since I was female I could not possibly be in the Architecture program. I vowed to never take him as an instructor again.

Along with my drawing classes and several required general education courses, I also had a Land Surveyor lab class. The old rod and chain system for measuring and calculating a plot was still in use. This was one of the classes I had together with my cousin Alan. We were instructed to form groups of three. Kirk, another redheaded boy who also lived in the Yosemite dorms, came and sat beside me, asking to join our group and complete the trio. The class met 3-6:00 p.m. Friday afternoons, and we were required to stand out in the agricultural fields and survey the assigned plots. The afternoons were the worst time of day for this work because it was so hot. To make things worse, the work was boring and it interfered with Friday's happy hour. We were not happy.

I was always asked to stand and hold the rod while Alan handled the measuring chain and Kirk worked the scope. Initially, Alan and I didn't mind letting Kirk work the scope because he seemed to know what he was doing. One afternoon, though, Alan decided to turn on the scope, and that was when he realized that Kirk hadn't really been checking the numbers on the rod and instead had been spending most of his time staring at me through the lens. Once we discovered this and gave Kirk a hard time about wasting our time, we were able to complete our surveys more quickly, allowing Alan and me the opportunity to head back to my dorm and make up a blender of margaritas, which we drank while finishing our calculations. Notice Kirk wasn't invited.

If we finished our surveys early enough, we often headed out to join the festivities with the ΔXA brothers, where I had pledged to become a little sister, thanks to my WOW counselor and her friends. They were a supportive group of super nice guys and fun little sisters. We had barbecues and many a beer-drinking contest together.

Along with my philosophy, English, and history classes, I regretfully and against the suggestion of my advisor signed up for calculus again. After taking it at College of Marin and receiving a D, I did not feel that grade was up to my standards, so I wanted to prove I could get a better one. It ended up being a completely wasted effort because I once again received a D. D for done, I figured, as I took my lumps and went on.

About halfway through my first term, a note addressed to me was slipped under the door of our temporary housing. It informed me that a bed had become available in the Sierra Madre dorms. I went to introduce myself to my new roommate; she was in Tower Two, on the second floor. I knocked on the door, and as it slowly swung open I found my new roommate sitting on the edge of her bed crying over the loss of her roommate. She didn't realize someone new would be replacing her so quickly, and she was surprised to see me. I walked in and sat on the other bed facing hers, and we had a long conversation. Her name was Trina, and she was a stunning ballet dancer with piercing blue eyes and long, wavy, dark brown hair.

My mother had given me her old European Melitta coffee maker, and one of the first things I did when I moved in was to set it up so I could brew my strong coffee.   I invited Trina to join me, and she quickly came to enjoy my coffee as well each morning.

Trina was always well put together and stylishly dressed, so you would have thought that she was a neat and tidy person. Nothing could have been further from the truth.   Our room usually looked like a fashion boutique had exploded. The floor quickly became a mixture of clothing, magazines, and textbooks.   Trina was a tenacious go-getter with a million things going on, but housekeeping wasn't on her list of priorities. As a Political Science major, she was usually up on the latest news. I was not.   One morning as I was stumbling to the communal showers, I happened to step on her latest issue of Time magazine, which was lying on the floor. She became enraged.

"Oh my God, I can't believe you — you just stepped on Jesse Jackson's face!"

I said, "Who?"

I defended myself by pointing out that there wasn't any clear walking room and I had no other choice but to walk over the debris. I proposed that we use stilts to raise our beds off the ground to create real storage space underneath; that way, we could clear the floor for walking.

The raising of the beds by three feet worked out better than I could have imagined. Under the beds we placed our small refrigerator, our dressers, and any additional items from home. Trina seemed to have brought everything she owned with her, or so it seemed, and she really packed that space under her bed.

One day, I arrived back at the room to find a note from Trina addressed to "Slyvia." She had flipped the first two letters after the "S" in my name; this had happened a few times before and I really didn't like it.   But after a brief discussion on the correct spelling, we both agreed to shorten it to "Sly," and from that moment, that's what she called me. I embraced it, perhaps because it made me think of my old movie hero Rocky. It didn't take long for others to catch on to my new nickname, especially Eric and Geoff, who spread it around to the students in the design studios.

They continued to tease me, saying things like, "How can you be called 'Sly' when you're so clueless?" I, in turn, nicknamed them Clueless One and Two. They went so far as to run a personal ad in Cal Poly's newspaper, the Mustang Daily.

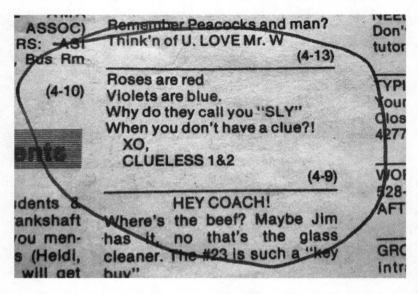

After a good laugh, I brought the newspaper home to show Trina, exclaiming, "See what you started!"

We took this as a sign of our unity and determination. Everyone enjoyed our company. We were both hard workers and very focused. And we played hard — we had so many invitations, it was just a matter of prioritizing which events we wanted to go to. Because we were in different majors, we had joined different fraternities as little sisters and had different circles of friends. When Trina and I showed up together, we often heard people (guys) exclaim, "No way, you two are roommates!" as if it was an unbelievable coincidence.

Most guys knew us both, independent of each other, and possibly they had crushes on one or both of us. That we were roommates seemed to throw them off. We were quite amused by the reaction. When I saw disbelief in someone's eyes, I would build on it by proclaiming that I was studying architecture. This information would really make their eyes bulge as they contemplated my tackling such a hands-on major with only one arm.

"Really?" they'd say, stumbling over their words. "I mean, wow, that's impressive and probably one of the toughest majors here..."

Trina knew my major, and with the reaction I got from most people, I wondered why she never asked me about what had happened to my arm. One day, though, I asked her why she hadn't inquired.

"I could never ask you that," she replied. She looked genuinely on edge, like this was way too sensitive a question for her to ask.

I laughed and said, "Well, I would have asked." I then explained about my cancer. Having an open discussion about it helped bring us even closer together.

Trina and I became the best of friends, and we were both impressed and unconditionally supportive of each other. We had both worked extremely hard to get here, and we were determined to achieve our goals no matter how hard it was going to be. It was wonderful to have a roommate who understood my drive to succeed.

I still enjoyed swimming, and I regularly invited Trina to swim with me at the pool. Cal Poly had only a small outdoor pool with the lap lanes set up in the short (wrong) direction. The pool tended to be crowded, and typically there weren't a lot of girls there swimming laps.

Trina and I quickly noticed that when we stepped on deck, we drew quite a bit of attention. A couple of guys would swim in the lane alongside us on a regular basis. It didn't take long before they began asking us out. At first we told them no, but they were persistent and we finally agreed to go out with them. I was paired with Chris, who had blond hair and a mustache; Trina with Pete who had dark hair. They were both third-year engineering majors and they seemed nice.

Chris and I hit it off for a while and dated until the holidays came around. He landed a temporary job over the winter break to help cover his spring tuition, or so I thought. He insisted on coming home with me for a few days to meet my family before heading off to his job, but I wasn't wild about the idea. I had never had a boyfriend come home with me before, and I wasn't that serious about him, so I was kind of uncomfortable. Thankfully he stayed only one night and slept in the den.

When I returned to San Luis Obispo for winter quarter, I got a call from Chris. He was so excited; he needed to see me immediately and asked me to come by his place. When I arrived, he swooped me up in his arms and spun me around. He proceeded to explain to me how he had worked hard over the break in order to save up enough money to reach his goal.

"Your goal? What is your goal?" I asked.

I started to panic when he got down on one knee and whipped out a small velvet jewelry box from his pocket. My eyes strained, nearly popping out of their sockets.

"It's a promise ring," he announced, handing me a small diamond ring. "Eventually, I'll get you a bigger, fancier engagement ring."

I was shocked. I had not seen this coming. After all, we had only known each other for a few months. In my mind, nothing serious was even going on. Evidently, we were not on the same page with our relationship. Agitated and not knowing what to say, I rattled on about how I had just started college and was not going to commit to any one person at this time. Settling down into a serious long-term relationship was just not on my radar at this point in my life.

Chris's reaction to my blathering caught me completely off guard. He began by yelling at me and calling me a selfish Marin County bitch! He claimed I was just a spoiled girl who got whatever my little heart desired. He then blamed my rejection of the diamond on my thinking it was too small and not good enough for me. None of this was true, of course, and I was becoming frightened by his rage. I wasn't sure how we had come to such different places with our relationship, but I was just not ready for a commitment, and I didn't have strong feelings for him.

My attempts to calm him and soothe his hurt feelings were not making any impact, so I just told him straight up, "It's over, I can't handle this drama," and turned and left.

He continued yelling in the background as I shut the front door behind me and fled his apartment. As I drove off, my heart was beating fast and I felt nothing but relief to have gotten out of there when I did.

To avoid the potential awkwardness of running into him at the school pool, I began swimming at the local YMCA. I didn't even mind the fee because it was a safe place to swim, the pool was much nicer, and open swim hours happened during the day, which I preferred. I luckily never ran into Chris again in town or on campus, but I did have one encounter with his roommate, who wanted to tell me how I had broken the guy's heart.

That was winter quarter.

By spring quarter, it seemed as if everyone had figured out that I was Danish.   I realized this when a fifth-year professor named Ron Batterson approached me, asking if I would teach a beginning Danish language class to the fourth-year students who would be studying abroad the following year.   He was the supervisor for the Danish architectural exchange program with the University of Copenhagen.

My first response was, "How did you know I speak Danish?"

"Everyone knows, and your blond hair and blue eyes also give you away," he explained.

I was a little taken aback that people who I didn't know seemed to know quite a bit about me, but I didn't let that stop me from accepting his offer.   The following Wednesday evening I was introduced as the new Danish teacher to an enthusiastic group of about twenty students. Professor Batterson made it clear to the group that I might be younger than them, but they were to pay attention and take the class seriously, as I would be reporting back to him directly.

Teaching this spring-quarter class was a paid job and lasted for the next few years.   Many of my past students would send me postcards from Denmark and other locations in Europe to stay in touch with me and express their gratitude for my lessons.   It was a wonderful experience.

I still have many of those postcards.

Chapter 21

~ The Grass Is Always Greener ~

Academically, my first year at Cal Poly was incredibly difficult. When it was over in June, I felt totally spent and a little discouraged. I had been put on academic probation for the second time. Now, for the first time in my life I experienced moments of self-doubt. I wondered if I was going to be capable of finishing my degree and was considering dropping out. I wanted to run away and do something different, so I booked a one-way ticket to Denmark.

The cheapest flight I could find landed in Hamburg, Germany, and I planned to take the train from there to Denmark. My uncle Hermann had relatives I could stay with for a few days when I arrived. After receiving a hearty welcome from the Germans, a tour of the sights of Hamburg, and a trip to the local carnival, I took the train north to Copenhagen.

When I arrived, my cousin Merethe was waiting to greet me as my train pulled in. Merethe lived in what the Danes call a three-room flat on the fourth floor of her apartment building in the Amager district in

Copenhagen. Her place was decorated sparsely in the Danish modern style and had a pleasant aroma of pine and teakwood. The kitchen was small and located right off of the entry, with a fold-down table hung from the wall. A tall, narrow window at the sink overlooked the courtyard below. This sink was the only one in her apartment. She had removed several lower cabinets to install a small clothes-washing machine. Everything was very compact. A bedroom with two single beds pushed together lay at the end of the corridor. A modest-size living room featured a large rectangular window looking out the front of the building. A small room for the toilet was tucked off of the corridor (communal showers were in the building's attic). It was cozy, and there was plenty of room for the two of us.

During my time staying with Merethe, I enjoyed learning my way around the streets of Copenhagen and getting to know the locals. I spent a lot of time sitting in cafes enjoying a cappuccino or a Pilsner, depending on the time of day, and people watching while making sketches of the scenery or surrounding buildings. One afternoon, I was spotted by several of the exchange students I had taught Danish to at Cal Poly.

"Hej Sylvia, hvad laver du her?" They were asking what I was doing there!

I was thrilled that they were using the Danish language skills I had taught them. They told me that they were extremely grateful for my course and invited me to a private tour of their studios at the University of Copenhagen. The university was beautiful, and I met many interesting faculty members and students. After our tour, we all went out for a few liters of beer.

Merethe worked at a local bank. While she worked, I would routinely handle the daily shopping by visiting the butcher, grocer, and cheese shops. On the weekends I introduced her to my fellow American architecture students; we'd meet for drinks at the Mouse & Elephant Bar. Merethe, surprisingly, had never heard of this quirky little bar. Upon entering a single door from the street, you proceeded up a narrow staircase to the second level, where a larger-than-life elephant's head sat mounted on the wall. The tusks operated as draft handles — when pulled, beer flowed! This was the only place in Denmark where you could get Carlsberg Elephant Øl on tap. Elephant Øl has a higher alcohol content than your average beer and tastes delicious!

I had promised Anne-Grethe and Kristian I would also come to Morsø and spend some time with them. I was afraid of disappointing them; I knew they would ask my reasons for leaving college. But after spending six weeks in Copenhagen, I knew it was time to face the music. We had always been so close, and I didn't want to hide anything from them.

As expected, my aunt and uncle were completely dispirited to see me taking a defeatist attitude. They counseled me to try and dig deep to find my depth of character and enthusiasm for life. They had never before witnessed me holding back and not going for any challenge that life put in front of me.

My cousin Mariane had heard the news from her father about why I was in Denmark, and she came one evening to take me out on the town to cheer me up. I wondered how much there was to do in the small town of Nykøbing, but Mariane had things figured out. We visited a number of local haunts, finally ending up at a western bar. It was dusk, which came quite late (the summer sun didn't set until 10:00 p.m.), and the dimly lit bar sported comfortable, three-legged saddle-style stools.

Mariane began confiding in me how envious she'd been of me all these years. She felt it would be much more exciting to live in California instead of being stuck on her small island all her life. I responded that I had been envious of her because it would have been wonderful to grow up on Morsø, to live life in a small community where everyone knows each other. With all my wonderful memories from my time spent on the island, I had a completely different perspective on what life would be like living on Morsø. I reflected that the grass is always greener on the other side.

Mariane expressed that she'd felt uncomfortable around town ever since her brother Lars Christian committed suicide the previous year. People react to tragedy in different ways, and the death had unsettled the relaxed flow of life in the town. Sadly, my uncle Søren had been the one to find his son hanging in his house. He was never the same happy person he had once been after the loss of his son.

It had always been perplexing to me: Why would someone consider taking his or her own life? I never could understand how any circumstance could be so extremely bad for someone to not want to live. After all that I had been through during my two-year battle for life, I felt that nothing in this world could ever be so terrible to entertain such thoughts, let alone to execute them. Life has so much to offer. The possibilities are endless. Surely taking a new path would be the better option rather than ending things.

Enhanced by the effects of the Elephant beer, our conversation turned to contemplation of our philosophical views on life, and we reached that slurring-of-speech stage where we were unsteady on our stools. We thankfully realized that we should make the wise choice and give Anne-Grethe a call to come and pick us up. Our ride home was appreciated, but the extremely loud lecture we got from her the entire ride back to Søndergård was not.

I did not awaken until the next afternoon, with a horrible headache. As I lay in bed with my hangover, I realized that I needed to get my ass back to America and finish college. My conversation with my cousin made me look at my life back home with fresh eyes, and now it didn't feel so overwhelming. Later that day I called my mother and explained that I had decided I needed to come home and get my life back on track. She was excited to hear this and offered to wire me the money for a flight home. This was appreciated because I was in fact just about out of money.

I stayed on the farm to help Anne-Grethe and Kristian through the harvest and then took the train back to Copenhagen. At the tourist bureau in Copenhagen, they were able to help me find a cheap flight as long as I was a student. I was never happier to say that I was a student.

Once back in California, I felt I had been given a new lease on life. My trip had invigorated me, and I was ready to hit the ground running. I knew I had my work cut out for me at school, but now I felt up to the task. My first challenge was to find a new place to live in San Luis Obispo.

The University Union housing board on campus was my best option. I had only a week to find a place before school started, and it wasn't going to be easy. I wrote down a few possibilities and started to make calls from the payphone in the corridor. While struggling with the payphone, I saw surfer dudes I knew in the student union and waved them down. I asked if they knew of anything available.

"Yeah, we have a room available," they responded. They lived only two doors down from the main entrance to campus on Grand Avenue, a perfect location. I could have taken the room, but after visiting the place I learned that I would have six — six! — male roommates with only one bathroom. No thanks! The dishes looked as if they hadn't been washed all summer long. There was no way, even if they were cute surfers, for this to be a good idea. I let it go and continued with my search.

I made an appointment to meet a few girls about a shared room in a duplex off North Chorro Street. It was in the upper unit of a pale-yellow stucco box with parking in front. It had two small rooms and a single bathroom. It was perfect. I told them I would take the room, and I headed back home to Marin to gather my stuff from my mother's garage.

Two days later, my cousin Bruce helped me move back down to Cal Poly, driving his dad's old cream-colored VW Squareback loaded with my belongings. My brother's old white bicycle was strapped to the roof. It was a cool beach cruiser that he'd purchased from the Newport Beach flea market on one of our summer trips to SoCal. It took an hour to unload and carry my belongings up the stairs and stack them in my new room. Once the car was unloaded, Bruce declared that he was ready to head back home.

My new roommates were two Filipino gals, and they spoke to each other in their native tongue. I shared a room with a Mexican gal named Evangelina. They were the sweetest girls and we all got along really well. Now that we were living out of the dorms and had a kitchen, my roommates did a lot of cooking and I was the recipient of many good meals. Because we were students on tight budgets, we ate a lot of rice and beans.

Evangelina often would accompany me to Pismo Beach. I had a friend teaching me to surf and needed to practice on my own occasionally. Evangelina wouldn't go in the cold water because she didn't have a wetsuit like I did, but it was nice to have her along for the company. She would cheer me on when I actually caught a wave.

On one occasion when I wasn't able to get up, I got too close to the shore and the fin on my longboard hit the sand, which sent me flying off the front end, head first into the sand. There I lay in the sand, embarrassed, while she couldn't stop laughing. After a moment, I couldn't help but join in the laughter, because it really was pretty funny, especially after the next wave washed the surfboard on top of me.

Second year was starting, and I was excited to be back in school. I needed to buy textbooks and supplies, so I spent time at the El Corral Bookstore checking off my list of new and used books, plus the architecture books that I wanted. I would flip through the pages of the numerous architecture books, deliberating whether I had any extra money for them. Then I strolled back down the hill toward the Architecture Department to confirm the locations of my new classes.

As I walked around the beautiful campus I wondered how I ever could have thought that I was not up to this challenge. I figured that doubting yourself was normal but that it was more important to forge ahead and shoot for your dreams. I was in my own world, having a moment with my thoughts, when my reverie was pierced by someone calling my name. A tall, wavy-haired Lambda Chi brother who was an Architectural Engineering major was shouting and waving at me.

"Hey, Sylvia; Who did you get for second-year design?"
"Denel, Professor Denel" I replied.

"Oh no, he gasped as he came jogging up alongside. I feel sorry for you." He tried to catch his breath.

"Bilgi, as everyone calls him, is the meanest, toughest design professor here at Cal Poly. You are in trouble now," he repeated.

"You are in trouble now."

Oh my gosh, maybe I should have stayed in Denmark. This thought briefly flew through my head as I collected myself.

"Why, what makes this 'Bilgi' so horrible?"

"He is a short, heavyset man from Turkey — oh no, you're in trouble now." He continued, "He doesn't like anyone or anything!"

This is absurd; this guy is just trying to scare me, I thought.

But he must have read my mind, because he then assured me that he was not joking.

Chapter 22

~ Two Worlds Collided ~
(And they could never tear us apart)
Lyrics by INXS

Upon arriving at the large classroom on the first day of my second-year design class, I paused at the door, as I typically did, to observe the situation. I noticed the tall drafting tables lined up in pairs lengthwise down the center of the room with the stools situated so that students would be facing one another. I was excited to see my old musketeers Eric and Geoff sitting in the center of the room waving at me. They had saved me a table next to them in hopes that I would again be in the same design studio.

There was a loud buzz in the room as the students shared distressing stories about our impending professor. When silence fell suddenly, as Bilgi entered, one brave soul attempted to spark a cheerful tone, shouting out, "Good morning, Professor Denel!"

"What's so good about it?" replied a gruff voice. "There is nothing good about mornings."

That struck us all dumb again as we waited to see what would come next. Bilgi continued to stroll silently around the room, placing his attaché on a desk while he passed his gaze over his new batch of students. I got a shiver when I noticed Bilgi noticing me, and I smiled at him. Many years later, he confided to me; that when he had initially noticed me, his first thought was that here was a lovely girl, naturally blond, blue-eyed, slender... and then he got the shock of his career! This young lady with the cheerful smile had only one arm! He wondered how I could cut, draw, and build, as these were difficult challenges even for those with two hands!

After his initial shock passed, Bilgi gathered himself and proceeded with the rant that served as an introduction to his class. He warned us that we could expect him to be politically incorrect and chauvinistic, and that he had already decided that he was not going to like any of our work. The class was silent with fear, but I could tell that this was all bluster. He once again noticed that I was smiling, in contrast to the other students who sat with their mouths hanging slightly open. He decided then and there that he would treat me like any other student. As the quarter went on, he also realized that I had developed my own techniques to draw and assemble projects as well as anyone else.

Second-year design studios met for three hours a day, five days a week. Bilgi's lectures provided great insight into design and philosophy, and all of us impressionable second-year students took notes as fast as we could, trying to get it all down in our sketchbooks. He was both brilliant and intimidating.

I will never forget his first lecture after he finished sizing us all up.

"Your first decision in architectural design is arbitrary, and your second decision confirms your first."

He further elaborated, "Your first decision is never justified. However, all the rest of your decisions must relate back to the previous one."

The more experience you have, the better your first arbitrary decision will be!

This was only the beginning, as Bilgi's lectures would push me and teach me new ways to not only grasp new concepts but visualize them. He made me think harder than ever. If you justify each step, through a process of elimination, to confirm your initial arbitrary decision, this can become a lengthy process until you have gained that experience. It is a very satisfying process in the end.

Most of us grew to adore Bilgi. He would allow us studio "free time" to begin working on our projects. This did not stop him from continuing to address the group, by attempting to break the tension with explaining his system of what he called "punishments." This was basically choosing one student at a time for mistreatment so that no one in the class felt singled out. We would all be "punished" at some point during the quarter.

A person could be punished for smiling, or not smiling, for being on time, or being late...

The person assigned for punishment would have to bring homemade cookies or cake, enough for the entire class. One day, I was assigned punishment for smiling too much. Bilgi asked the class what I should bring, and they asked for cake. At the time I really did not know how to bake a cake, but I remembered a delicious rum cake my aunt Sonia used to make. I called my mom for the recipe and then took the liberty to add a little extra rum. Everyone thought I had just bought an angel food cake and poured a bottle of rum over it. When they found out it was homemade and deliciously intoxicating, the word spread, and everyone wanted a piece.

By this point, I was becoming known on campus, not only for my now-famous rum cake, but also for my outgoing personality and my ability to accomplish things with only one arm. People called my name and waved at me as I rode around campus on my beach cruiser, which was fully loaded with my drafting gear. I had mounted a rack to the back, and on this, I strapped a pair of light-gray saddlebags with red trim and leather straps. I was able to transport all of my drawing tools and books, plus my sketchpad and lunch.

The bike was very handy, as I didn't have to worry about parking or walking with all my drafting supplies. In second year, we still had an architectural drawing/drafting class. This class was all about drafting details, primarily door and window details. By this time we all knew how to draft quite well. Some people were still amazed when they saw me setting up my piece of vellum, aligning it with my parallel rule on the bottom, then with my triangle to square it, holding it all in place using the side of my palm and reaching up with my fingers to the corners of the sheet to tape it down with my drafting dots.

I rode a couple of miles each way to get from my apartment to campus. There was only one significant street I had to cross, which was also Highway 1. The rest of the way, I rode the back trails and lastly had to pump my cruiser up the hill to reach campus. Once on campus, it was easy cruising down the promenade that bordered an expansive lawn, passing the Engineering West building on my way to the Architecture building. The second floor of this building was lined with windows that opened off of the classrooms where my peers had their design studios. As I rode up on my bike, they would lean out of the windows and holler down to greet me. I would release my one hand to wave enthusiastically at them, smiling as I pedaled past.

My roommates and I got along pretty well when I was home, which wasn't that often. When I did come home, I usually found them in the kitchen cooking. Sharing the kitchen caused some issues between the three of them. One day, poor Evangelina couldn't find her masher to make refried beans and became very upset over the loss of this important utensil. We all tore the place apart looking for it, but we had no luck. She seemed to think the other girls had taken it. I couldn't bear her crying, so I went straight to the grocery store and bought her a new one. It wasn't exactly like the missing one, but it restored the peace. After that, I looked for a different place to live.

A friend of mine who was a fifth-year architecture student would soon have an opening at her place in the Woodside Apartments, where I could have my own room. I jumped on it. When I returned from the holiday break, I moved in with two graduating seniors, Chris and Kathy. The apartment had a small kitchen and living area just inside the entrance, and then a staircase leading up to a large landing area with a double sink and mirror. Three bedrooms and a shower room opened off the landing. I was happy to find that I knew an amazing number of other students living in this dark brown, wood-sided complex known as "Woodside."

Kathy worked at a little café downtown and brought home stories about five very cute Australians who came in every day for breakfast. They were in town for a few months on a work visa while on an extended trip around the world. They had found employment at a local landscaping company. Though she encouraged Chris and me to come to the café and meet them and maybe join them for breakfast, it never seemed to work out.

One late afternoon, I was with a fellow architecture student, who I was dating, and we dropped by my apartment to pick up something I had forgotten and found all five of the Australians in our living room. Kathy introduced us all and we chatted for a few minutes before heading out. We were in a hurry and just needed to pick up materials and get back to our design studio at school. The next morning, my roommate Kathy wanted to know if they had made an impression on me...

"What did you think of the Australians? Cute, huh?"

"Yeah, they were pretty cute, and I love their accents!" I replied.

"What about Glenn?" She asked.

"Glenn...?"

"Yeah, he was the sweet blond one sitting on the back of the sofa," replied Kathy with a smirk. "And. . . he would like to know if you might consider being his girlfriend for the next few months while he's in town."

"What?"

That was rather presumptuous, but I'll admit I was intrigued.

I told her to tell the Australians that if they wanted to get to know me better, they could meet me on Saturday at 10 a.m. in front of the Architecture building, and I would be there with a friend.

The upcoming weekend was Cal Poly's annual open house, Poly Royal. Tess was coming down, and I had promised to give her a tour of the campus. On Saturday morning Tess and I waited in front of the Architecture building to see if any of the Aussies were going to show up. We waited a good fifteen minutes and then decided to go;

we had waited long enough.   As we began walking down the promenade, I heard someone calling out with an Australian accent.

"Hey mates, wait up! I'm here!"

We turned.   Running toward us was a guy, not much taller than me, with soft, tight blond curls, a boyish smile, and a mischievous glint in his eye.

"I'm sorry I'm late," he apologized as he tried to catch his breath.

"Is it just you?" I asked.

"Yeah, my mates and I were out late last night and they were too hungover to get up this morning," he replied.

But you showed, I thought to myself. He must genuinely want to get to know me.

"Let's go. I hope you can keep up."

I turned and continued down the promenade with my two guests following through the crowds.   Lining the promenade were student kiosks and booths promoting clubs, selling food and drinks.   We traipsed over the many hills of the campus exploring the different sites. Wherever we went, there were people I knew and I would introduce them around.

Tess and Glenn were quite impressed, and he remarked, "I can't believe you know so many people." Tess nodded in agreement.

"I get around," I replied with a wink and a laugh.

By the time we looped back around to the Architecture building, the poor guy's hangover seemed to be catching up with him, but he had been a good sport. I thought it was sweet that he made such an effort. I was especially happy that Tess loved the campus and was now hoping to be accepted into the Civil Engineering program. The three of us had

had a terrific day. Glenn invited us to join him and the four other Aussies that night at Spikes. The local bar saw us partying until late into the night, hitting it off quite well — especially Glenn and me.

Tess hit it off with another Aussie named Mic, and we all made the most of the weekend before Tess went back home. Glenn was adorable; he had an awesome accent and just wanted to have fun over the next few months with no strings attached. I was a bit free-spirited, so this sounded great to me. I was tired of every guy wanting a more serious relationship than I was interested in. This was school mode and fun mode. I wasn't interested in bringing any relationship drama into my life. So, this was perfect.

Glenn and I just clicked, and it seemed like we had known each other for years. Our personalities meshed better than I could have imagined. He was compassionate, considerate, and attentive — in tune with what I needed without my having to ask. I was very focused on my architectural projects, and when I worked at home he would come over and keep me company while I busily sketched my designs and built my models.

One of his many charming qualities was that he would take my pulse because he was concerned about the large quantities of caffeine I consumed throughout the day. I drank coffee or Diet Coke to help me stay up late most nights working on projects. If my heart was racing, he would help me to calm down and relax by rubbing my neck and back. If my stress was related to a deadline, he was the first to offer help with cutting or gluing. We often worked until late even though Glenn had to get up early for work.

On the weekdays, in addition to helping me out, Glenn worked with his mates doing landscaping for a local company to earn extra cash for his travels. When I returned home from class, I would sometimes find him waiting outside my apartment to surprise me. Otherwise, we met at Spikes and drank our way around the world in beer. Sometimes we would party at his place with his mates or, when we had time, go to the beach. We really enjoyed each other's company and had more fun and laughs than I thought possible.

After several months had passed, it was time for Glenn and his mates to continue their travels. He told me he would write to me. His goal was to reach Santorini, Greece, as his final destination before heading back to Australia. I was sad to see him go and tried to console myself with the thought that I had known all along our relationship would only be a temporary thing. We said our goodbyes, and he headed off to Europe.

Around that same time, Tess called me, excited. She was barely able to contain herself.

"You want a new roommate?"

She all but shouted into the phone, announcing that she'd been accepted to Cal Poly and was moving down to SLO. We would have to find a place that would take Shasta, her dog, which was going to be a challenge. The timing couldn't have been better, though. Both of my roommates were graduating, and I was going to have to move anyway. I was so excited. Tess came down the following weekend, and we began our search for a new place.

As the weeks passed, my mind periodically drifted off, thinking of the wonderful times I had spent with my Aussie friend. I wondered where he was on his travels. Thankfully I was still preoccupied with finishing up my final design projects and preparing my presentations. When the quarter ended and finals were over, I stayed in town waiting for Tess to arrive.   With alone time, I realized that I actually missed Glenn. A lot! I didn't know what to do with these emotions. I had not experienced such feelings for any of the other guys I had dated.   He understood me and always seemed to do just the right thing or say the right words.

I tried to put Glenn behind me, letting the excitement of moving in with my best friend occupy my mind.   Tess was on her way, and I couldn't wait to get settled into our house together.   She borrowed a truck from a friend and loaded it with all her furniture and belongings, which were considerable.   She and Shasta, her black-and-white mutt that was part coyote, headed south to join me.

It was the summer of '85; we were both now 21 years old and primed to have a good time.   We rented a little three-bedroom, steel-blue, turn-of-the-century house with white trim and a small front porch on the corner of Pismo and Beach streets.   The house needed a lot of TLC.   We got to work right away painting and fixing the wainscoting on the walls, the trim around the windows, and the railings on the front porch.   I got the double-hung windows operable again while Tess whipped out her sewing machine and made curtains.   Her mother came down and helped us do repairs to the electrical wiring.   We fixed up the front yard, mowed the grass, and planted flowers.   We even planted a large vegetable garden along the side of the house.

Once Tess and I had completed our renovations, I headed home for a few weeks to spend some time with my mother and Steve.   I arrived to find that I would received a postcard from Glenn.   It was a picture of the Loch Ness Monster; he was in Scotland.   I wanted to write back but was uncertain where I should send a letter.   Glenn was still traveling and wouldn't be back in Australia for months.   I began checking our mailbox on a daily basis, hoping for another postcard, but nothing came.

I would be driving around in my black Scirocco, and the Swedish rock group Roxette would come on the radio. It seemed as though the songs they sang were describing me. I cranked up the volume and sang aloud to "The Look" and "Dangerous." Then later, when the group released the song "It Must Have Been Love," I listened to the words and wondered if he had forgotten about me.

> It must have been love
> But it's over now
> It must have been good
> But I lost it somehow
> It must have been love
> But it's over now
> From the moment we touched
> Till the time had run out.

~

I could not get this song out of my head. I couldn't understand it; typically these kinds of thoughts didn't even enter my mind, but I had certainly not forgotten about him. I kept hoping for another postcard because my imagination was carrying on about the great adventures he must be having as he traveled through Europe. I hoped he was also still thinking about me.

I stayed busy with family and friends, and soon it was time to return to SLO. I convinced my group of high school friends to return to

SLO with me to celebrate Cat's 21st birthday, and I invited everyone to stay at the new place I shared with Tess.

The day before heading back to SLO, a second postcard arrived from Glenn. He had finally made it to the Greek isle of Santorini, just as he'd said he would. I was thrilled for him and envious at the same time. What great adventures he must have had, and now he'd be heading home to Australia. He had given me his address in Australia, so now I knew that I would be able to write to him.

The gang met at my house to caravan down to San Luis Obispo for Cat's birthday celebration. The group included Cat, her sister Liz, Kirk, Sandy, Staci, and me. When we piled out of our cars, Tess and Shasta were standing on the front porch waiting to greet us. Everyone was extremely impressed with how nice and homey our place was. My room had a built-in loft elevated about six feet off the ground. It had a straight-up ladder for access that was a little tricky to navigate with one hand, especially in the middle of the night. The previous tenant had built the loft, and I put my mattress up there, giving me an office space below, now set up with my teak drafting table, my dresser, and an extra chair and table.

We had a fantastic time with our friends and showed them all of the reasons we loved living in SLO. We spent our days at Avila Beach soaking in the late summer rays. We showed them the quaint downtown including the creek, the old mission, and Bubblegum Alley. We even took a trip to Solvang.

For Cat's 21st birthday, we had a fabulous spaghetti feed that Tess cooked up at our place. We all sat around the large kitchen table eating heartily before heading out with the intent to take Cat to every bar in town for her free birthday drinks. Tess was a firm believer in "getting a good base in your stomach" before drinking a lot, so we all chowed down. First stop was Spikes. I had not been back there since Glenn left. When we walked in, I noticed Glenn's old boss from the landscape company. He was happy to see me again, giving me a big hug and somehow managing to ask me out on a date. I ignored that and turned the conversation to ask if he'd heard from any of the Aussies recently. I told him that I had received a couple of postcards from Glenn.

He sharply responded, "You might want to just forget about Glenn. He has a high school sweetheart he's already promised to marry as soon as he gets back to Australia."

I could not believe what I was hearing. I was in complete disbelief. If this were true, then I must have been just a fling to him! I couldn't get myself to believe that. I tried to shake my doubts off and move on. I needed to stay focused on my path. He was thousands of miles away in Australia, and I didn't have much hope of ever seeing him again. If he was going to get married, I certainly didn't want to cause any problems for the guy.

Although I knew in my heart that we really had had something special, and that it wasn't just a fling, hearing this news created a seed of doubt. Maybe these feelings I was having were only in my own mind, and he never felt the same way. So, I put him out of my mind and decided that even though I had his address and phone number, I would not contact him. It was simply time for me to move on with my life. The postcard from Santorini was the last one I received.

Although I was shaken by the news about Glenn, I put it aside and focused on celebrating Cat's big day. I wasn't going to let anything ruin this special occasion After drinks at Spikes, we hit McLintocks Saloon, McCarthy's Irish Pub, then our favorite dive bar called Bull's

Tavern, where a gin and tonic was only 25 cents and we knew all the bartenders by name. When the lights flickered for last call, we ordered one more round before staggering home.

Somewhere during our night's escapades, we seemed to have attracted the attention of a couple of followers. These guys wanted to party with us, and as we left Bull's they continued to trail us out the door. Tess turned, putting her hand out in front of them in a stop-right-there gesture, saying,

"Where do you think you are going?"

"With you," they replied.

"No, no, we are going home now; the night is over. See you guys later."

Unfortunately, that didn't stop these two. As our group continued walking down the street toward home, laughing and cackling, we didn't notice that a car was following us.

Once back at the house, Liz said she heard something outside. With everyone a little impaired, we all brushed it off as nothing and got ready for bed. Then, we all heard the voices in our front yard. Everyone ran to the windows to look out.

"Shut the lights. They can see us!" I yelled.

"There is someone running through your yard!" Kirk called out.

"Oh, no, it's the guys that wanted to come with us," Tess said. "They followed us?"

Tess, Kirk, and I went outside and told these guys to get off our property and leave, or we would call the police. They shouted back, "No, we want to come in," but then turned, ran, and jumped into their car and started the engine. It appeared as if they were leaving, but instead they started revving the engine, with the headlights pointed straight at the side of our house. We all ran screaming away from the windows, as we thought they were going to come crashing right through the wall.

The car did come thundering toward us, up onto the curb, going full speed and then smash! straight into the seven-foot hedge in the side yard. They were stuck in the giant bush! They tried putting their car into reverse, but the tires spun as they continued to gun the motor. It was crazy. When they realized they were stuck and just spinning their tires, they got out of the car, leaving the doors open, and began to run.

Good riddance, we thought! Their car was now stuck in our hedge, which made us uncomfortable, but since they'd run off, we just went to bed. The next morning when we finally awoke, Cat looked out the window and saw the two goofballs lying passed out on the lawn! A tow truck was called, and we were finally rid of the intruders. This was definitely a memorable 21st birthday for Cat, and for the rest of us, too.

It was a crazy end to a fantastic summer. My third year of design was about to start. In third year you finally get your own workspace in your design studio — a place where you can be as creative as your mind allows, and set up the space to be personalized however you like. It would become a home away from home, some students even sleeping there. I would no longer have to haul my drafting board, drawing tools, equipment, and books back and forth on a daily basis. After two years of carrying my gear back and forth each day, it was wonderful to set up my own workspace at last.

Chapter 23

~ Life Is Good . . .

My design professor this quarter was Terry Hargrave. He was the coolest professor on campus. He had this shabby-chic look with scruffy blond hair, and he wore John Lennon–style round tinted glasses. He had attended MIT for grad school. I was so impressed.

I arrived a few minutes late on my first day, and most of the other students had chosen their workspaces for the quarter. Although there were few left, I found one I liked toward the front of the classroom. It had potential. The student in the next workspace was a fellow named Kurt. It was a bit strange that I had never seen or met him before. I thought I knew everyone in my year. He turned out to be a great guy, and we got to know each other quickly in our new design studio setting.

The area was too open for my liking, so I created a private entry between my desk and my new neighbor Kurt's desk, stringing up a sheet as a canopy that enclosed our two work areas together in an intimate fashion. Kurt and I both loved this because people could see us only if they entered through the doorway I had created. We were free from most distractions. I had transformed this ordinary classroom space into a unique and inspiring workspace. Ensconced in our tent area together, I quickly figured out that Kurt had a crush on me.

When Professor Hargrave gawkily entered the studio that first day, he seemed hesitant and uncertain as he looked around the room observing his new batch of students. Usually an instructor had a more commanding air when surveying a class. He was the bumbling professor as he assigned our first task, and when he used the term "design esquisse" we were all a bit perplexed as to what he wanted. Although I was confused, I could tell that he was a professor I could really learn from. This would be a challenging and fantastic class.

Professor Hargrave briefly described the design project for the quarter. It was to be a residence for the philosopher Bertrand Russell. We were to use Russell's philosophical ideas as a tool in designing his house, and the property had a creek running through it. Before he would provide us with the full requirements or take us to visit the site, we had the weekend to complete our esquisse. I was still baffled as to what this was or what I was supposed to do. After a long, silent pause, with the students beginning to murmur and look around at each other, he finally explained to us what an "esquisse" is.

We were relieved to have it explained but daunted by the task ahead. A design esquisse is a preliminary sketch or design concept drawing for a project. We were each to paint our idea onto a 4-foot by 4-foot canvas, and by Monday morning each student's esquisse was to be on display in the classroom. Wow, a 4' x 4' canvas. That is really big, I thought.

That's when Kurt asked me, "Where will we get a 4' x 4' canvas?"

"We also need paint, gesso, and brushes," I said.

Kurt suggested we work together and share the expenses, which was fine with me. I had an idea where we might get the canvases, hopefully for free. There was a construction site near my place. I suggested we talk to the crew and see if they would donate a 4' x 8' sheet of plywood for our projects.

They were more than happy to help out and cut it in half for us. So we each had a 4'x 4' square piece of plywood on which to make our work canvases.

We carried our heavy boards back to my place, along with the other supplies we had bought at Law's Hobby Center, the only art supply store in town. My roommates were out of town for the weekend. So, I told Kurt we could spread out in my living room with our canvases and paints and not disrupt anyone with the mess. We laid a few old sheets over the floor and covered the furniture and began setting up. With our supplies ready and our blank canvases in front of us, we wondered, now what to paint?

Four feet by four feet is a big canvas. I had done some painting in the past, but Kurt had not, and he was at a total loss. We discussed what our professor had described and started brainstorming. I finally came up with an idea and began sketching on my plywood lightly in pencil. I then used gesso to lend a three-dimensional quality to two cliffs flanking an ocean scene. I wanted to bridge the gap with an abstract bridge over the waters below. I built a three-dimensional cube out of quarter-inch wire mesh and spray-painted it fire-engine red. I attached the bright red cube to the painting to create a bridge connecting the rocky cliffs. I finished with a beautiful blue sky rising above. Kurt was impressed.

"How did you come up with that so quickly?" he asked, as he continued to struggle with his painting.

I explained how I let things percolate in my subconscious for a while. Then I pull from things I like. For example, I like geometric shapes, especially the square with its four equal sides and ninety-degree corners. And I enjoy the beach. But I chose to make it a rough ocean scene with rocky cliffs because we did not know what to expect from this class. When Kurt finished straining over his concept, he eventually came up with a very organic and fluid design of his own. After the paintings were done, we had a quiet, roommate-free weekend together, and things got pretty hot and heavy between us.

When Monday morning arrived, we all managed to have our paintings perched up on desks, propped against walls, and a few suspended from the ceiling as Professor Hargrave entered the studio. Looking around the room, he addressed the images on the giant canvases. I was fascinated by his interpretations. He noted that all the paintings by the males in the class were organic in nature, sensual and curvy, whereas the females' paintings were geometric in shape. Mine definitely was geometric, with my 3D, red cube protruding. Professor Hargrave also commented on how these paintings would be a direct inspiration for our projects.

A half hour later, we were walking the site for our project. Surprisingly, it was a rather remote location, completely overgrown with wild vines and foliage climbing upward and hanging all over the many live oak trees. The terrain was rugged; a hillside sloped from gradual to really steep in spots. A dry creek ran down the center. It was filled with dried twigs and brush, but it appeared to be the easiest way to traverse the site. I began taking photos with the Canon 35mm camera my mother had given me, and making rough sketches. Now that I could see the area, my mind was overflowing with ideas.

It was the fall, and warm, so I was wearing a short skirt that day. With all the leaves missing from the twigs, I initially couldn't understand how I contracted the worst case of poison oak in my life. It was from walking through the dry creek. I had it all over my legs, and in between. I have always been extremely allergic to poison oak. I couldn't even walk. I finally made it to the on-campus health center where I received a shot in my buttocks! Which cured it almost immediately. I have never had it since. Beware of the dry scrubs!

The project took the entire quarter and consisted of numerous conceptual sketches, perspective drawings, a rendering, and a scale model. In using Russell's philosophical ideas, I developed a concept using a rotated cube as my form generator.

Based on my interruption of Bertrand's idea;

> "To act on probability,
> To act with figure,
> Not with complete certainty.
> So, if you think you're right, you're probably not."

By using the simple form of a square and rotating it, then stacking squares upon one another in a three-dimensional form, I came to a simple, yet complex puzzle: What is the probability of the square being rotated? It would depend on where you were standing in the house, and on what axis you were facing.

Then a central spine spanned the creek connecting to an additional, isolated cube housing Russell's private library. A red front door distinctly announced the entry. All the windows were organized in groups of four small squares, together creating larger squares. The skylights above were also squares. The image of the cube was strongly represented in its purity throughout the design.

My project was well received, with much praise from the jury panel made up of other professors and guest lecturers. Kurt had been watching and listening to my critique and he rushed up to me, rattling on about how he had never heard anyone get such rave reviews from these critics. He seemed genuinely happy for me, but equally conflicted because his own project did not fare so well.

Elated from my positive critique and feeling quite pleased with the outcome of my project, I walked back to the design studio to clean up my workstation. Upon entering the classroom, I stopped and noticed my painting from the original esquisse. Gazing at the image I had created, it dawned on me with a burst of recognition that it really had influenced the design of my final project. I turned and looked around the room at the other student paintings on display. The direct correlation from paintings to projects shocked me. We don't realize how the images in our daily lives impact the decisions and choices we make on a daily basis. This was a turning point in my thought process. As I became more aware of my surroundings, I understood how visual elements contribute to my impressions, observations, and actions as I deal with life as a whole.

When Kurt approached me the next day, he wasn't looking just for reassurance on his project, but was mainly concerned about the status of our relationship. It hadn't crossed my mind that the difference in our critiques would affect our relationship. He had always been insecure and hesitant with our relationship, and now things had come to a crisis point for him. He told me that he had an old girlfriend who wanted him back.

"Okay," I said. "So, what do you want from me?"

I could tell that he wanted me to fight for him, but I wasn't going to do his thinking for him. I finally had to tell him that if he wanted us to stay together, that would be nice, but he should decide what he wanted on his own. I had realized he was insecure with me throughout our relationship, and so it seemed that we had come to an end.

Kurt was not the first guy to have a problem like this with me. My confidence and independence intimidated some men. That was fine with me; I did not need someone who was looking for a clinging vine of a girlfriend. It was my time to shine and focus on my achievements. Next quarter, I was heading into a highly competitive and creative studio. I knew both my professors and peers would watch me closely because of my previous accomplishments. I was going to have my work cut out for me.

I always felt, when I was in my design classes at school, that I could keep up with most of the other talented students, and that I was a part of the mainstream. We were a competitive bunch, and it was a lot of work to stay original and true to your own beliefs. It wasn't until years later and reminiscing with the old gang that I was told I had always been considered a whole person, and that I fit in the same as anyone else. It was never an issue of having one arm to me, so it was never an issue for my peers.

But I was confided in that, at the same time, it did set me apart. Why? Because I was a person with one arm who could not only mysteriously draft, but also cut and glue models together very precisely with extremely square and straight edges. Because I could do everything equally well, but with only one arm. This also made me intimidating and considered a threat in the design studios. It was something I had not realized.

On a visit to show my kids around Cal Poly, I ran into an old classmate who had become a design professor. I must admit I was a bit jealous of that. Then he revealed something.

"I hope you don't mind," he said...

"But when my students begin hemming and hawing over the difficulties of designing and building their projects, I break into a lecture about you, and how capable you were with one arm, and you set a new standard that they must follow."

I was flattered.

Meanwhile, Tess and I were having the time of our lives enjoying the SLO life, as people called it. We continued making new friends. We were often at Bull's on the weekends, and would stop in there after the Thursday night farmers market, which, to this day, I believe to be the best farmers market anywhere. San Luis Obispo closes off Higuera Street, one of its main streets that run through downtown. It is always packed with people from both the town and outlying areas. The local restaurants set up their smokers and giant grills to smoke their signature beef ribs. If you have a sweet tooth you can find the local bakeries setting out their delectable wares. Local farmers come in with their vibrantly colored fresh produce, and street vendors and musicians entertain the crowds at every corner. The merchants, even those without a sidewalk booth, stay open late. One vendor made particularly good pulled pork sandwiches, and I would get one every week.

One night after sitting on the curb along Higuera enjoying our pulled pork sandwiches, Tess and I began strolling back up the street through the hundreds of people toward Bull's. I spotted a guy with short, wavy blond hair wearing a white tee and blue jeans and leaning against a light post. He had movie-star good looks and I couldn't help myself from staring at him.

"Tess, Tess. Look at that guy, he looks like James Dean," I said, tugging on her arm. "Wow, he is gorgeous," I continued, as we walked past nonchalantly, and then I turned around to get another glimpse of him.

"Damn, he's gone." How did he disappear that fast? "Boy, was he sexy though," I said aloud.

"Not my type," Tess stated flatly.

Probably one reason we got along so well, I thought to myself.

The next night, Tess and I were invited to some friends' house for a party. In our typical style, Tess with her tequila in hand, the two of us walked over. When we entered, I just about knocked Tess over trying to alert her. There he was again! James Dean, as I called him. The mysterious, sexy guy I had seen leaning against the lamp post.

Little did I know, he had also noticed us back at the farmers market the previous night. I walked through the crowded room attempting to greet everyone, and before I realized it, James Dean was approaching me. He introduced himself (of course James wasn't his real name; it was Tim) and, as it turned out, Tim was also good friends with the people having the party, and he had been informed that Tess and I would be attending.

Subsequently, I learned that Tim went to the farmers market only to get a glimpse of Tess and me. He had spotted me previously at school, and wanted to make sure he and his friend were talking about the same blond girl. Tim and I continued chatting throughout the night as if no one else was at the party, until I began feeling a little odd. I initially thought I had had too much tequila.

I told Tess I wasn't feeling well and needed to go home. When she asked if I had eaten any of the brownies out on the table, I admitted I had. She told me they were "special" brownies and consequently I was flying high.

"I was not ready for this," I told Tess, "and I need to get out of here now." Tim came over and asked what was going on. I told him I had to leave. He asked for my phone number. I couldn't even remember it, and Tess stepped in and explained that I had eaten the brownies. She gave him our number and said to me,

"Let's go." We began our journey home and about halfway there, near Bull's, I said,

"I need a drink."

Tess replied, "I don't think you need any more to drink tonight."

"No, I'm really thirsty, I just want some water. I am so thirsty."

We entered the crowded bar, everyone cheering at our arrival. We headed straight for the end of the grimy bar, pulled up a pair of stools, and shouted at the bartender.

"Two waters, straight up!"

"What, no gin and tonic tonight?" he responded, setting two glasses of water in front of us.

"No, Sylvia's had too much already," Tess replied, as I drank my water and continued to feel higher and higher.

Then without warning, I broke out into my hysterical laughter for no reason at all. I was laughing hard, so hard that when Tess and the bartender turned to see what was so funny, I was gone.

"Sylvia, where did you go?" Tess exclaimed.

She looked down when she heard my cackling continue and saw me laughing on the floor! "I think it's time for me to take you home," she said, as a cute guy helped me onto my feet.

"Thanks." Still laughing uncontrollably, I attempted to get my bearings. Tess tried to hold me up as we stumbled out the door, making it the few blocks over to Pismo Street. When we realized we had to pee, we had four more blocks to get home. After about two blocks, we realized there was no way we were going to make it. We began crawling, as we couldn't even walk, we had to go so bad.

"Let's get past the houses," Tess said. "And go in the bushes in the church parking lot up ahead."

Still laughing while trying to crawl, with me feeling like a three-legged dog and laughing even more, we tried not to pee our pants as we approached the nearest bushes. But then we heard noises from up ahead.

"Do you hear something?" I asked.

"Yeah, shhh; it's coming from the trash dumpster," Tess exclaimed.

The noises became louder, clang, clang, along with a growling sound. The two of us screamed simultaneously, uncontrollably, when suddenly a dark shadowy figure popped its head up out of the garbage. Our shrieks and screams turned into hysterical cackling and laughing once we realized it was Shasta, Tess's crazy dog who had once again escaped and was going through the trash. There he was, staring back at us with his paws perched on the edge of the dumpster, happy as a clam with a huge beef rib bone in his mouth.

There was nothing stopping the two of us. Life was going well, between school, boys and... then our mothers came to visit. They were also good friends back home and felt we were having too much fun!

They decided it was time to check up on us girls to see what kind of mischief we were getting into. As if we were still capable of such a thing! Haha.

Tess and I thought we should show our mothers the town. It was our families, after all, who had taught us how to party and have a good time. We began with happy hour at Spikes because they served tasty potato-skin appetizers. I knew my mother loved those, and this way we'd have some food in our stomachs if we were to keep up with these two ladies. As the night went on, we had hoped to bring them to Bull's to meet a few of our friends, but it got late, and to our surprise they were tired from the drive down earlier in the day and preferred to go back to our place and relax. They told us to go on; they would head back to our place as it was only a few blocks away. As we watched them stumble off, we hoped they knew where they were going. Tess and I headed over to Bull's to let them know they wouldn't be meeting our legendary mothers this time and ordered our usual. A few hours later, Tess and I were approaching our front walk when we noticed the front window wide open with the curtains blowing out and all the lights off.

"Oh no, our mothers! What happened?"

"Hurry up, open the door!"

We fumbled with the key, Tess and I both falling into the living room as the door swung open. There we discovered the two of them sound asleep on the sofas. Our mothers had arrived back to our place only to find themselves locked out! Managing to pry the double-hung window open, they then crawled in and over the sofa and forgot to shut the window.

Tess and I looked at each other and simultaneously stated, "We cannot let them go anywhere by themselves." We all got a good laugh out of it.

What a quarter! I was living with my oldest and dearest friend in our quaint little home, and we were having the time of our lives. I also had my best project critique to date and went out with James Dean (as I referred to him). Well, James Dean turned out to be as dumb as a post, so that didn't last long, but my design mojo was in full swing and I finished the quarter strong.

I was really looking forward to going home for vacation and to get re-energized. Being home for the holidays and my birthday with my family and all our wonderful traditions would give me a sense of love and belonging. I always had a home base, a place of security, full of people I knew I could count on. It was touching that my old roommate Trina and my good friend Eric drove all the way up to join me for my birthday on New Year's Eve, where we would typically head into San Francisco, dance till midnight, and toast to the new year and all the new adventures we were going to have.... I was feeling like I could conquer the world and was excited and energized for winter quarter.

My new design professor, Joe Burton, had a reputation for being very avant-garde in the design world. He was new to Cal Poly; I hadn't even met him yet. The buzz among the students was that he would push us beyond our limits. It was an added bonus that I would be in the same design studio with Eric again.

The studio was located on the second floor of Engineering West, where rows of windows overlooked the promenade and Dexter Lawn. I was able to grab a desk next to a window, and now I could see why this was such a great people-watching place and how visible I must be when riding my bike through the area.

My design studio was going to require a considerable amount of my time this quarter. Joe expected a lot from us. Luckily we had a great group, especially since we would all be working long hours into most nights on our projects. We became like a second family.

This was difficult for Tess. I was not home much anymore, except to sleep and eat my late-night quesadilla. It became increasingly challenging for Tess after one sad day when Shasta, Tess's beloved coyote dog, once again escaped. She was driving home down Pismo Street and witnessed him being hit by a car ahead of her and killed. Tess was devastated.

I felt really bad for her, but I was still incredibly consumed with my design projects and had everything set up at my studio at school. I wasn't able to be there as much as I should have been. As winter quarter continued, I spent most of my time at my design studio working on projects. It was my most challenging quarter thus far. But it was no excuse for me to abandon my friend in her time of need. Needless to say, Tess met someone else who she became very serious about in a short time.

Since architecture students spent a lot of time in their studios, we got to know each other and learned who was in which studio. If you had time during a break, you might wander into one of the other studios to see what their projects looked like or possibly get some inspiration if you needed it. Although I rarely left my studio except to get a cup of coffee or a Diet Coke across the lawn in Dexter Hall, I did tend to have a lot of visitors. There was one in particular who began stopping by rather frequently. He claimed he was visiting another friend in my class, but he always seemed to get stuck at my workstation.

This started becoming more of an interruption to my concentration. He would ask me what I was doing, which seemed pretty obvious, and normally such a thing wouldn't bother me, but this guy was from a second-quarter calculus class I had taken the previous year. Back then, I had asked him if he wanted to study calculus together, and he took this to mean more than I wanted. Now he was pestering me, and I was not interested. Eventually, after about a half dozen visits, he got to the point and asked me out to get a bite to eat with him. I told him I was too busy. I still thought of him as just a jerk from the calculus class we'd had together last year.

However, he didn't give up easily. He claimed he had met me a few years back while stopping by my dorm with a friend who was interested in my roommate Trina. I did not recall this. I did tell him that I remembered him from the ever-so-difficult second-quarter calculus class the previous year.

Like several other architecture students, I had really struggled in our last calculus class. Knowing we had to pass the class to move on, we would visit the professor during office hours for help, and frequently requested he use alternative explanations for us architecture students. Desperate to pass, I had vigilantly studied with anyone who knew what they were doing, anyone who might help me through that nightmare of a class. So one day as I approached the classroom with dread, I noticed this fellow, sitting in the corridor waiting for class to start. I asked him how he was doing in the class and he shrugged nonchalantly and said, "Fine."

Oh good, I thought. Finally someone who really knows what they are doing here.

"I'm really struggling, do you think we could study sometime?"

To which he replied abruptly, "I have a girlfriend."

What? "I am not asking you out on a date. I just would like to study, if you actually know what you're doing," I retorted.

"Well," he came back. "You know what that usually means…"

I thought, What an asshole. Then I realized that he was also an architecture student. I had never seen him or had any classes with him previously, and it turned out that he was actually struggling more with calculus than I was.

Fast forward one year, and this same guy is now coming around wanting to go out with me, and he proceeds to tell me that he's been watching me from the windows as I ride my bike past carrying my gear and making it all look easy. That part was nice to hear; it was easy for me. A lot of people view someone with one arm as handicapped and make the assumption that things must be difficult for that person — because they themselves cannot see how they would be able to perform the task without struggling.

In reality, we all adapt to our own personal struggles in the given environment that we live in. Just as we develop a daily routine, the adaptations become second nature to us. Each of us has our own inner learning process, and with this we attempt to set ourselves up to succeed. Not to say that we don't stumble and fall occasionally. I strongly believe that falling down is an important part of the process, and from our mistakes we learn how to improve.

This guy was probably attempting to flatter me, but I thought it was kind of strange that he was telling me how he'd been watching me. There was no way I was going to go out with him. The next time I saw him, I was preparing to enter Engineering West on my way to my design studio. I had just been up at El Corral Bookstore, so as usual I was carrying loads of supplies to make my newest model. I saw his reflection in the glass door as he approached. He was attempting to rush forward and rescue me from having to navigate the door carrying all my supplies with one arm. I quickly maneuvered myself in front of him so I could open the door, and I held it open for him to pass through first. He was completely disarmed. He told me later it was that moment when he knew I was the one.

He became even more persistent about stopping by my design studio. Day after day, he came by asking me if I would like to do something together sometime? Anytime I wanted, he added. I think he held onto the hope that I had tried to hit on him back when I asked him to study for that calculus class. Finally, he wore me down with his relentless pursuit, and I said that after finals I would go out and have a drink with him before I went home for spring break.

On the last day of finals, he came by my workstation again. I was packing up my things to move out of my studio space.

"Are you staying around for spring break?" he asked.

"No, I'm going home tomorrow," I replied.

"You promised at the end of the quarter you would go out with me," he said.

He insisted we go to the Rose and Crown pub and have a beer and a game of darts.

"Okay, but first I'm going to go home to get my car packed up so I'm ready to leave in the morning. I'll call you later and we can meet," I replied.

I had been stringing this guy on for so long, I really had figured he would have forgotten about me and moved on. Boy, was I wrong.

The next morning, after our date, I left for home. It was Easter weekend, and my whole family was gathered at our house for Easter Sunday. Seated around the table, everyone wanted to know how school was going, and if I had met anyone interesting.

"Well... I've got a good one for you," I replied.

I proceeded to tell the whole table about my date, and how this guy had been coming around all quarter asking me out. I finally agreed to go out with him, I said, just for a drink to celebrate that finals were over. We went to the Rose and Crown in downtown SLO for a pint of beer, and I emphasized how I thought his family was tied to the mafia!

Roars of laughter erupted at the table. I described my date as a guy with big brown puppy-dog eyes. He told me that his family was from Sicily, and they were related to the mafia, and he mentioned several people who had disappeared and others who'd received death threats. Then he proceeded to tell me that I was not to repeat any of the things he was telling me, not to anyone.

The story was just too good not to share. The rest of the meal's conversation circled hilariously around jokes about me and my mafioso boyfriend and our future together.

When my family was assembled, we always had a good time, even if I tended to be the center of the joke. I didn't mind. It was great to be home again. My friend Staci had recently returned from travels in Europe, and she said that if not for hearing of my adventures and my encouragement to go off and travel, she wouldn't have gone. She went on to tell me that she almost came home with an Italian boyfriend. All I could say was,

"Make sure he's not in the mafia!"

Staci was considering attending Cal Poly, and I was thrilled. She had applied without even telling me. She wanted it to be a surprise and was awaiting her acceptance. Staci would start summer quarter if accepted and was hoping we could live together. The timing couldn't have been better, as Tess was getting married and would be moving away.

Chapter 24

~ One Good Margarita ~

I returned to San Luis Obispo for spring quarter. I was so excited about Staci coming to Cal Poly. I also planned to stay on in SLO that summer to make up several structures classes that I had fallen behind in. I wanted to make sure Staci and I would have a nice place to live, so I began scoping out the housing situation immediately. A little duplex became available on Johnson Avenue. It was closer to campus than where I was living on Pismo Street with Tess. It would be the perfect spot for Staci and me.

The only problem was that the place was available now, and I didn't want to miss out on getting it. I called Staci to let her know that if we wanted to secure this place for the summer, we needed to act quickly. Thanks to her grandmother's help, Staci was able to provide her part of the security deposit for us to get the place. I went ahead and began slowly moving my stuff over to Johnson Avenue before Staci moved down.

Since classes were underway, I was already busy with new projects. It was slow going for me trying to move my belongings to Johnson.

Eric helped me at first, but then he had too much to do with his projects, and everyone else I knew was busy with their projects as well.

Chad, my mafioso date from last quarter, was quick to figure out which design studio I was in now, and he continued to stop by, hoping we could go out again. I told him that I had a lot going on with school and I was also in the process of moving. As I previously mentioned, he was persistent. I couldn't help but admire his tenacity.

Once he heard I was moving, he began offering his help. I started to think, here is a big strong guy with a vehicle, wanting to help me — am I crazy? This move would go a lot faster if I had some assistance. So, I finally agreed. Not only did Chad help me with the heavy lifting, but he also set up my stereo and TV and took care of numerous other handyman jobs for me. This was not so bad, I thought. I could get used to having this guy around.

Chad always seemed to time his visits around the dinner hour; this way it worked out conveniently for us to get a bite to eat. We slowly got to know each other and, as things progressed, did more things together. He liked taking a Sunday drive out to the coast, which was something my family had done on many occasions when my father was alive. We made this a regular event if we didn't have much schoolwork.

Chad was several years older than me and was putting himself through college. He was the eldest of five siblings raised in a military family. His family never lived in one place for more than four years at a time when he was growing up. Most of his father's tours were in Europe and Asia. He enjoyed talking about his travels and the adventures he'd had as a child. He especially loved racing small Japanese cars off-road with his group of friends.

Chad had a very serious side to his personality. He claimed this was because he was the oldest. Next in line were his three brothers, and then, with a twelve-year gap, a baby sister. He'd had to take care of himself from a young age, he told me, and began working at fourteen. He explained to me that his family was not supportive and did not help him financially. Everything he wanted or needed, he had to earn himself, including food, cars, insurance, and college. Chad loved cars, driving and racing them off-road. To afford this, he learned how to repair them. His parents had actually told him that since he was so mechanically inclined and really liked cars, he should just become a mechanic and not go to college. Chad wanted more for himself.

He seemed very interested in me, and curiously enough always seemed to show up wherever I was. I couldn't figure out how he always knew where I would be, but I was busy and didn't put much thought into it. He was very supportive, although he did have a bit of a problem with my open-minded, confident nature, and he disapproved of what he considered exhibitionist behavior. As we grew more attached, he became fiercely jealous and protective of me. I first noticed this when he started to shut the window shade in my bathroom every time he came over. The bathroom in my new place was upstairs and faced the main street but wasn't really visible because the house was located slightly up a hill. The window was only 12" wide, full height, and made up of slatted, louvered glass panes. The way the panes tilted, they really did obscure the view. Still, they bothered Chad, and every time he came by, the first thing he would do was go upstairs and close the shades in the bathroom.

One of our favorite things to do was enjoy long talks while sitting on the small, narrow staircase in my apartment. We would talk into the wee hours of the morning getting to know each other better. He

reminded me of a lost puppy with his big, sad, dark eyes. I thought he
was cute, and he reminded me a bit of my hero from the movie Rocky.
For the first several months we were the best of friends, just talking
night after night for hours at a time and hanging out.

I felt there was an attraction between us, but Chad never tried to
make any advances.   The only thing he would do was give me a
goodnight kiss. That was it, and then he would leave. I found this to
be kind of refreshing but, at the same time, concerning. I was not sure
why he was holding back.

Eventually, my mother became curious about who this guy was,
and she planned a trip down so she could meet him. My family still
referred to him as the mafioso guy that I had told them about at Easter.
They were quite surprised that I was actually still seeing him because I
had not represented him in the best light.

My mother and I were sitting in my living room having a glass of
wine when the doorbell rang. My mother jumped up and opened the
door to find Chad standing there sweetly holding a small bouquet of
flowers and wearing a pale lavender, polyester suit. My mother — the
fashion police — and I looked at Chad, then at each other, and back at
him again. Where did that suit come from? It looked like a leftover
from a 1970s prom. My mother and I couldn't help from bursting into
laughter.

"Where on earth did you get that suit?" I asked.

He explained that he'd had it custom-made for himself in the
Philippines for his prom, and it had a ruffled shirt to go with it (this,
fortunately, he opted not to wear). He said that when his family was
stationed in Asia, the suit was the only nice clothing he ever owned,

and he had kept it for special occasions. He felt this was a special occasion and was hoping to make a good impression on my mother. Well, he succeeded in making an impression, that was for sure. My mother confided in me later that evening that when she first met my father, he was also going around in polyester suits. It wasn't the end of the world, she said.

My mother was surprisingly accepting of Chad even after the polyester suit incident. I, however, was still on the fence. Like most of my previous boyfriends, Chad was rapidly becoming too committed. I would tell him, as I had told others, that I didn't have time for a serious relationship. I needed to stay focused on school and my goals. To my surprise, Chad's response was to tell me that I was just afraid of commitment.

"First of all," I replied. "I am not afraid of commitment. I just don't want it yet. That's why I am telling you this now."

He proceeded to tell me I was full of shit! He said, "Everyone wants a commitment, and I am not going away."

We would have this conversation every time I had a deadline, needed to get projects done, and needed my space. Chad was persistent and was not about to get lost, no matter how many times I told him to. I felt that this meant he was different from other guys I had dated, because he didn't run away. Maybe he was someone I would be able to count on.

One thing that I didn't see coming was from my classmate, and good friend Eric, who called Chad "Chad-o." We had Architectural History together all through second year and now third year, and we always sat beside each other, twice a week in the back row of the large lecture hall. Eric would lean over and write funny comments in my notebook — if he wasn't sleeping through the lecture, that is. Then, one afternoon in class, he leaned over to scribble, "WTF Chad-o" in my notebook! I gave him a puzzled look, because I didn't understand.

What did he care? It never seemed to make a difference to him who I went out with in the past, or at least I never thought it bothered him. I was totally baffled by this comment. I waited till after class was over and we were walking outside, then I immediately questioned him.

"What's your problem with Chad?" I inquired.

"My problem is," he retorted, "you never gave me a chance! You always have one guy or another after you and you never stopped to think about me?"

"What about you? You're one of my best friends," I replied. "Besides that, you told me you are gay!"

Eric just sighed, and said he still would have liked a chance. From that point, my friendship with him began to languish, which saddened me — we had always been such good friends. I sensed our friendship was threatening to Chad because we were so close, and I worried that Chad had a problem with him being gay. Chad was not very friendly toward Eric, and that no doubt added to the distance.

Chad knew how to make it up to me and put a smile back on my face. When I walked into my studio, I began finding intricate handmade notes with embossed images left at my workstation — little reminders of how he felt about me. It was sweet, and the notes seemed to be increasing as the end of the quarter approached. This was probably because he was worried about our pending separation. He had accepted a summer job in Alaska prior to us dating and would be leaving soon. He was concerned because he knew I was a free spirit and was going to be having a wonderful summer in SLO together with one of my best friends, Staci.

Chad's parents were stationed on a small island off the coast of Alaska. His parents were allowing him to move home for the season, as he had secured himself a well-paying summer job. This way he could make his next year's tuition, room and board. He could not afford to pass up the opportunity.

I wasn't sure how this whole long-distance relationship was going to play out, so I tried not to think much about it. I was really excited that Staci was on her way to join me in our quirky little place on Johnson, and I kept my focus on that. The duplex had been converted from a 1930s house and sat perpendicular to the road. When you pulled into the driveway, there was an entrance into both units through a small alcove in the center of the old house. We lived in the unit on the right, which included the second story of the old house. The lower level of our unit consisted of a living room, dining room, and very small kitchen. A dark wood, narrow staircase off the living room led up to a second floor, which had been converted from the old attic and transformed into two bedrooms. A tiny bathroom with a claw-foot tub was directly at the top of the stairs.

The bathroom is the one I have previously mentioned, with the full-height louvered glass window. This window was great for letting in the summer breeze. And that summer, it was like an oven up on the second floor. The old attic ceiling sloped with the steeply pitched roof, and you had to be careful to stand where you wouldn't bump your head. Staci and I had our rooms set up to work around the sloped ceiling, and we ran fans to keep the air circulating.

It was summer session prior to my fourth year, and it was going to be tough. I had a full load, which was not unusual, but my schedule was typically a mix of design classes, core curriculum classes, and maybe an elective or two. This summer, I needed to retake a third-quarter structures class from second year. I had not done well in the class the first two times I took it. Yes, to be honest, I had failed it twice. It was always during spring quarter when I had a full load, and my design classes had taken priority. The first time I failed probably also had something to do with a certain Australian who was in town. However, since I had not passed my third-quarter, second-year structures class, I had not been allowed to take any of my third-year structure classes during my third year.

Now I was once again sitting in Associate Dean Zweifel's office being told that to continue on to my fourth-year design classes, I was required to take my second-year structures class simultaneously with all three third-year structures classes. If I did not pass all four structures classes during summer session, including the concrete lab, then I would not be allowed to continue to fourth-year design in the fall. Associate Dean Zweifel concluded by reminding me that he had met with me at the end of freshman year when I was on academic probation, and that if he were to see me in his office a third time, it would be the last. So, the pressure was on, and this was not going to be easy. It was summertime, though, and if you have learned anything about me by now, it would not be all work and no play.

Although I was determined to vanquish the evil structures classes, I knew it would be difficult because I like to maintain a healthy balance of fun and work. Now living with another one of my best friends, and living so close to the beach, you can only imagine where this was going. Chad was working in Alaska, leaving Staci and me free to enjoy the summer and good times.

Every day started with a good cup of coffee, the local radio station, and Steve Winwood's latest release, "Higher Love." As soon as we heard that song blasting from the radio, Staci and I dropped everything and danced wildly around our apartment. *"Bring me a higher love..."* The song became our anthem of summer.

After our classes were done for the day, we would usually head down to Avila Beach to soak in some rays and pretend to study. Later, since we were both over 21, we would hit the town. We both enjoyed Mexican food and a good margarita.

Staci and I often visited Los Hermanos, a favorite local spot. One day, we walked in, called to the bartender for a couple of margaritas, and took our usual place by the window. When the server approached our table to deliver the margaritas, chips, and salsa, he was not our regular waiter; he was this absolutely gorgeous human being who we had never seen before. Staci and I could not take our eyes off him as he placed our drinks down. Then we looked at each other with our eyes wide open. He asked if he could take our order, but we were both speechless and staring.

Embarrassingly enough, he realized this and said, "I'll give you two a few more minutes to decide," before he walked off.

We just looked at each other, still in complete awe, and exclaimed simultaneously,

"Wow! Is that the most beautiful guy you've ever seen?" and began laughing at ourselves, at how ridiculous we were acting.

Really, he was just another guy, but we couldn't stop talking about his good looks as we sipped our margaritas and ate our chips and salsa. When he returned to take our order, Staci was so flustered, looking up at this handsome fellow with goo-goo eyes, she didn't even realize her elbow was in the salsa bowl! The gorgeous waiter was trying hard not to laugh as he asked us if we needed more time. I couldn't hold it in any longer and busted up laughing as Staci very nonchalantly removed her elbow from the salsa and began wiping the red mess off her arm. My laughter in turn made the waiter laugh, and eventually Staci joined in, too.

A few nights later, I was not sure if I could take Staci anywhere after her salsa incident, but I wanted to go back for another margarita. Staci wasn't ready to show her face there again, so we headed down to Bull's for our usual gin and tonic, hoping to unwind after our midterms. We settled into a booth in the back corner and hopped up to sit on the top of the seat with some friends. About an hour later, we noticed our handsome waiter from Los Hermanos strolling in. Staci immediately slid down, attempting to keep from being spotted by Mr. Gorgeous. Too late, he had noticed us and was walking toward our booth. He looked right at us and asked if he could get us a drink, possibly a margarita and some more salsa? It broke the ice, and we began laughing hysterically.

"That would be great," I replied, still giggling.

Staci couldn't really speak and her face was as red as the salsa she had put her elbow in.

Drinks in hand, he jumped up to sit next to me on the back of the booth. Brent was his name, and he was not only extremely good-looking but a super nice guy. We hit it off immediately and chatted till the bartender flickered the lights for last call. Brent offered to walk us home, but we declined, to avoid any further temptation. I walked out ahead of Staci and stood waiting for her, leaning up against a tree in the sidewalk, when Brent came out, and Staci heard him ask me for my phone number as he leaned in, just about to kiss…. Staci promptly broke it up, saying I had a serious boyfriend who was working in Alaska for the summer.

I was so pissed off at Staci, although she was probably right. Chad and I had been seeing each other for only three months, however, and before he left, we never made any sort of agreement about not seeing other people. This made me wonder if I was committed to him, even though it was he who had left for the summer. Although he didn't know what was going on back home, he would no doubt be happy that I had a roommate like Staci to remind me about him when faced with the ultimate temptation.

Chad wrote to me on a daily basis from Alaska, but I guess the military didn't pick up mail every day because some days, I would not receive any cards or letters from him, and on others I would get three or four at a time. I would write back once or twice a week. He also called me every few days to see how I was doing, and how I was surviving taking all of these structures classes at one time. I did not want to keep secrets, so I told him about Brent asking me out after meeting him with Staci and the now famous salsa incidence.

Although he was happy to hear that I didn't give Brent my number, he was quite disturbed at the thought of men asking me out. His response was to begin calling me every night, and the frequency of the cards increased. He told me that whenever he heard Belinda Carlisle's new release "Mad About You" on the local radio, he knew it was our song because that was how he felt about me. I thought that was really sweet; no one had ever said we had a song before, although it occurred to me that possibly a song was something chosen between two people during a special moment.

My friend Eric was also in town taking summer classes, and he was ecstatic to learn that "Chad-o," as he called Chad, was gone for the summer. He wanted to get together before he and a handful of other architecture students left for an exchange program at Virginia Polytechnic for their fourth year. One night, after Eric and I had been out to dinner, he started up.

"Why didn't you ever give me a chance?" He pointed out how good we could be together and how much he admired me.

Then out of the blue he blurted,

"Why don't the two of us just get married? You can just dump Chad-o."

"Because you are gay!"

To which he replied, "You could help me change."

"Life doesn't work that way," I explained to him.

"You have to live your own life and stop trying to be somebody you are not."

Meanwhile, Chad was working construction in Alaska. He had earned enough money to invite me to fly up and visit him and to meet his parents. I had never been to Alaska and was rather curious about what I would encounter, and by this point in the summer I was missing Chad, so I decided to go. I really needed to get away after toiling through four structures classes and a concrete lab. Fortunately, I had learned how to study and be efficient at it, so not only did I pass all four classes, I actually received A's in all of them. It felt awesome to have that behind me. I returned home for a quick visit with my little brother and mother before flying off to Alaska. My sense of adventure outweighed my nervousness about meeting his parents. I felt that meeting his parents was a major step in our relationship. I hoped that they would like me.

Once I arrived in Anchorage, I needed to transfer to what Chad said was called a puddle jumper. It was a small plane that held about eight passengers, four on each side of the aisle, plus a jump seat for the crew. But it was only me and three other passengers for this flight out to the island. We all had window seats. The flight was a bit bumpy, but the view was spectacular over the other volcanic islands.

Chad was eagerly awaiting my arrival on the tarmac while his mother waited inside the small terminal. Although it was August, Alaska was cold, and as we walked over to meet his mother I was glad I had brought my down jacket. She greeted me with open arms and made me feel welcome.

Driving to their house, Chad suddenly stopped the car.

"Look!"

He pointed in the direction of a large outcropping of rock. I turned to look and saw a rock face with words spray-painted seven feet high:

W E L C O M E

TO ADAK . . .

S I L V I A

I MISSED YOU

<u>REAL</u> BAD !

I couldn't believe it! Wow, I was speechless. His mother filled in the awkward silence by explaining how Chad had worked hard painting the rock. He'd had to wait till the last moment before my arrival in hopes that someone else would not paint over it, as this was the welcome rock used by all of the military families stationed on the island when loved ones came to visit. This was his explanation as to why he had spelled my name wrong. He said he had used part of the previous writing to adapt the message for me. In spite of his spelling my name wrong, I was touched by the gesture.

The island was spartan, with few buildings. The homes were primarily modest single-story cinder block structures, built to withstand the harsh climate and strong winds.

We arrived at Chad's parents' place to be greeted by a frightening, hissing Persian cat they called Big Boy. Chad told me to just ignore the cat, who was very disagreeable, but his parents loved it. They had always had cats growing up, but the felines usually came with the military housing. Then the cats would be left behind for the next tenants when his father was transferred. Big Boy was the first cat they actually chose to adopt.

I followed Chad closely as he carried my suitcase in. This hissing cat frightened me.

"You'll be staying in this room while you're here," he said, pointing out that his room was the one on the left at the end of the hall.

As I walked down to check out his room, there was a closed door on the right, which I opened thinking it was the bathroom.

"Get out of there," Chad said abruptly. "That is my parents' room; we are not allowed in their room."

"What? You're not allowed in your parents' room?" I exclaimed.

"No, never as kids, and we are still not allowed to go in," he responded.

"Come on and get out of there before they find out."

When his father arrived home that evening from work, he had a very reserved manner about him. The next morning, he loosened up and generously offered to show us the sights. He showed us most of the island except where he worked. The landscape was quite barren —

primarily rolling hills of frozen tundra — apart from a small grouping of trees called the petrified forest.

Having quickly exhausted the sightseeing on the island, Chad and I flew on another puddle jumper to Anchorage to get some alone time. Anchorage was beautiful. We toured an amazing glacier park and watched as the sun loosened large chunks of blue ice causing them to fall crashing into the waters below. We took advantage of the long evenings to enjoy romantic dinners and strolled through the rustic frontier of Anchorage, which was really quite charming, before I headed back to California for Tess's wedding!

I would be, of course, her maid of honor. Tess was absolutely radiant in her wedding gown. The ceremony was held at an old stone church with the reception at her mother's beautiful Victorian home in San Rafael. It was quite an affair. Then Tess transferred schools, as the newlyweds were moving to Southern California for her husband's new job, and I was sad to see her go. It was really hard having her move away after we had been reconnected only a few years. Our time in San Luis Obispo together was time well spent. I knew from that point on, though, nothing would ever change the bonds of our friendship. It was stronger than ever, and still grows stronger to this day.

Chapter 25

~ Let's Go to Holland ~

Once back in San Luis Obispo, Chad and I picked up right where we had left off. We were able to get into the same design studio, which was great and saved Chad a lot of time from walking back and forth to see me... haha.

I am sad to say that the fourth-year design class was off to a horrible start. The main reason? Our new design professor, a visiting professor from Virginia Polytechnic, was a terrible chauvinist, and when I looked at him, he reminded me of a turtle. I just kept waiting or rather hoping for him to tuck his head into his shell and go back to Virginia. He was the worst design instructor I'd had thus far at Cal Poly. It was incredibly disappointing. Every time this man spoke with his heavy Southern accent, it reminded me of my friends and fellow classmates who had gone to Virginia Polytechnic on their exchange program. I missed them, especially Eric, and hoped the design professors they had were better than this guy.

The only good thing was being in the same design studio as Chad. This allowed us to have similar schedules. Which was nice, since we were spending most of our time together. Chad lived in a house with a few other fellows near the Madonna Inn. Every day I would drive over to his place and make our daily top ramen soup with a poached egg sprinkled with cheddar cheese for lunch while watching a portion of a movie. I guess I found comfort in our routine.

The following two quarters Chad and I had separate design studios. Winter quarter, I once again had another rather chauvinistic male professor. It was all about model making, and size. Cal Poly did have several women professors but, for some reason, I never seemed to be in their studios. Since I unfortunately did not have the same ideology as my current design professor, I referred back to my old sketchbooks and notes from my second-year design classes with Bilgi.

This always gave me inspiration. One day while going through my old sketchbooks — I always bought the ones with the black hardcover and soft, slightly off-white blank pages for both note-taking and freehand sketching — looking for inspiration, I noticed something written on one of the last pages that I thought I had left blank. It was a little handwritten note, in the upper left corner of the right page, that I had never noticed. It was from Glenn. It said,

It had been two years since Glenn was in town. I guess I hadn't used those last few pages in that sketchbook so I never saw the note he left me.

Knowing him, he probably figured I would have used up the book by the end of that term and his note would put a smile on my face, as it always did when I saw him. It still worked, two years later. It immediately sent me back to that wonderful time we had together — the chemistry and the connection between the two of us. I sat there, leaning back in my chair with a smile on my face and a twinkle in my eye, and imagined seeing Glenn. It made me wonder what he was up to and contemplate that maybe one day I would go to Australia and try to find him.

Daydreams of going to Australia were truly wonderful, but the reality was I still had another year to complete my degree, and I was planning on going abroad to Denmark for my last year. Cal Poly's architecture program is a five-year curriculum. Chad knew I wanted to attend the University of Copenhagen, but he really wanted to go to Holland to the University of Delft for his fifth year.

At first, I thought it was great that we would both be in Europe. Chad had lived in Holland as a young child when his father was stationed overseas. He really wanted me to go to Holland with him. He had done the research and explained that he had an old friend of his family that we could both stay with until we found our own housing.

One requirement to attend the University of Delft was proficiency in Dutch. We would need to go to Holland for the summer prior to school starting to study the Dutch language. It wasn't that different from Danish, except for the accent, and I had also studied German for a year. So I figured I could probably handle learning Dutch, too. I was always up for a new challenge and adventure. I finally conceded.

"OK, I'll go! Let's do this!"

Chad had researched the process to study in Holland. But he had not actually done the paperwork for acceptance into the program at the University of Delft, and he had not made sure that Cal Poly would accept classes from a foreign school that was not on their exchange program list. To make this happen, I realized, we would need to overcome a lot of obstacles. I got started immediately. The first task was to write to the University of Delft, asking for acceptance into their architecture program. We also needed permission from a fifth-year design professor at Cal Poly. The professor would need to accept the credits we earned from the classes taken at the University of Delft as a direct exchange for our required units at Cal Poly.

I went to speak with Professor Batterson, for whom I had taught the Danish language class to his exchange students. He was disappointed that I wouldn't be attending the University of Copenhagen, but he understood. Professor Batterson filled me in on all the necessary requirements we would need to fulfill in order to still graduate with credit for our fifth year from Cal Poly's program. We also applied to renew our passports and student visas for the two of us to stay and live in Holland.

Once all our documents seemed to be in order with both universities, we bought our airline tickets. We arranged for a few days' layover in New York. I had never been to New York, and Chad had family living nearby who we could stay with. His family was wonderful; they showed us all the sights, including a trip to the top of the Twin Towers and the Chrysler Building, which architecturally speaking makes a lot bigger statement than the Empire State Building. We also visited the Statue of Liberty and Central Park.

After our whirlwind tour of New York City, we were off to the Netherlands. It was a stressful trip mostly because I did not know what to expect upon arrival. Chad had made arrangements with our host family to pick us up, and had told them that we would be landing at 6:00 pm. After we boarded our flight, we realized that Chad had misread the itinerary, and we would be arriving at six in the morning. Since we were in flight, we had no way to contact the family, and we felt it would be too early to call them once we landed. So, we dragged our 80-pound suitcases onto the train, which traveled through the beautiful countryside but took hours to reach our destination. I was so tired.

The confusion continued after we arrived in the small town of our host family. It was really rather awkward, as I don't believe the family understood the complexity of our situation. In spite of the inconvenience of having house guests, our host was very friendly and accommodating.

Little did I realize that Woerden was about two hours away from the University of Delft where we would be attending school, so our first priority became searching for housing closer to campus. Each morning we set off on a pair of traditional Dutch bicycles they so kindly loaned us for the twenty-minute bike ride to the local train station. Then we boarded the train for the hour-plus ride to the town of Delft. From there we continued our search for housing on foot, walking the remaining half-hour to campus. We would check the campus housing board and the local newspaper in search of a place to live. If we were lucky, there might be a listing. Usually we came up empty-handed but still needed to take the train back to our bikes and ride home to our temporary housing again.   It made for long days, and school was starting in a week.

The family thought we were only staying a few days or maybe a week till our summer classes started, so as time wore on we were imposing on them further which did not feel right. I was getting more anxious by the day as the start of our language class drew closer (the class was required to attend the university). Finally we were forced to start class, making the long commute from their home daily. The class took up most of our day, so it limited how much time we had to search for housing. This continued for weeks, and the longer we stayed with the family the more challenging things became.

Our host mother was a very kind, sweet lady.   She had four children, three of them living at home — a boy and two young girls. I adored them and spent a lot of time playing with them. The challenge was the father. He was an alcoholic who came home every night and drank until he started yelling and fighting with the mother; then he would go into the bathroom and puke his brains out loudly, into the wee hours of the morning. I don't know how he managed to get up and go to work, but he was typically gone by the time we got up and were sipping our morning coffee.

This scenario played out over and over again each night, and it was horrible. I felt so bad for the wife and her three wonderful children. The mother seemed embarrassed and ashamed, which increased the tension.   I could not comprehend how she could put up with this behavior night after night with three young children in the house, but she would make excuses for him. She also had an older daughter who didn't live with them and never came around, which made her very sad.

I initially thought the older daughter did not come around because of the alcoholic husband, but as time went on, I learned that the older daughter was the one who Chad had been going out with when we first met during our calculus class. The mother finally admitted to me that her daughter was not coming around because she did not want to see Chad, which added yet more tension in the house.

Even though living with this family was less than ideal, we still managed to have good times with the kids and fun adventures in our travels around the Netherlands. We made the most of our free time by visiting the many famous museums, Anne Frank's house, and my favorite — the Rietveld Schroder House by Dutch architect Gerrit Rietveld in Utrecht. One day, walking down the main pedestrian street in Amsterdam, we passed by the Hotel California, which brought back old memories of my time spent there after high school. What a glorious, carefree time that was, just Chris and me on our big adventure alone in Europe.

Spending time in Holland was wonderful. I loved riding my bike through the beautiful countryside and quaint villages, over the many drawbridges and dikes, along the countless canals... The unique vernacular architecture that had developed throughout the country was charming. And every day along our bike route to the nearby train station, we passed the most adorable pair of black pygmy goats, which we befriended. Since then, I have always wanted a pair of pygmy goats.

The two-hour trek each way to Delft was leaving me exhausted. Chad had not made preparations for our move to Holland, as he had led me to believe. I was getting frustrated, so I set up a meeting with the administration office at the University of Delft to help us get a better handle on our enrollment process and housing search.

The meeting was encouraging, as they explained that if we passed our proficiency test in the Dutch language, we would be able to start classes in September and all our credits would be transferable back to Cal Poly. Half the problem was solved. The remaining problem was still to find housing. The school was no help with this, and they explained that they did not have an exchange program. We were on our own just the same as any other students enrolled at the university. They continued to explain the difficulties of finding housing in the Netherlands in general, even for their own citizens, especially in college towns.

All I knew was that I was not going to continue to commute two hours each way to get to school and keep imposing on our host family. The summer session was winding down, and we needed to get settled in before the full term began in the fall. If housing was such a challenge, I realized, our time in Europe might be a lot shorter than anticipated. To escape the stress in Holland, we took a trip to Denmark to visit my family.

We took the train to Copenhagen, and my cousin Merethe was waiting to greet us at the station when we arrived. We stayed a few days with her, as she was centrally located in her quaint little apartment out on the Amager, where I had stayed with her after my first year at Cal Poly. Then we headed over to stay with my other cousin Laurids and his new girlfriend Ninni. They took us to an ancient Viking Village, and on a canoe trip across the lake. Then there was my favorite — a tour of the Carlsberg factory with the beautiful, life-size elephant statues flanking both sides of the gateway to the factory, along with the impressive statue of the Norse god Thor on the roof.

I was hoping to see the Panduro boys, but they were still up on Morsø enjoying their summer. We did stop by the University of

Copenhagen and were able to catch up with a few of my students from the Danish language class I had taught at Cal Poly. I loved seeing how well they were doing. We also met with an old family friend of my father's, Flemming Jacobs, who was the head of Mærsk, a huge shipping company. He took us to the Crystal Palace restaurant in Tivoli Garden for the most delicious — and fanciest! — smørrebrød I had ever eaten. In the numerous courses, we enjoyed herring, shrimp, beef tenderloin, and smørrebrød topped with all the special garnishes, along with the traditional Danish snaps (akvavit), and øl (beer). This was the most memorable smørrebrød ever. Thank you, Flemming!

Unfortunately, time and funds didn't allow for a trip to visit my family on Morsø. Instead, we decided to take the "scenic route" through East Germany on our way back to Holland. We boarded the train at Copenhagen's main station, toward West Berlin. It wasn't long before the train boarded an East German ferry to cross the Baltic Sea, as this was the only way in 1987. The Cold War was still underway, and the Berlin Wall separated West Berlin from the Eastern Bloc area of Germany known as the DDR (Deutsche Demokratische Republik). Once we docked in East Germany, we were required to show a special visa and a day pass before continuing on to West Berlin. Believe me, this ferry was no luxury liner like the well-equipped ferries I had taken elsewhere in Europe.

The boat docked in East German territory, and we immediately went through the intimidating passport control process. A full inspection of all the train cars commenced with armed guards checking our visas and passports, and German shepherds sniffing our bags. Some passengers had their luggage rummaged through. We looked out the train's windows at soldiers walking in high step, wearing bellowed jodhpurs and steel helmets, keeping watch from catwalks high overhead.

We were aware, the entire time we were stopped at the DDR train station, that we were surrounded by tall, barbed-wire fences. Guards armed with machine guns in the towers were on the lookout for runners. Just before the train left East Berlin, we made one final stop, similar to the last, and went through the whole security check again prior to leaving the Eastern Bloc. At last, they let us go into the West.

The moment the train passed into West Berlin, there was color! The buildings had color, and bright neon lights radiated through the night air. We could hear the sounds of a vibrant nightlife, with music and people laughing and having a good time. It was as if the city had been brought back to life. It was an incredible contrast to the dreary appearance of the rundown countryside we had just passed through on the train. We checked into a fantastic youth hostel in the heart of West Berlin and headed out in search of Wiener schnitzel with pommes frites.

To my amazement, in the center of the city there were several buildings in ruin, including what they called the "Lipstick" church. It was the lone tower of a long-destroyed church left as a monument to WWII. It resembled a woman's lipstick (hence the name). Much of West Berlin had been rebuilt after the war, but this monument remained in remembrance of the devastation and to remind the people of the West what had transpired here and how fragile life can be. To me, it was such a powerful statement to mankind; it evoked feelings of empathy for the losses that people endured and simultaneously gave me feelings of happiness to be alive now and be able to enjoy life without war.

The next morning, we headed back out to see East Berlin via "Checkpoint Charlie," but this time we were on foot. We arrived at

Checkpoint Charlie to find a small tollbooth. This tollbooth was the only portal allowing people from the West to pass through to East Berlin. Upon check-in, we were also required to exchange a set amount of Deutsche marks into East German currency. The DDR money was made of tin, and it was so light, you couldn't even feel that you were holding it when the East German guard put it into your hand.

The moment we passed through Checkpoint Charlie into East Berlin, an odd sensation came over me. Seeing the empty streets, and the dingy, dirty, gray buildings, it was obvious that nothing had been cleaned or repaired since WWII. I had a tense, eerie feeling, as if we were in an old spy film, and I kept looking over my shoulder as if someone was going to jump out of an alley and snatch me.

After we walked for what felt like hours, we finally stumbled upon an East German history museum that was open. It was only open a few hours a day, and it was the only place that was open, as we had passed by many closed businesses, including shops, markets, and restaurants. We joked about how they made us exchange our German marks for East German currency, and yet there was no place to spend the money. Even the history museum was free. The only exhibit in the museum was propaganda showcasing Berlin's 750th anniversary.

After the small museum, we were hungry and searched for a place to eat. Finding no place open, we decided to begin heading back toward the West. A few blocks before we reached Checkpoint Charlie, we came upon an open restaurant. It looked like a cafeteria, and we could see a few people inside. It was very spartan, no frills, and only a few items on the menu to choose from, but we decided to check it out. Everything was so incredibly cheap, but the food was bland, and the service not very good. When we finished, we left a nice tip since we hadn't been able to spend any of the money we were required to exchange. As we left, the server came running after us to give it back and explained that she wasn't allowed to take tips. She could get in a lot of trouble and even be fired from her job if she accepted our generosity! We took the remainder of our tin coins back to West Berlin with us and figured we would keep them as souvenirs. Once again, the moment we passed through Checkpoint Charlie back into West Berlin, the oppressive atmosphere was lifted.

The Berlin Wall was approximately 12 feet high, made out of reinforced concrete with a thickened and rounded concrete top. The wall had towers and bunkers spaced equally along the entire distance surrounding West Berlin. An open area on the east side of the wall was known as the "Death Strip" and could be seen from certain vantage points in the West. The West-facing side of the wall was covered with vibrant graffiti depicting hatred toward the Nazis and making political statements. There was one spot where you had a visual sight line of where Hitler's bunker once was.

Upon reentrance to West Berlin, it did not take long for us to follow the sounds of life to the Tiergarten (park), where the real celebration of Berlin's 750 years was taking place. The festive sounds of accordion music played, and people were dancing the polka, singing, and clinking steins of beer — just like life should be celebrated. It was glorious.

The next day, we got back on the train to the Netherlands. When we returned, our host family left on their annual summer holiday and wouldn't be back for another two weeks. We slipped back into our routine, with daily treks back and forth for our Dutch immersion course at the university, but now we also had to do all our own shopping and cooking. As our search continued for housing, the closest we could find to the school was still over an hour away.

"This is getting ridiculous,"

I stated to Chad one day as we began our two-hour trek to school. We were riding our bikes in the pouring rain on our way to the train station. We were running late and did not realize it was going to rain. So we had not brought our raincoats and by the time we reached the station you could wring us out, we were so wet. We stayed wet and cold and uncomfortable all day. I insisted we leave early from school to return home, as I was shivering. It was a miserable ride on the train for over an hour, and then there was our final leg of the journey home on our bikes. Throughout it all, it was still raining.

I couldn't take it any longer, so I told Chad,

"I am returning to California to finish my fifth year at Cal Poly."

He could stay in Holland and commute two hours each way in the cold if he liked, but I was going home!

Needless to say, he also abandoned the idea of ever finding reasonable housing and said he would return to California with me. However, before we left he wanted to take the Dutch language proficiency exam since we were so close to completing the course. He took the exam but only received a score of 69 percent whereas he needed a 70 to pass. His score would not have allowed him to study architecture at the University of Delft. So I guess it was a good thing he was coming back with me. I didn't even bother with the exam; instead, I went to the administration office to receive a refund on my tuition. I applied that money to my ticket home. The cheapest route we could find was through London. So we sailed to England and spent a few days sightseeing.

We booked a dorm room at the London School of Economics. The century-old dorms were built of red brick, with ivy growing on the exterior. An enormous group bathroom was down the hall from our oversize dorm room. The room had two single beds that were narrow and very tall; I had to climb up to get onto the bed. It was so tall that the first night I rolled over and fell out, landing on the floor with a loud thump. My fall woke Chad, and he came running over and swooped me off the floor. He was so worried I would fall out again so the next night he stacked all his pillows up against me. I slept well until I woke to the smell of a delicious breakfast. It was in the student cafeteria and consisted of thickly sliced bacon, eggs, and stewed tomatoes, along with a strongly brewed cup of English tea.

With stomachs full, we set out to tour the magnificent sites of London. We rented a car and drove out to see Windsor Castle, which was magnificent. We also stopped by the University of Oxford, which has a beautiful campus. Soon after, we flew back to California.

It was wonderful to be back home with my mother and younger brother. I couldn't say "little" brother anymore, as Steven was now 6 foot 6 inches tall. He had just graduated high school and claimed he was in love and very happy. I was glad to see him feeling so good about himself and life. My mother was extremely happy that I had returned to California to finish college and graduate. After a brief visit, I packed up my Scirocco with my clothes and school supplies and drove back to San Luis Obispo in anticipation of starting my fifth and final year.

I found myself in the position of having to quickly find a new place to live. Staci and I, unfortunately, had given up our cute little place on Johnson when I had left for Holland. That was my fault, and I totally regretted it now. So, it was back to the housing board at the student union for me. Looking on the giant board once again, I fortunately spotted a post by a girl I knew from my AXA little sister days. Her name was also Staci; she lived in the mobile home park on the outskirts of town. It was a little farther away from campus than I preferred, but I couldn't be too choosy at this point. The place was roomy and cheap, and Staci was a great gal. Okay, one problem was solved.

It was a whirlwind change in our plans, but I couldn't complain too much since Chad and I had enjoyed our summer for the most part, essentially because we were together on a big adventure. We were able to travel to Denmark to visit with my family; we toured all the corners of Holland and a bit of Germany and England.   It was a trip to remember and brought us closer together in spite of all of the frustrations we had encountered.

As a side note, regarding my life: I have always felt that things work out for a reason, and I believe that if I had gone to study in Copenhagen for my fifth year, I probably would have stayed in Denmark to live permanently. In the end, of course, I was glad to be back in California. I felt I was in the right place to complete my degree and graduate. Besides, I loved living in San Luis Obispo.

Chapter 26

~ Cal Poly, SLO ~

Fifth Year

Fifth year, wow. I couldn't believe I had made it to this point. Cal Poly's architecture school is a five-year program from which you receive a Bachelor of Architecture degree. If you know Cal Poly and the rigors of the program, you understand what an accomplishment this is. As I reflected on how I got to this point (and I had thought junior college was difficult after high school!), I really couldn't believe it. Even though I had almost been one of those many students who drop out after their first year at Cal Poly, I now felt both empowered and humbled to realize how far I had come. I had never imagined how challenging this would be...

To add to the tension, since I had gone to Holland with Chad, we missed early registration and had to scramble to get our classes. As a fifth-year student, you typically get priority registration, but we had given that up to study abroad. Neither of us had signed up for a fifth-year design studio, and the choices were rather limited this late in the game. I had hoped to be with Ron Batterson, the professor whose

Danish language course I had taught for his exchange program, but his studio was already filled.

Your choice of fifth-year studio was based partly on the emphasis of the professor. Both Chad and I were able to join David Brodie's studio, whose concentration was Urban Design. The only problem with Professor Brodie's studio was its location way out on the back side of Engineering West. It was far, far away from the Architecture building and most of the other fifth-year studios. I felt disconnected from my fifth-year peers.

Professor Brodie was an older gentleman with a gray beard and mustache who had been brought up in South Africa and spoke with a slight Afrikaans accent. He created a supportive atmosphere in our studio and we became a tight-knit group, in part because we were so isolated from our fellow architecture students.

Brodie took us on field trips to Southern California to see great architecture and show us examples of good and bad urban planning layouts. He figured we were all familiar with the success and beauty of San Francisco, and gave us the fail example of Rohnert Park just 42 miles to the north. It was an urban experiment to diversify a city without a downtown area or central meeting place for the community. He felt we did not have to witness this firsthand. (Three decades later, Rohnert Park is finally adopting a new master plan with a central downtown. There is still hope.)

Los Angeles offered a variety of examples — the J. Paul Getty Villa and museum in Malibu, the thoroughness of details in the residences designed by Frank Lloyd Wright, the Gamble + Gamble craftsman-style homes, the outdoor spaces in Watts. The recent building of the Bonaventure helped bring a skyline and people back into downtown LA. Brodie's intention was to have us experience them all firsthand and understand the how's and why's that made open spaces work or in some cases fail.

Success was apparent when you walked around a corner in a busy urban area to see an open space filled with people sitting and enjoying music, or kids playing. In contrast, a beautifully designed sitting area might have no one in sight. What makes a space work? To achieve a well-utilized open space, it first must be accessible to the community. It offers something for everyone: cafe, easy walking paths, open green area, ample sitting spaces. Its hierarchy of space is simply understood, and it's adaptable over time. This hands-on approach was extremely helpful for understanding of the challenges we would face when choosing locations for our Urban Design projects and fifth-year thesis papers.

Professor Brodie gave us the freedom to select our project location; it could be anywhere in the world, within certain parameters. It had to be a site that was currently underdeveloped or not making good use of open space. We were required to find an existing building that could be renovated into a multi-use facility, and to design a new building somewhere on the site to help improve the lifestyle of the community. The only caveat was that we would need to be able to document the area — by including maps, photos, and statistical information and data to back up our designs.

A few of my classmates chose to use their hometown; others chose more exotic places. Globally we ranged from Paris, France, to Detroit, Michigan. There were sites in New York, Seattle, Reno, and Clovis, California. I chose my project to be in the Christianshavn area of Copenhagen, Denmark. This area was originally used by the military and the trade industry. It was prime land on the waterfront, close to the heart of Copenhagen.

To make sure this would be possible, I called my cousin Laurids, who was a land surveyor in Copenhagen, to enlist his help. I explained what I was trying to accomplish and the concept that I was developing for my project. I asked him if he would be able to send me maps of the area. I couldn't believe it when, the following week, I received a long tube in the mail, postmarked from Denmark. Laurids had sent me maps of Christianshavn and the entire region of Copenhagen, plus photos and original drawings of the various centuries-old towers, along with the survey documentation I needed. I could not have had a better resource to help with both my urban design project and my fifth-year thesis paper, which was on "Towers and Monumentality."

The quarter had begun and I was still looking for classes to round out my schedule. I heard that my two all-time favorite professors, Bilgi Denel and Terry Hargrave, were teaming up to teach a fifth-year thesis seminar class by invitation only. They did not realize that I had returned from Europe and welcomed me in with open arms, excited to have me join their seminar. I asked if Chad could also be in the class. Bilgi at first hesitated, stating that he did not think that was a good idea, but in the end, he agreed. I found his hesitancy a little odd but didn't pay much attention to it. I always enjoyed listening to Bilgi's philosophies on life and architecture, and I still can listen to him for hours, as we have remained in touch over all these years.

Now that I had all the classes I needed, I was saddled with the task of figuring out how to manage my new schedule. My stress level was high, and my anxiety was off the charts, and it wasn't all school related. I was worried about my health. I had been experiencing pain on the upper-left side of my chest. I discovered there was a lump there on my chest wall. Once again I was faced with the overwhelming worry of the unknown, which made my mind go crazy.

One thing I have learned over the years is that facing an unknown situation is like facing your fears. No matter how afraid you are — and I have been incredibly scared at times — standing up to those fears and getting answers allows you to move forward.

If you're lucky, it's good news, or maybe it was only your shadow that scared you. Either way, you will be overcome with joy. If the news is not so good — or really bad — you at least know what you are dealing with and can figure out a solution to make it better, and then the unknown is gone.

So, that being said, I immediately called my old oncologist, Dr. Ablin. He was now working only at UCSF, primarily researching pediatric oncology. He was very happy to hear from me but surprised at the same time. He did not expect that my original cancer would appear on my left side so many years later. To help relieve my anxieties, he said I could come in and he would take a look.

Chad said he would like to come with me and meet Dr. Ablin, as he had heard so much about him. We left the next day and spent the weekend with my mother. Chad and I drove to San Francisco to the Parnassus campus at UCSF. As we turned left from 19th Avenue onto Judah Street toward the hospital, I had flashbacks of this place, and they were not helping my anxiety. This was the same hospital where I'd had my last two surgeries. I never thought I would be back here.

But it was really nice to see Dr. Ablin again. He had not changed from the way I remembered him — still wearing his half-glasses with a big smile, walking with a slight limp as he reached out and gave me a big hug and told me how I had grown. Obviously, his sense of humor was still as sharp as ever. If you recall, I was told that my growth would be stunted by the chemotherapy. I have not grown since the sixth grade, except for the bone growth that caused my last two surgeries.

He had me jump up on the examination table and began palpating the lump on my chest. He said that to make sure to ease my mind I should get an X-ray taken, but he felt confident that the lump I was feeling was only my rib. He continued to explain that it was unlikely to be painful if it was cancer. He suspected I had probably done something to pop my rib out of place. He pressed it back into place and said it was just aggravated and for me to take it easy, if that was possible, and let it heal. The X-ray confirmed his hunch.

Dr. Ablin concluded by saying that I had been cancer-free for over ten years now. My risk of getting cancer now was just as likely as the next person. Chad was so relieved, and I walked out of there with a huge weight lifted off my shoulders. I felt I was given a whole new lease on life, and nothing was going to stop me now!

We quickly drove home to tell my mother the good news. She made a celebratory dinner and loaded us up with leverpostej (paté), frikadeller (Danish-style meatballs), and a few other Danish goodies for the road. You can't even imagine the relief I felt as we drove back to SLO.

My mind was still racing, but now I was able to refocus my attention to getting through the school year, my last and final year. This was the home stretch. I walked back into Professor Brodie's fifth-year design studio and saw that he had laid out a schedule for us that was going to be intense. The requirements for our Urban Design projects were to develop an entire geographical area into a much-needed, desirable usable open space and provide a sense of community with housing and a multiuse facility.

This would be a different process for me. I typically designed buildings from the inside out — in my opinion a more practical way, and a better use of the interior space. Not to say that I ignored the aesthetics or exteriors. For this application, though, we were to design the urban plan first, then create the design of a building from the blocked-out urban forms. The urban concept was going to take some time and thought, at least until I could wrap my head around what my concept would be.

I grew to appreciate that my new living accommodations were on the outskirts of town. Having to drive, even only fifteen minutes to and from campus, provided me with a nice mental break from school and the challenges of my design studio. The drive home each day helped me to clear my head, and then later I would find I had gained clarity and perspective on the challenges I was facing.

Our mobile home was really quite spacious, with your standard layout of entering at the side of the unit directly into the living room, and having a giant kitchen off to the right. A corridor to the left led to a bathroom and two large bedrooms; I had the bedroom at the end of the hallway. Chad had found a studio apartment in the home of a Cal Poly professor of City and Regional Planning. Although it had a separate entrance, the room was very small and he usually ended up staying at my place.

One night around 2:00 a.m., my hotline rang (the red desktop push-button telephone my mother had given me). It startled both Chad and me out of a sound sleep. I panicked, afraid something had happened to my mother or my brother. But when I answered, to my surprise there was a familiar Australian voice, one I hadn't heard in several years.

"Hey, is this Sly?" the voice said. "It's Glenn... Remember me?"

I was trying to wake up to the reality that the voice on the other end belonged to my old boyfriend.

"I know it has been a while, but how has your life been going?" he asked.

"Good, yes, yes, of course, I remember you." He was actually calling me from Australia after all these years!

He continued. "Has it ever been as good for you, as it was when we were together?"

I was so taken aback, and still reeling that this was my Aussie calling after so much time had passed. I was happy to hear from him again, but... how to react to this?

I was now in a serious relationship with someone who was extremely jealous and just happened to be lying right beside me, listening to every word I was saying. So I was in an uncomfortable situation.

"What did you say?" I asked, thinking I must have heard him incorrectly.

Glenn repeated, "Has it ever been as good for you as it was when we were together?"

Then he proceeded with, "I'm getting married, and I just wanted to know?"

"Wow, congratulations," I answered. "When are you getting married?" My head was spinning. I couldn't believe what I had just heard.

"Tomorrow. But, have things ever been as good for you, as they were for us?" he asked again.

I was shocked to hear that Glenn was getting married. I had thought he was already married, based on what his former boss had told me. I was dumbfounded. So he hadn't been married for the past three years as I was led to believe? I couldn't wrap my mind around all of this. What was I supposed to do with this information now? My head kept spinning; I figured whatever I said probably wouldn't make any difference at this point, so I did what I thought was right. I wished him all the happiness and a great life, without really answering his question. But, in my mind, the truthful answer was

"No, it's never been as good as when we were together!"

After hanging up the phone, Chad began the inquisition.

"Who was that, and what did he want?"

I explained the story of meeting Glenn and how I was told, when he went back to Australia, that he had already promised to marry his high school sweetheart. So I never gave him another thought.

But that was not entirely the case, and now I couldn't stop thinking about him. The phone call really had my mind reeling, filling with What if's. What if I had called or even written to him after that last postcard from Santorini?

I was never really sure why he called me that night, the night before his wedding, or what he was expecting me to say. What if. What if Chad hadn't been there and I answered honestly, would that have changed things? I will never know…

I did find out later that he had been calling my home numerous times, and my mother told him I wasn't there, which I wasn't. I guess she finally got tired of the calls and gave him my new number. I asked her why she hadn't told me before that an Australian guy was calling looking for me, and she admitted that she hadn't told me because I was in a relationship.

Regardless, it was nice to hear his voice again with that Australian accent. I just sincerely hoped that he was happy, because that unspoken answer kept ringing in my head — we had been really good together, and I did care about him.

After having all those feelings stirred up, it made me question where I was in my relationship with Chad. Chad and I seemed to have a pretty good thing going; we worked well together, and he made me feel secure, but we lacked the strong chemistry I'd had with Glenn.

I felt that our different qualities complemented our relationship and made it stronger.   Chad was a great guy; he was attentive and affectionate, and he completely doted on me. My friends saw how he had me on a pedestal and thought he must be the one for me. I felt at times, though, that his image of me was hard to live up to. I had always been so carefree, and this relationship felt constraining. I was happy being by myself and being an independent woman. I didn't like the feeling that I had to report to someone all the time about what I was doing.

One morning, driving alone in my little black Scirocco on my typical route toward campus, I suddenly had this realization, an epiphany of sorts, about my future. I realized that if I continued with my life the way things were going — meaning, if I stayed with Chad — I would never become the famous architect I envisioned becoming. I knew that I was at a crossroads, and I felt I had to decide between focusing only on my career or possibly having a family in the future.

Conversations I'd had with Professor Denel (Bilgi) over the past few quarters kept resonating in my mind. He had warned me that if I stayed with Chad, he would hold me back. Now, I understood why he hesitated to let Chad enroll in his Thesis Seminar with me. Bilgi had made it very clear that he felt Chad was not good for me, and he could see the distraction in my work. My designs and program analysis didn't have the same ingenuity that they used to have. He felt I had so much potential and I should not let it go to waste.

I enjoyed spending time with Chad, though, and he provided me with a sense of warmth and security. As you can see, I was somewhat conflicted, but my positive attitude led me to focus on the good aspects of our relationship. I shoved my doubts to the back of my mind and told myself that was enough speculating on relationships, I needed to focus on school... .

My fifth-year final presentation was only a week away. I had worked on this project for the past eight months. Living, eating, sleeping, and discussing it with Professor Brodie and my fellow classmates, I felt I had my description and concept pretty solid in my mind, though I needed to begin practicing my oral presentation.

Luckily for me, I was also taking an art elective with another architecture professor. She let me draw a series of pastel renderings to depict my concept of a tower, and these renderings would complement my fifth-year thesis paper. The catch was that she required I put on a special exhibit of my renderings for her students and explain my vision and process with a Q&A after. I was more than happy to do this; it provided me with an audience for a practice run of my final presentation. I would later have to present it in front of the College of Architecture and Environmental Design faculty, advisors, and guest architects who would sit on my jury panel along with numerous fellow architectural students.

The final presentations were given in the fishbowl, as it was called — a large, glass-enclosed presentation space on the lower level of the Architecture building. A crowd had gathered, and to my surprise, it appeared to be standing-room-only. I took a moment to glance around and identify who my harshest critics might be. I saw Bilgi, along with several other design professors I'd had, sitting in the front row. I closed my eyes briefly and took a deep breath, getting ready to begin, when I spotted Chad's smiling face.

I began by welcoming everyone, introducing myself, and thanking Professor Brodie for the opportunity to have studied Urban Design under his guidance during this past year. I prefaced my design presentation with the requirements for our projects. Then I explained the site I had chosen.

The site is in Christianshavn, one of the oldest existing foundations in Copenhagen, originally laid out by King Christian IV in 1618. It is situated along the major harbor that separates the islands of Sjælland and Amager, with smaller canals surrounding the other edges. The site has been used for light industry and trade over the past centuries. The city of Copenhagen wished to restore the area and bring housing and a sense of community back to this unused land near the center of town.

To introduce housing into the area, I explained the necessity of creating a sense of place, with a central gathering point for the community. Since the only link was a bridge at the south end, I added a small drawbridge near the east side in an attempt to create a larger sense of community with the existing neighborhoods. Traditional Danish courtyard-style housing was used to optimize the views of the main canal while, more importantly, allowing maximum light into each apartment. I also developed an open-market concept, allowing local retailers to sell their wares, along with spaces for new retail shops for the convenience of the new community. A central open space was created as a visual connection for the community and a way to easily access the bakery, cheese shops, smørrebrød shops, and grocers while keeping an eye on children and the community at the same time.

On the west end of the site, along the water's edge, an observation clock tower would be placed as a landmark and historical tribute to King Christian IV for his dedication to architecture and his contribution to the majority of towers in Copenhagen. The tower would also be the entrance to the new community center, allowing the community to continue social interaction during Denmark's long winter months.

To create a visual impact while describing my project to my audience, I had placed drawings of the site plan, floor plans, sections, and elevations mounted onto several 30"x40" presentation boards so they hung on the wall behind me, with the three different scale models I had built. Two models were of the site, the first representing the overall area, which included Christianshavn's neighboring vicinity. For this model, I had learned how to use a hot wire and cut Styrofoam to create what is called a massing model.

For the model of the island where my specific site was located, I used chipboard — an eighth-inch-thick brown board — laid under my parallel rule to secure it and allow me to measure out the pieces and cut them with my Exacto knife and a straightedge. I would then use a hot glue gun to assemble the pieces and create the buildings. Both site models also involved replicating the water in the canals, the tiny drawbridges, and all the buildings in a blocked-out form to scale. A final, enlarged scale model of the Community Center with the clock tower was constructed out of an off-white Strathmore paper for the main body, with balsam wood for the tower. This model was more detailed to help illustrate the overall function of the building; it had a removable roof for viewing the design of the interior floor plans.

I brought in additional easels to mount the series of abstract pastel renderings of towers, and flanked the sides of my presentation with them. The towers also tied in directly with my fifth-year thesis paper titled "Towers and Monumentality," which I gave a brief synopsis of during my presentation but had not yet completed writing.

As I wrapped up my presentation, I nervously asked if there were any questions. Multiple hands went into the air. Although I was primarily commended for my ideas, along with my ambitious endeavors for such a large-scale project, I was also questioned about the choice for my site — why I would attempt someplace so far away without having control over the area, and why I would stay with the traditional style of Danish architecture. In the end, the jury felt that given the scope and program requirements of the project, I had illustrated a solution that was fitting. Some members of the jury felt I should have shown more initiative, but they were all impressed with my model-making abilities and drawings. For the most part I was pleased with the outcome of my critique and learned that there are no simple solutions, and working on a project of this scale by oneself, it is impossible to answer all the questions.

This made sense to me because doing things with one arm, I have learned there are typically many different solutions to any given situation. I have struggled many times with how to approach a project or even a simple task. After evaluating my options, I must choose. And I've had to make many hard choices.

I do not regret any of them. Even the bad ones. I have learned from them. It is unfortunate, but we tend to learn the most from our mistakes. When I get questioned about a choice, I try not to take it defensively but look at it as an opportunity — an opportunity to look at the bigger picture, to get out of my comfort zone, to learn more.

As for the critique of my final project, I would typically reflect on this for days or even weeks to absorb all the comments. There was so much to learn from both the praise and the constructive criticism I received. I would have to wait to ponder these ideas, as graduation was fast approaching and the stress of finishing up writing my fifth-year thesis and studying for my final exams continued weighing on me.

I wanted to have everything wrapped up as much as possible before my family's arrival for graduation. They had all been to visit several times during my years at Cal Poly, but I wanted this time to be special. I wanted to show them how much I appreciated their support that had allowed me to complete this journey.

I was so proud to show my Mother, Nanna, and Uncle Hermann that I was graduating from Cal Poly's Architecture program and receiving a Bachelor of Architecture. I still couldn't believe this was actually true. I was the first member of my family to be born in the United States and the first to graduate from college. After facing all the tragedies and adversities that my family had to overcome, we were all still standing strong, standing together, and celebrating our accomplishments united as one.

My cousin Alan and I had reserved rooms at the Embassy Suites Hotel for our families. The first night they arrived, we began our celebration at my place. This was the first time my family was able to meet Chad's parents. His father offered to cook up a huge pot of his signature Fettuccine with Clam Sauce. I had made a large salad and garlic bread to go along with the pasta. There was plenty of wine for toasting. Everyone joined in the festivities, including my dear friend and old roommate Staci who had begun dating Todd, another Architecture major. Todd won everyone over with his enthusiasm for the fettuccine and clam sauce; he ate four huge servings and was given a huge skål!

The next day, I awoke to the sun shining on the Central Coast with all its glory. And as I got ready for the day's festivities, I couldn't help but flash back to that moment when I arrived on campus looking for housing. I was so excited, scared, and nervous all at the same time, but mostly, I was glad that I had my mother alongside me. I do not think that anyone actually knew how nervous I was, except my mom. My enthusiasm for life was more apparent.

To me, just being on campus was the promise of a new beginning. It was a place where no one knew me or my story, a place where I could show the world that this independent, happy-go-lucky girl with one arm could be whatever she wanted. I had not wanted to fail, and I certainly didn't.

Yes, I struggled, and I still needed my family. I made mistakes, but I learned — I learned a lot. Not only about architecture, and how to maneuver through an economics or calculus class, but about myself and about life.

Cal Poly's Mustang Stadium was nearly filled to capacity with families and guests. I emerged from the passageway onto the field, securing my cap onto my head, and headed straight into the overwhelming buzz of excitement. In front of me was a sea of black gowns, my gold tassel shimmering as it dangled from my cap in the sunlight. Students were gathering, to be seated with the various colleges, and flags waved from each section, denoting Business, Mathematics, Agriculture...

I continued walking toward my fellow classmates of the College of Architecture and Environmental Design, and as they assembled, I noticed they all had huge smiles on their faces. I realized I had the same goofy grin, and it wasn't going away. We were all so glad to have completed the 249-unit flow chart that we had been handed as incoming freshmen. I could not have been more thrilled.

I was moved by the ceremony, especially the inspirational speakers. When we got to the valedictory announcements, and the university's president began announcing each college and recognizing us for our outstanding achievements, I felt the pride bubble up inside me. We all stood as President Baker congratulated the California Polytechnic State University Class of 1988!

The roar of the cheering graduates escalated. It echoed in the sky, along with the thousands of caps being tossed into the air. Tears began streaming down my face, I was so overwhelmed by emotion. Our future was now, and all I could think of was ...

"I did it! I really did it!"

Once the waves of cheering died down, a surreal feeling came over me. Not only was this the beginning of my future, it was also the end of a community I had been a part of with these incredible people for the past five years. Many of us had become like family. It was a bond we would always share.

Then it was as if an awareness took over, and we all began hugging and kissing one another, offering congratulatory words and goodbyes to our friends and fellow classmates on the field. The celebration continued around us, the crowd thickened and grew louder with laughter and tears, and all the friends and families swarmed onto the field to find their graduates.

I saw my mother approaching, attempting to wipe the tears as they rolled down her cheeks, while reaching out to wrap her arms around me. She said how unbelievable this moment was, and how proud she was of me, that in her excitement to get ready, she had forgotten my present! I could care less about that, I said, I was just glad she was here. Then my Uncle Hermann told me that that was not the only thing she had forgotten — that in her anticipation to come and see me graduate, she had forgotten to pack and had brought an empty suitcase! We all laughed so hard, but that empty suitcase revealed volumes about how much my family cares.

That was my family, and I love them.

Now it was time to get this party started. We all headed out to the San Luis Bay Inn at Avila Beach for a beautiful meal with plenty of skåls! and stories, mainly about me growing up. There were tales of my struggles and of my determination, and of my family wanting to help me and my mother telling them to let me figure it out.

I always knew they were there for me. That is what let me be me.

What had comforted them, amid my horrible treatment, was when I found my laugh again and resumed my characteristic cackle. Then they knew I was going to be okay. And then when I stepped outside to play stickball with the neighborhood kids, even Dr. Ablin said,
"There is no stopping this one…"
As we continued to reminisce, we watched the magnificent orange glow of the California sunset reflecting across the Pacific Ocean. I could not wait for the adventure to continue. I believed I could do anything I set my mind to. And I really have done just that. Anyone who knows me is sure to tell you...

I still am!

I DID IT!

CAL POLY
SAN LUIS OBISPO

The Trustees of
The California State University
on recommendation of the Faculty of
California Polytechnic State University
have conferred upon
Sylvia Rolighed Larsen
the degree of

Bachelor of Architecture

Given at San Luis Obispo, California, on the second day of September,
nineteen hundred eighty-eight

George Deukmejian
Governor of California and President of the Trustees

Marianthi Lansdale
Chair of the Board of Trustees

W. Ann Reynolds
Chancellor of The California State University

Warren J. Baker
President of the University

Message from the Author

~

Thank you for this opportunity to share my story with you. I hope that by coming along on this journey with me, you have been able to see that even though I have dealt with sorrow and pain and have struggled, again and again…

I continued to face my fears.

Along with the difficult times and adversities, I have loved, and I have experienced the joy of accomplishment and the happiness of family. Over the years, one thing I have learned is that everyone has a story.

We can all overcome challenges, no matter how traumatic they may seem, and still enjoy life, be happy, and find success.

Just like when you watch a good movie, and it makes you laugh and cry. It is this wide range of emotions that allows us to experience life to its fullest. Sometimes we stumble and fall, and when this happens it is the feeling of getting up again and moving forward that makes us feel alive.

I have learned that the easiest way to overcome bumps in the road is being able to share both the good and the bad with friends and family, or even sometimes with a complete stranger. By doing this, you create bonds, everlasting bonds that you will cherish forever.

These connective bonds will fulfill your life going forward and make you want more out of life. No matter how big or small your support group is, you must find the courage and face your fears from within, and knowing your family and friends are there to catch you, this lets you be you.

Be kind and keep smiling. Remember, friendship is a powerful thing.

Love,
    Sly~

~ Acknowledgments ~

As I mentioned in my dedication, my family and friends have ALL always been there for me. Especially the ones you have just read about in my story. Most importantly, my mother, my little brother Steven, Nanna, Hermann, my cousin Bruce, and my Mormor for being my constant rocks. Words can not express my overwhelming gratitude for ALL they have done in their unwavering support of me for the past 45 years.

I would also like to give an extra acknowledgment and special thank you to those who, not only supported me growing up but have been there for me in the most recent years. (going through cancer for my third time and helping me with this enormous task of writing this book). A special thanks to Kristianna for her professional editing, analysis, and incredible input to help me complete my manuscript, and allowing my story to convey my message as best as possible.

To my entourage of friends: Tess, Staci, Sandy, Cat, Val, and Trina for not only being by my bedside through my surgery and recovery but also making me laugh and continue to enjoy life even through the bumps in the road. These girls are the best friends anyone could ever ask for.

To Staci for helping me to set up the outline and giving my story the structure it needed to allow me to begin telling my story. The countless dictations I sent her along with the research on childhood cancer and her overwhelming enthusiasm, support, and understanding when I was trying to find my voice. I could never have done this without you.

To Tess, for the countless hours insuring I was telling the stories of our incredible friendship, from walking to kindergarten together to being roommates at Cal Poly, sharing vacations and our love for dachshunds and a good party! I honestly don't know what my life would be without you and your family. My gratitude to you and your wonderful husband Kurt, as well as your father Norm, your mother Anna and your sisters.

This has been and continues to be, an amazing journey together ~.

~ Friendship ~

Friendship is one of the greatest gifts in life. I have been incredibly fortunate to have met so many wonderful people in my life. As many of you know, when you meet a special person, a true friend, something insides you just clicks, you immediately feel a connection, and you cannot break that bond. That is when you know you have a friend for life.

Sometimes in the course of life's ups and downs you may lose contact with one or a number of these true friends for a period of time. But, you know in your heart that they will always be there. When you reconnect, it is as if no time has even passed. That is the true test of time and friendship.

∾

~Musical Compositions~
&
~Lyrics Acknowledgment~

Appendix

~ Danish Kinship Terms ~

In Denmark, each relative is identified as to their connection to the family. For example in English we identify a son and daughter, meaning we know the son is a boy and the daughter is a girl. The Danes take family identity to a whole new level.

In Danish, a son(søn) and daughter(datter) are similar to the English identity, as is the same for your immediate family.

However, the grandparent, aunts, uncles, and cousins are identified as to how their classification fits into the family. Grandparents, aunts, and uncles can be categorized 3 ways depending on whether they are on the mother's side, on the father's side, or related by marriage.

Parents   Grandparents

Mother's Parents~

Mother = Mor   Mother's mother = Mormor

Father = Far   Mother's father = Morfar

Father's Parents ~

                       Father's mother = Farmor

                       Father's father = Farfar

Generic for Grandparents ~
Meaning it can be on either mother's or
father's side

Mother = Mor	Bedstemor = Best Mother (Grandmother)
Father = Far	Bedstefar = Best Father (Grandfather)

Great Grandparents
Mother = Mor   Oldemor = Old mother
Father = Far   Oldefar = Old father

Likewise, for grandchildren
Child = Barn
Children = Børn

Therefore my child's child is my grandchild = Barnebarn
My child's children is my grandchildren = Børnebørn

Siblings
Sister = Søster   Brother = Bror

Uncles ~
Mother's Brother = Morbror
Father's Brother = Farbror
Uncle by marriage = Onkel

Aunts ~
Mother's Sister = Moster
Father's Sister = Faster
Aunt by marriage = Tante

Cousins ~
Girl cousin = Kusine
Boy Cousin = Fætte

~ About the Author ~

Sylvia Larsen

S ylvia is a graduate of California Polytechnic State University, with a Degree in Architecture. Throughout her initial struggles, she very quickly embraced the process of learning to do things with one arm. Having a growth mindset has contributed to her being able to think out of the box and be extremely innovative in her process. Sylvia has been recognized as being in the top 3% of the population for her inherent ability for initiative allowing her to problem-solve tasks before she attempted them and has given her the capabilities to move forward.

After working in the Bay Area for approximately ten years, she started her own Architectural firm in the historic town of Sonoma, California amid the wine country. Where she became quite the wine enthusiast, and also the proud mother of two recent graduates of NYU, one in the field of music, the other in film.

Now a three time cancer survivor, Sylvia has taken time off from architecture to write her book and has begun lecturing as a motivational speaker. Where she has developed the abilities to work and educate others to succeed. Sylvia currently lives in her hometown in Marin County with her miniature dachshund Luna.

∽